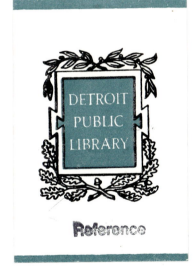

GIRLS, GANGS, WOMEN and DRUGS

GIRLS, GANGS, WOMEN and DRUGS

Carl S. Taylor

Michigan State University Press
East Lansing
1993

Printed in the United States of America

Michigan State University Press
East Lansing, Michigan 48823-5202

00 99 98 97 96 95 94 93 1 2 3 4 5 6 7 8 9 10

Library of Congress Cataloging in Publication Data

Taylor, Carl S.
  Girls, gangs, women, and drugs / Carl S. Taylor.
      p.   cm.
    ISBN 0-87013-320-9 (alk. paper)
    1. Gangs—Michigan—Detroit—Case Studies. 2. Afro-American
  women—Michigan—Detroit—Case Studies. 3. Drug Use—Michigan—Detroit—Case Studies. 4. Afro-American teenage girls—
  Michigan—Detroit—Case Studies. I. Title
  HV6439.U7D68   1993
  364.1′06′0977434—dc20
                                                          93-24037
                                                              CIP

Dedication

To my grandmothers Mollie Jenkins and Mattie Taylor.

To my mother Mae Taylor for giving me the sense to know and appreciate that women and men are equals.

To Mayor Unita Blackwell of Mayersville, Mississippi, you certainly are the symbol of strength and integrity that has always been the backbone of our richness.

To Ann, thanks for always listening.

Acknowledgments

First and foremost, thank the Creator for all the blessings. Thanks to everyone in my family for understanding. My deepest appreciation to the Harry Frank Guggenheim Foundation for supporting this project, especially Ms. Karen Colvard whose understanding and knowledge gave this work a comfort zone that allowed us to do our "thang." Thanks to my colleagues at Grand Valley State University, the entire faculty and staff in the School of Criminal Justice; to all my friends at the Michigan State University Press for their support and special attention to my work; to Ms. Martha Bates for her editing and friendship; to Sgt. Anthony Holt of the Wayne State University Public Safety Department, Timothy J. Mitchell, and Paul Franklin for all their hard work in research and fieldwork; to Virgil Taylor, for always reviewing and assisting the team, you are the best brother; and to Linda Folmar, Dwain Love and his family for giving me an oasis in the city. Special thanks to all those on the research team, interviewers, investigators, and to the crews for being tolerant during all those questions. Love and happiness to Brandy, McGinnis, Killa, Spider, Malik, Randallator, Barry Michael C., William Sparks, Valerie S., Sherronda, Natrese, Viola K., Tracey Kirkwood, Remo, RiAnn, E.A., Dollar Bill, Slick Y, Medium Shaq, Medium Charles, Alphonze Ali, and Mo. Thanks to the Coke Girls, without your word, this wouldn't have had the flavor. And a million thanks to everyone who contributed in making this project a success and to those who spoke and can't be named.

Contents

Foreword

As Carl Taylor's powerful new study of female gang members in Detroit demonstrates, the crisis of the inner city does not discriminate between genders. By taking us into the lives of a number of girls and young women who are confronted with the same hopelessness and lack of options as their male counterparts, Taylor shows us that the American epidemic of guns, gangs, and drugs is not solely a male phenomenon.

The females interviewed include honor roll students and mothers. They are you and I. They are our daughters, our nieces, our girlfriends. Most importantly, they are the mothers of our children—the nurturers of our future.

Taylor persuasively demonstrates that it is not solely a question of low self-esteem or needing to belong to a group that motivates these women and girls to be involved with gangs and drugs. For too many young people, selling drugs or joining a gang has become the only chance they see for achievement. Drugs and gangs are merely symptoms of the neglect and abuse we, as a society, have inflicted on an entire generation. We act as though these young people are invisible and leave them to fend for themselves in a world that worships materialism and money but offers them no means of inclusion.

I can only imagine and guess at the fear, anxiety, and loneliness of DeWanna, Erica, and the other young women in this book as they navigate each day in a dangerous world of drugs and nervous gunslingers seeking to preempt death by first strike. How can we expect our young people to survive without the hope that someday things in America might be different? How many more children do we have to lose to gunfire and drugs before you and I say, "enough"?

All of us must listen and respond to the cries for help and despair coming from the children and youths in our neighborhoods, on our street corners, in our schools, in our families. We must work together to change these young women's vision for the future. We must stop the proliferation of guns. We must implement a range of violence-prevention strategies including anti-violence curricula and such positive alternatives as after school service, recreation, tutoring, and mentoring

1

opportunities. And we must confront our cultural obsession with violence hawked in the media, television, movies, and advertisements. Finally, we must examine the deepest values of our culture which measure success by things—things we kill for—rather than by community strength and mutual support. We will all pay now and later if we continue to ignore our youth's fight for survival. *Girls, Gangs, Women, and Drugs* provides a powerful insight into the problem we *must* all tackle now.

Marian Wright Edelman, President
Children's Defense Fund

Preface

Until recently, the complex lives of young, inner city, black females have gone unnoticed and unexamined. The obscurity these young women in the eyes of urban anthropologists, ethnographers, journalists, and social scientists in general has much to do with the 1980s preoccupation with the sociocultural and economic predicament of their male counterparts. Highly visible in the illegal drug economy (the new occupation replacing unskilled manufacturing employment opportunities), young black males are most frequently associated with the moral decay and deadly violence of America's inner cities. It is within this context that social scientists and other observers have focused their undivided attention and research.

Likewise, the black community—its clergy, civil rights leaders, elected officials, social service providers, and grassroots community activists—responded to the collapse of civil society in urban communities by sounding the black male "endangered species" alarm. With Reagan-Bush social conservatism and urban neglect shaping federal response, soaring urban homicide rates, alarming inner city unemployment rates, disproportionate rates of drug addiction, and ultimately an urban pandemic of HIV infection, the black community desperately sought to marshal its limited resources toward saving young black males. Young black females, in the midst of all this urban decay and social crisis, were visible only as teenage mothers.

Although organizations like the Children's Defense Fund and black women's social and professional groups undertook important teen pregnancy prevention campaigns, young black girls in distressed urban communities felt invisible and neglected by the "save black males" social agenda. My personal experience organizing youth in New Haven, Connecticut revealed the extent to which black girls felt abandoned both by society and black leadership. Frequently consumed by the dysfunctional realities of poor families and neighborhoods, the young women I befriended told stories of emotional abuse, domestic violence, incest, and rape. Abandonment by parents addicted to alcohol and drugs, the unhealthy competition between young mothers and daughters for the love and attention of men, and

3

the emotional stress of daily violence, all seemed to undermine the healthy social development of so many young black girls. As I listened, it became clear that for many of these young girls having a baby was in some way a therapeutic act—a search for love and understanding. Teenage pregnancy, understood correctly, is a condition symptomatic of much larger societal ailments. And yet, for many of these young women, it seems that few who address the issue really understand their pain and silent suffering.

Black clergy, for example, preferred to lecture young girls about keeping their panties up and dresses down, while middle class black professionals preached good girl abstinence/bad girl damnation. Even fewer encouraged young teenage mothers to complete their education and continue striving to reach their personal and professional goals. Consequently, many young black women began to internalize their stigmatization, referring to themselves when pregnant as "just another statistic" with no husband or boyfriend just "my baby's father." In their profoundly stigmatized, alienated worlds these young women—isolated by race, poverty, age and pregnancy—are now growing angry and resentful toward society. It is this hostility that is now commonly described by educators, social service providers, and potential employers as "negative attitude."

I will never forget being approached by a group of black, female high school students terribly upset that the superintendent of schools in New Haven had organized a Young Men's Leadership Group at their school. Jealous and hurt by the attention, perks, and activities provided for this group, the young women informed me that they intended to organize their own Young Women's Leadership Group. It was not fair; they argued, that boys should get all the special attention. I knew then that the exclusive focus on saving young black males was damaging the self-esteem and psyche of young black girls.

It was, however, the crack epidemic of the late 1980s that ultimately brought to the surface the pain, alienation, hopelessness, and despair felt by so many of these girls and young women . In their description of the potency of crack cocaine, many urban journalists acknowledged the addictive qualities of the substance by observing how it was capable of overpowering the "natural" instincts of motherhood. As images of abandoned crack babies have filtered through the popular press and news stories of grandmothers raising grandchildren who were abandoned by crack addicted daughters proliferated, some social service providers have begun to acknowledge the dire straits of poor, young black women. With crack cocaine and heroin addiction fueling an upsurge in urban prostitution and multiple sexual encounters in crack houses, the AIDS epidemic now paints a horrific picture for these women's futures.

Around the same time the crack epidemic revealed the despair of these inner city women, a bold group of black female rap artists proudly announced the arrival of "Ladies First." This black female explosion in hip-hop underground culture served to assert the identity and presence of young urban women who had previously been hidden by the largely masculine, misogynist hip-hop explosion in American popular culture. Black female rap artists like Salt-N-Pepa, Queen Latiffah, Yo-Yo, Monie Love, and MC Lyte all symbolize the emergence of an independent black woman capable of "getting paid" in a man's world. Proud, defiant, strong, and independent, this hip-hop version of black feminism is a direct response to the outrageously "raw" disrespect, inequality, and unabashed abuse promoted and practiced in hip-hop culture.

With domestic violence and physical assault rampant in urban communities, women had no recourse but to get tough. Borrowing the bravado, styles, posture, and attitudes of male-dominated popular culture, the "block girls" of the inner city took the late 1980s by storm. Black female teenagers became more visible in public spaces, especially in shopping malls, roaming in gangs or "posses" like young males and parroting the same profane language usually associated with young men. Like their male contemporaries, these young women marked territory (i.e. boys and neighborhoods), some entered the drug trade and, increasingly, they began to carry weapons. Preferring razor blades and knifes, these young girls unleashed their anger and alienation by randomly fighting and maiming people. Because more young black males have access to, and prefer the use of, semiautomatic weapons, their violence tends to be more deadly, attracting both police and media attention. But inside depressed inner city communities, many are equally aware of, and deeply disturbed by, the number of young girls habitually slashing each other's faces.

The "rawness" and violence of this female culture in the 1990s is a new phenomenon. Although teen pregnancy, urban poverty, and carrying razor blades is nothing new for most city girls, the masculine bravado so widely accepted in the construction of contemporary black female identity is a distinguishing characteristic for this generation. To be sure, there are few predecessors of these '90s combat boot wearing, sagging crotch, baggy blue jeans, gold jewelry laden, large designer pocketbook carrying, jeep driving, unbuckled belt hanging, drug dealing "around-the-way-girls" with beepers, cellular phones, athletic gear, and weapons of their choice.

Similarly, the new generation of black college girls who exclusively date drug dealers and intertwine street culture with educational upward mobility is just another example of this new breed of young, black, urban females. Whereas in the past, traditional norms defined female identity and adherence to Victorian morals distinguished the so-called good girls from the bad girls, female identity in the ghettos of the 1990s is blurred by the masculinity of hip-hop culture and the moral decay of black civil society. In short, poor black girls and boys behave and think in a similar manner because their socio-cultural and moral influences are often identical.

This ethnography of young women in the inner city of Detroit is a long overdue glimpse into a world of emotional damage, harshness, violence, sex, and drugs. Much of what this ethnography reveals does not fit a traditional definition of female behavior or identity. Because this research captures the voices of young women on the cutting edge of the demise of black civil society, it offers important evidence that both poor, urban, young black women and men are in serious trouble—deeply alienated from the American mainstream and in desperate need of national attention and direct action. Like the newly proclaimed "manchild," his female counterpart is raw, spiritless, violent, and without hope or compassion.

By examining the world of inner city girls, this effort may help social scientists begin to identify those common themes which recur both in the lives of poor black females and males. In the long run, comparable attention to the psycho-social, cultural, and economic crises facing our young black females in impoverished inner cities may just help the nation develop a comprehensive agenda for saving all urban youth-at-risk. Policies and programs for boys which neglect the dilemmas facing their female counterparts can only lead to a failed effort. Quite simply, the plight of both genders demands our attention, compassion, examination, and immediate action.

Lisa Yvette Sullivan
Black Student Leadership Network
Children's Defense Fund
Washington, D.C.

Introduction

In the rustbelt city of Detroit, the feminization of poverty has become a reality for more than half of African American, female-headed families. Life in the inner city has changed to one of survival. The plight of these girls and women, particularly in Detroit, cannot and should not be ignored. The violence and destruction of their environment, though typical of other inner cities in the U.S., often rivals that of international combat zones. In recent years this violence has become readily apparent to all who care to recognize it. What has not been recognized, however, is how women are reacting and acclimating to this "way of life."

Drugs, violence, and hopelessness are just some of the demons confronted daily by the people of central cities. Notwithstanding their surroundings, many of these young women have found success, happiness, and independence. This powerless populace has found vehicles for survival that middle America may not accept as means for expressing success, esteem, and power. And just as Americans in the 1980s discovered the new manchild, in the 1990s they will find females entangled in webs of criminal enterprise not seen before. These changes should not be dismissed as simply gang development; they also reflect a change in the attitudes of inner city women. The disenfranchisement of these young women and their social isolation and neglect have left lasting impressions not only on them, but on all people of the inner cities. In response, some are attempting to survive by pursuing traditional paths of education, civil rights, and better jobs. However, the reality of decades of neglect and inferior status has taken its toll.

Women in this study are drug dealers, victims, abusers, and the leading destroyers of their own selves and futures. The reality of women in gangs pales in comparison to a world populated with young women with children becoming addicted to crack or bringing children into this hell of civilization. If young men are considered endangered in Wayne County (Detroit), more so than in any other county in the U.S., what are we to conclude about the young women of Wayne County? The notion of mothers as dope dealers and drug

abusers should be just as abhorrent as the idea of fathers as dope dealers and drug abusers. During one interview a young crack addict was
asked how she could abandon her children. Looking befuddled, she
answered, "Just like the men do, why can't I be no good like a man
. . . women can be messed up. I'm a dope fiend. I ain't proud of the
shit, I'm thinking 'bout gitting high just like a man who is in the same
situation like me, okay? What 'bout the daddy, y'all don't ever ask him
how come he just left his baby?" The path some of these young
women have taken may not be acceptable to many Americans. Theirs
is the perception that the world is harsh and cruel. This perception is
derived from a daily existence of blocked avenues, broken dreams,
and distorted images.

The socioeconomics of Detroit have erased the hope of many people. Social workers, academicians, and policy makers debate about low
self-esteem and hopelessness in the inner city. This study amply
demonstrates the fact that not all African American, inner city women
are debilitated by low self-esteem. Living apart from society, they simply feel they have limited choices and have chosen the path that
seems, for them, to lead to success. They represent the outcome of
Robert Merton's Strain Theory.[1] The double bind has doubled back on
itself; these women are acting on the distorted view presented to
them and forging ahead with their lives.

As the cultural definition of women changes, areas that have traditionally been male-dominated are also changing. Women, both young
and old, are demanding to be part of the "American Dream." This
dream includes being able to make choices both good and bad. The
young females presented here are participating in the same struggle as
their male counterparts in urban Detroit. Their isolation is at least
equal to, if not greater than, the isolation of African American males.

Even in the area of criminality, Americans have double standards.
Culturally, women are defined as very different from men—but we
have found that females are just as capable as males of being ruthless
in so far as their life opportunities are presented. This study indicates
that females have moved beyond the status quo of gender repression.
There are many strong and capable young females in Detroit. They are
heard throughout this book, giving their views. But they have been
impacted indirectly by young women in the illegal world. The standards by which many young females and males live in urban America
are set by the subculture of illicit narcotics, violence, and an undercurrent of materialism.

Gangs have been an element of industrialized cities since at least
1927 according to sociologist Frederick Thrasher's study of Chicago.[2]

However, his study, as well as others, have paid little attention to the role of females in gangs. Field studies of male gangs in Detroit conducted from 1980-1986 lead me to realize the overwhelming need for a significant study to address the intricate position of women in gangs. My previous research found females to be more than traditional auxiliary partners. For the purpose of this study, gangs are defined as: transfamilial social organizations that can include ethnic families, groups, and clans, but are not exclusive to these entities. The analysis of gang types and infrastructure include: 1) structure, 2) function, and 3) motivation. This definition of gangs is not the traditional one which focuses exclusively on criminality.

Field studies of female gangs reinforced the data from my previous research; there is evidence of females in non-criminal gangs. It is the broadening of the definition of gangs in this study that allowed the research team to paint a fuller picture of the underground and overground experience in the urban arena. Policies cannot be formulated until this complex culture is understood. Criminality is only one part of gang culture.

The status of celebrated role models whose business is selling narcotics has had a tremendous impact. The dope business has empowered young and old, female and male, in many major cities. What we found in the field were various small groups, sets, crews, poorly conceptualized associations of females, nameless entities that have group processes, and new types of urban criminal organizations that are hybrids of traditional and new definitions of gangs. Some professionals say that there is no multigenerational gang situation in the city, however examination of the roster in the state correctional facilities might argue otherwise. While some groups that were observed do not qualify as gangs within some definitions, the data cannot be ignored. The fact is that organized and unorganized political, social, and criminal groups, crews, and gangs are in the city. Definitions can be debated for years to come, but the test for a gang is behavior. The spectrum of gangs ranges from those barely making a criminal living to those who have become criminal celebrities. The city's political position concerning its reputation and its fear of chasing away potential tourist and convention business is understandable. Yet, the fact that Detroit is not Los Angeles nor Chicago does not mean it has no gang problem.

The innovative blueprint for the new wave of organized gangs was drawn by gangs like Young Boys, Incorporated in the early 1980s. Critics have contended that YBI was an organized crime operation and not a gang. Yet the Young Boys, Inc. infrastructure was comparable to that of General Motors or any other legitimate corporation. Their function was strictly the business of selling narcotics, not social interaction. Former YBI member Marvin Webster stated during an interview, "Selling dope was our only business. Sticking your nose in other matters would be dangerous; our business was selling dope, that was it." YBI employed large numbers of juveniles. Most of those juveniles were male, but some were female. These members have referred to themselves as gangs, crews, posses, etc. There may have been adult leadership and their intent was serious criminal enterprise, but they were a gang.

In 1982, girls did not play a very visible role in corporate gangs like Young Boys, Incorporated. However, the evidence presented in the book *Dangerous Society* showed that females were involved and this involvement was not simply secondary. In fewer than ten years, females have arrived on the scene. In this study we found evidence that girls were always in the "classroom" of criminal education. Today, without much fanfare, women are participating in gangs and in crime as never before in urban America. And, this is not exclusive to Detroit.

Hopefully, readers will begin to understand other dimensions of gangs. This is not an attempt to balance good gangs vs. bad gangs within sociological definitions. It is, rather, an effort to show another dimension. Society repeatedly ignores females in criminal, compatriot, and non-criminal gangs, as well as in social and political advocacy networks in Detroit. This book addresses the issues of female gangs and females involved in illegal drug enterprises in this city.

Does Detroit have a gang problem? Do gangs exist in Detroit? Some in the city say that gangs do not exist. Gang activities have been dismissed. Yet, the community has a responsibility to deal with this issue.

Michigan is a prime example of a place where politicians, public polls, and public policy collide. There are now fourth and fifth generations of welfare families in Detroit due to welfare politics. The thirty-five-year-old grandmother and her daughter, who is having babies and nurturing them with poor education and in poor health, with no socialization and no spiritual guidance, are here and must be dealt with. The criminal justice system is overburdened, locked on opposing theories and not designed for what society needs it to do. Detroit, despite the indignation and retreat of the middle and the upper middle class, cannot hide from the results of over seventy years of urban apartheid. There is fragmentation and tribalism, and the nation refuses to acknowledge the problems and that its domestic policy is lacking integrity and substance.

This book is about more than gangs; it is about poverty, teen pregnancy, protracted unemployment, crime, illiteracy, and drugs. It is about battles lost; it is about hopelessness; it is about taking control; it is about women.

Notes

1. Robert Merton, "Social Structure and Anomie," *American Sociological Review* 3, no. 5 (October 1938).

2. Fredrick Thrasher, *The Gang: A Study of 1,313 Gangs in Chicago*, (University of Chicago Press, 1927).

1

Methodology and Gang Typology

The means by which we conducted this study was crucial in obtaining accurate data. One of the most important aspects of data collection was site selection—we went directly to our subjects. The field study also demanded that we focus on the language and intent of those being interviewed. Interviews were conducted in their surroundings, in their homes, in their clubs, at local shopping malls, etc. Not only did this provide a more relaxed environment for the subjects, but it also allowed us to see the diverse circumstances of the individual women.

Interviews were conducted at many different locations in the greater Detroit area. The core of the city, of course, was the most important site for the field team; however, many of our interviews took place in remote places—dope dens, crack houses, public institutions, middle class neighborhoods, suburbs, and hotels. The flexibility of being able to meet at different locations proved essential in the target community. The best locations for conducting interviews were those free from distractions; they also provided the maximum amount of privacy.

It is critical to remember that the women presented in these interviews represent a diverse cross-section of class, age, and values. Confidentiality played an important part in the conduct of successful interviews. The women were very sensitive to our purpose. Who were we? Was this for the police? Their distrust of adults was very prevalent. We had to insure complete confidentiality for all subjects before any aspect of trust could be developed. Our reputation as trustworthy—gained during the first study (*Dangerous Society*)—was beneficial in attempting to gain the women's confidence for this study.

13

The following guidelines were used during interviews to help assure the women of confidentiality:

1. Guarantee (or at least make a strong promise) the subjects that no names would be recorded or used. This included nicknames which often identified individuals in gangs better than their birth names.

2. Guarantee that this study was for research to understand women in the inner city only. As researchers, we had no other motives. However, if the interviewees were worried about our intent, they should refrain from giving any information they considered critical or possibly damaging to themselves, since our study would be released to the public.

3. Give the subjects a 24-hour, 7-days-a-week, telephone number to use in the event that they had any questions.

4. Guarantee all subjects that no hidden tape recorders would be used. Investigators would inform subjects that interviews would be taped. If subjects objected, no tape recorders would be used.

5. Guarantee that all conversations and interviews were confidential. (We emphasized guideline number 2.) Investigators promised under no circumstances to name sources to other gangs or internally to fellow gang members.

FIELD TEAM

Initially, we debated whether or not the entire investigative team would have to be composed of women. To our surprise, we found that gender became secondary in establishing solid communications. To gain acceptance, race or gender was not enough; trust, developed through time and action, was the primary key in developing an open dialogue. We did find however, that a gender-integrated field team was best—both for the interview process and interpretation of the interviews.

The lines of communication have been working for our research team relatively well since the early 1980s. Some of the youths who were interviewed in *Dangerous Society* have grown into adults. One of the most vital dilemmas in ethnography is the element of consistency. The research team never severed the lines of communication in Detroit's inner city. We kept in touch daily with many of the families, youths, and social institutions that dealt with these neighborhoods. The critical factor in our association with those we interviewed was our consistent presence in their lives—this gave us credibility. It is important not to be an outsider, foreigner, or worse, invader. The field team was headed by a key investigator who participated in the previous study on male gangs. The team leader is from the east side of Detroit—one of the primary areas for interviews—and is well connected with the residents and their lives. The investigative team also consisted of a senior project manager and a police consultant, who designed our daily, weekly, and monthly field strategy based on the team leader's assessment of street activity. Other consultants, investigators, and interviewers rounded out the field team.

The interviews were arranged by the field team at the convenience of the interviewees. The number of interviews for each subject or subject group varied from one to seven. Interviews for the case studies were conducted over several months with subsequent follow ups. Telephone interviews were used occasionally, but this was primarily to set up interviews and to keep in touch with the women. Telephone conversations helped us to become part of the subjects everyday life rather than one-time-visit researchers. This was crucial in obtaining realistic views, feelings, and experiences. It has been our experience that consistent communication breeds an element of trust and allows the subject to feel comfortable and familiar. If an interviewee did not trust us, it was not unusual for them simply not to show or to leave abruptly in the middle of the interview. Our pre-interview relationship was based on having the subjects comfortable with the process prior to the interview.

INTERVIEW QUESTIONS

The field team developed a set of questions for each gang type before the process of the field survey took place. These questions were designed to gain both the confidence and affirm the specific group and/or gang. The following questions were given to potential interviewees.

1. Are there any female groups, crews, gangs, or similar organizations to your knowledge? [Note: It was explained that the gang did not have to have violent acts, criminal behavior, or other traditional gang definitions to qualify in this survey.]

2. Are you or any associate, relative, friend, or acquaintance in any type of gang? If yes, what type of female gang? [Note: this question gives the interviewee the typology used for this survey.]

3. Do you know of problems caused by female gangs anywhere in the city?

4. What are females doing outside of gangs, the females not in the gangs? [Note: introducing the concept of social and political groups and compatriot gangs.]

5. Is there any dope business in your community or anywhere in the city that you know?

GANG TYPOLOGY

As discussed in the introduction, gangs, for the purpose of this study, are defined as transfamilial social organizations that can include ethnic families, groups, and clans, but are not exclusive to these entities. Structure, function, and motivation must be analyzed to determine gang type and infrastructure. I must emphasize here that the typology I have developed is not a universal one, but a typology based on my field studies. As a result of my research, four different gang types have emerged: scavenger, territorial, commercial, and corporate.

Scavenger Gangs

The scavenger gang has caused many questions in various circles. There is the continual question, "Is this really a gang?" It has been my experience that scavengers are the gangs that no one is particularly concerned about. Frederick Thrasher first documented this gang type in his 1927 study.[1] Scavengers represent the first wave of gang membership. This gang draws those who, unlike the other gang types, are almost exclusively from lower classes. When scavengers come together within their circle of problems and organize, they become gangs. They may engage in criminal acts, or they may engage in acts which are immoral but still legal. An example of this may be standing on public streets and freeways soliciting work, food, or money by design. These scavenger gangs are civil gangs rather than criminal gangs. There is little, if any, concern for such gangs. In the 1990s, collective groups of all ages, ethnicity, and gender are bonding for survival.

Criminality is not essential in becoming a scavenger. They may be a gang of crack addicts or heroin addicts. There are gangs of thieves that share their booty and are not successful in their enterprise. (Scavengers who are unsuccessful commercial gangs). The level of accomplishment should not dictate their existence of definition. Scavengers are existing by whatever means are available. Their collective process is what gives them power. If they decide to Jack Roll someone, it is the gang's decision. Any gains are divided between the members. The decision of scavenger individuals in the gang can at times become conflicting. Discipline, focus, and other talents are generally lacking in this gang type. The predicament of scavengers has been short-lived and generally it has been those short term objectives that have doomed their success.

Vickie, 20, discusses her life on the streets as a member of a gender-integrated gang. She dropped out of school in the eighth grade and lives with a gang of eight men and three women. She says she has a juvenile record for shoplifting and prostitution. She is a multi-drug abuser. Her mother put her out when she was fourteen; her father was shot and killed in front of her at the age of three or four. The X-gang adopted her at the age of fifteen, and this gang has, over the past several years, become her family.

> *Well, this is my crew, family, my people or whatever you wanna call it . . . in a way it's my everything, it's a job, and these fellas look out for me, and we look out for them. What's a gang? I've been down wit these fellas since I was real young. This is a gang if you say we making monay. Is this a gang thang, 'cause we out here gitting paid or is this a gang thang 'cause we run together all the time? Hell, we live together, me and Cookie take care of these guys . . . if I didn't have these fellas and my girls, I wouldn't have nuthin'. . . without these guys, they my people! Bobby, taught me everythang 'bout everythang . . . he is the one that got me and Cookie away from all those old muthafuckas that I used to have to fuck to git enuff monay to eat. Shit, me and DeLori was starving and everybody was fucking us fo change. That's when Bobby and his boys took me and Cookie in and didn't let nobody mess with us, treat us like we was his people. That's why we do anythang fo these fellas, they save me from all them old fuckas out there in the street. Girls got only two choices out here; one, be a sacker, or git rolling . . . That's it, sell yo sweet ass pussy, or work with somebody rolling, somebody reeling in that big monay!*

Territorial Gangs

Territorial gangs are those which have taken position within a particular territory and claim ownership. This ownership is collectively the gang's property, territory, or person(s). The protection, maintenance, and identification of gang ownership is the bonding force for members. Territorial gangs have existed since the early days of industrialization in the U.S. In fact, territorial arguments, battles, and wars can be traced throughout the history of our species. This gang type is prevalent in certain regions of the U.S. In the west, Los Angeles gangs are notorious for their territorial wars over gang turf. Territory, in general, means physical land, ground, or neighborhood. This general ground may have no other significance than symbolic value. The land is worthless to the outside world. African American gangs in Detroit historically never protected turf intergenerationally when compared to their counterparts in Los Angeles. Southwest Detroit Hispanic gangs have generally been territorial. Territorial gangs can be involved in criminal activity. Yet, there is no rule that crime is essential to their definition.

There are territorial gangs that continue day in, day out, drifting in and out of small criminal activities. Some are not successful in their quest of moving into serious crime. Yet, they will not relinquish their neighborhood fiefdom. Their power is their control over who can and cannot enter into their "hood." There is no debate that gangs often protect their interests, and sometimes expand that interest. The classic movie, *West Side Story*, depicted the conflict between rival territorial gangs. On the screen, the Sharks and the Jets were locked in the honor of membership, protecting their neighborhoods from hated adversaries. This was the extent of the gang's activities. Yet, sometimes a gang may evolve from a territorial gang to a commercial gang, such as the real life Jets (The Westies), who actually became a deadly commercial gang thirty years later.[2]

The territorial gang, the FS-4s, are a combination compatriot/territorial gang which has roughly seventeen young women as members. They range from ages 13–19 and consider themselves primarily compatriots; yet, they acknowledge their reputations as warriors in the neighborhood and show pride in their ability to defend themselves. Nici, 19, and Rici, 15, tell of their rise from the FS-3 into the strong territorial gang of the FS-4. Nici speaks,

> We all came up in the same blocks, we just hung out and didn't take no shit from nobody. When we was the first ones in the FS-3s, we was strong, we weren't soft or crying 'bout nothing, we all was getting it down, we got hard, they made us hard, and now we the ones slaying everybody.

Rici adds,

> People know that the FS-4s will get it on, we is buck wild, we will bust 'em up, stomp a girl or a boy [laughing]. There are lots of old people trying to scare us, we take 'em all . . . one of our girls is in the Youth Home. She told us how they dog her in there, but they don't know how strong she is, my girl is hard, she ain't soft. We is hard as any fella, and if you come into our hood

and you don't want trouble you had better come and give us some 'spect, cuz we run the hood, it's us and the fellas in the CV-23, they run the serious shit, and we're their girls. If you mess with them or us it's gonna be serious illing, somebody is gonna get popped, smoked.

Commercial Gangs

The foundation of this gang type is material gain. Their sole purpose is to make revenue of some type. Their collective strength as a gang is not as important as the individual's role in the gang. Commercial gangs such as the James Gang and the Younger Brothers were famous. Our folklore is rich with tales of commercial gangs—ranging from Robin Hood and Jean Lafitte to John Dillenger and Bonnie and Clyde—who have practiced their own version of free enterprise and the "American Dream." Unlike corporate gangs, commercial gangs may forge relationships based on gain only. They do not want to monopolize the market, just share it.

Anybody that says girls ain't getting it on either don't know or is just full of shit. This city got so many girls getting paid it's crazy stupid. The fellas is making it real large and girls is making it too! Look here, we ain't saying nothing 'bout who it is, that ain't happening, not with us. But, all you got to do is look 'round you. How much does it cost to go out to the clubs and to drive the rides, dress that way? Monay is large and just because some sucka from out there don't know, don't mean shit to us. Everythang is 'bout monay . . . We all out here getting it on, making that monay, that's what it's all about and that's what everybody is doing . . . It's 'bout getting that monay. Some do, and some want to do it, but it's still 'bout the monay!

Corporate Gangs

This gang type is well organized for specific objectives and goals. The bond for this gang is not comradeship nor socialization of its members, but financial gain by criminal action. While the commerce of illegal means has existed in such models as Organized Crime Syndication via the Mafia, it has been the trade of narcotics that has found other minority groups being brought into the mainstream of crime. The 1920s had young ethnic gangs in cities like Chicago, St. Louis, and Detroit moving into major crime as the corporations of corruption. It is important to remember that the intent of corporate gangs is to rule the business they have selected. These gangs dominate whatever enterprise they have designated. The infrastructure, fashioned in much the same way as legal corporations, is developed for the sole purpose of capitalism. The syndication of organized crime is not a new concept. In the 1990s, illegal drugs as a commodity rival that of boot-leg liquor in the 1920s and 1930s.

The 1990s have introduced a byproduct of corporate gangs that has caused a great deal of confusion. In Detroit, the Federal indict-ments of YBI in 1982 signaled the beginning of the visible entity of "corporate" gangs being dismantled. The colorful lifestyle of the gang and others like Pony Down were easier to follow in the 1980s due to their monikers and other activities. The fact was clear, law enforce-ment had a strong handle on gangs such as YBI. Unlike Los Angeles, where gangs had traditional names and legacies, the Detroit gangs' activities were more subtle. The names of Pony Down, 20/20's, A-Team, Wrecking Crew, and YBI were well known on the streets. Gold chains and exotic foreign cars dotted the streets, it was easy to see who was in a corporate gang. The demise of YBI came at the expense of their own popularity. Corporate means that gangs have become formidable in their dedication to organized crime. The method or means in which these gangs go about their business is gauged by deadliness and capitalism. The distinction between corporate and commercial gangs is the intent. A corporate gang monopolizes what-ever commodity is providing revenue for the organization. They will not tolerate any other competitor.

Toya, 29, heads the small female crew of an integrated corporate gang. She has been in gangs since elementary school. Currently, she is dependent on a large, former male crew that supplies her. While she is reluctant to talk about detail of their operation, she has no problem about the significance of their independence.

If you had been around long as me, you could work the shit the same way. I know the players in this game, and I am chilling with the action . . . people, especially men underestimate what a woman can do. It's only a few real girls that understand who is in charge. We got to do what it takes to make it work. Girls got to get strong and leave all the soft ho's alone. These girls know what time it is, we hate seeing some ho begging for clothes or a car. Get your own, have a fella respecting you, be the one. I can't see myself or none of these girls out there selling blood or pussy. Do you know how much they give a crackhead for blood, selling yo'self is tight. Ho's have it bad, and when everybody done fucked you real good, they just leave you . . .

It's easy when you got your own paper, fellas love ho's jocking them for anything. Look, I am almost thirty, and when fellas get tired of you, and young cuties is coming down the way, well . . . it's over if you can't do for yo'self. We know this real fine babe, she is a crackhead, a skeezing, low-down ho. My sister said she was the "one" a few years back, today she is sucking dicks in the crackhouse, the girl is nothing. Think your girl here is gonna go out like that . . . no way, not this girl, a ho waiting to get fucked at the crackhouse. The life is my social security, and let it be known these girls ain't down with no freak shit at the crackhouse. That's where fellas will leave you, strung out on dick and drugs. They want to give you a little dick and lots of dope. Then, BOOM, you is ugly, stanking, fat or skinny, but you ain't fine, don't care just another crack ho in the world. Got my own monay got my own way, we is the ones and that is the only way to go.

The covert entrepreneur organization has resulted because of the success law enforcement had on their operations in the 1980s. The break-up of big corporate gangs forced these gangs into covert operations. While gangs do not call themselves by the old names of the previous decade, many members have formed new alliances with former contacts and members from the corporate days of YBI. The covert stage grew directly from the success of the illicit narcotics commerce. The smaller, and more discerning crew, or gang, operated in the guerrilla like fashion. Invisible to most, these gangs tend to work with only those who they can trust. They sell or interact with certain selected clients. In many ways they are like the hybrid of the corporate and commercial gang. Females have become part of this method of operating. This type of gang is almost exclusively held by those in the narcotic enterprise.

Social and Political Advocates

These groups are built around social and political ideals and philosophies. There is no criminal dealings or intent. Groups may advocate violence as a means of self-defense or to impress upon those who are not sympathetic with the group's focus. These groups have an ideology of social, political, or civic concern that they choose to promote. They may dress and appear the same as gangs in certain environments. Many times these groups share the same cultural idiosyncrasies as gangs—they simply use legal means to express their concerns or protests.

Included in this typology is the terminology explaining the historical role of organizations that are closely associated to gangs in this study, yet they do not consider themselves gangs within our definition. Social advocates, or compatriot gangs, are groups concerned with social events such as dances, concerts, and entertainment for themselves or others. Political advocates are groups that promote the political ideology of certain beliefs. The advocate network has existed since the beginning of the industrialized experience in Detroit for

African Americans. This is not to say that Hispanics and other ethnic groups did not participate in similar networks.

There are strong historical roots in Detroit regarding females and social-political participation. Detroit's black middle-class is one of the oldest and most affluent in the U.S. Prior to the destruction of the black enclave known as Black Bottom, black Detroit boasted prominent attorneys, doctors, dentists, business persons, and a strong, working class.[3] The black church was the cornerstone in the community. Black nationalism goes back to the early days of this nation. During the course of interviewing and surveying the city, it became clear that some females were involved with social issues ranging from protest of racism to the problems of public schools.

There are groups of young women in the city who express their religious beliefs, political philosophies, and economic agendas. Today, the young women in the city are emerging as independent voices in the social protest from grassroots organizations that assert themselves on many issues to having political aspirations. While the typical image of social activism is that of Malcolm X, Martin Luther King, Jr., or Jesse Jackson, black women, such as Fannie Lou Hamer, Ella Baker, Dorothy Cotten, Rosa Parks, Septima Clark, and Unita Blackwell, have been involved in the social and civil struggles. From the early 1930s, Detroit (like Harlem) had women organized and acting in the political arena on behalf of the African American community. The emergence of the Housewives League of Detroit, a socio-politico organization that spearheaded economic protest for black businesses and other relevant concerns grew to a membership of 10,000.[4]

Women have been community advocates for years. The NAACP and Urban League, along with strong church organizations, have provided leadership with women well entrenched in the ranks. Rosa Graves was a prominent black leader who had the ear of Eleanor Roosevelt. Women such as social worker Geraldine Bledsoe in the 1940s (wartime Detroit) were major leaders in community concerns. Irene Graves, a retired school teacher, has been one of the strongest promoters of the NAACP over the past four decades. Clementine Barefield and Vera Rucker, members of the community group Save Our Sons adnd Daughters (SOSAD) have championed the fight against violence on both a local and national level.

Olivia Safford, a mother who has worked in the public schools and the community, shared her view, "I have always felt that many of these young girls needed my support. Some of these girls are caught in problems that we have to deal with at this point, in our community. If we don't, then the jails, and welfare will, at a much greater cost later."

The evolution of these females laid the foundation for the years to come when the role or purpose of females in gangs changed in the mid-1960s. One of the best examples of this transformation can be found in the autobiography of former Black Panther, Elaine Brown, *A Taste of Power*.[5] In the colorful chapter, "Who Are These Girls," the author sheds light on the attitude of girls in the inner city coming to terms with not only racism, but sexism as well. Brown tells the story of sexism in the Panthers that reflects the confrontation of the 1960s and 1970s for women of color in social advocacy. Whether in the Black Muslims, Black Panthers, or other social groups, the Detroit experience explains the pain and fight that these women had to endure in being heard—or more to the point—in being respected.

Hispanic Gangs

While this study centers almost exclusively on African American girls and women, the culture of other ethnic groups is a strong determinant of female gang activities. According to Angie Reyes, a Hispanic social worker and community activist who lives and works in Southwest Detroit,

> We have not had a problem with females beyond the scavenger mode. The larger problem is with male gangs in Southwest Detroit. We are beginning to see female problems in gangs, but not in the same sense of the male gangs.

The cultural difference is important in understanding the variety of gang types. African American female gangs have similarities and differences. While male dominance is shared by both groups, African American females in Detroit have moved into more serious modes of independence and operation. There are strong cultural variables in Hispanic culture that still plays a major determinant in what is accepted and expected by both male gang members and the Hispanic community at large. The influence of the drug commerce has played a key role in black female emanicipation. There is a great need to differentiate between the two cultures. The Hispanic culture is unique and should be respected on its own. The initial inquiry found that while there is some gang activity by Hispanic females, it is not in the same vein that the African American females are participating.

Notes

1. Fredrick Thrasher, The Gang: A Study of 1,313 Gangs in Chicago, (University of Chicago Press, 1927).

2. T.J. English, *The Westies: The Irish Mob*, (New York: St. Martin's Paperbacks, 1990).

3. Joe Darden, June Thomas, and R. Thomas, *Race and Uneven Development*, (Philadelphia: Temple University Press, 1987).

4. Darlene Clark Hines, ed., *Black Women in America*, (Brooklyn, Carlson Publishers, 1993).

5. Elaine Brown, *A Taste of Power*, (New York: Pantheon Books, 1992).

2

Female Gangs: A Historical Perspective

Research regarding African American female involvement in gangs has been very limited. While there have been numerous works on their participation in the criminal justice system, there is nothing of great length or substance on the subject of their role as gang members. Historically, female involvement in gangs and other criminal activities has been defined as subordinate and secondary to their male counterparts. The illegal activity of females was limited to a set of preconceived crimes, with a distinct concept of what females did and did not do.

There are studies that theorize about the female participation in crime. *The Class Structure of Gender and Delinquency: Toward a Power-Control Theory of Common Delinquent Behavior* examined the social basis of gender-delinquency. This theory rejects the contention that gender is a factor in delinquency.[1] Anne Campbell underlined this notion as one of several myths in female gang research.[2] The power control theory implies that gender is of reduced importance as class is factored into juvenile delinquency.[3] However, some researchers argue that traditional models, such as the power control theory, are not sufficient for examining female crime or delinquency because they ignore gender as a major factor.[4]

In 1977, W.K. Brown did research on an autonomous, female African American gang in Philadelphia.[5] Research to date speaks of females participating in gang activity within one of two roles. One identifies them in sexual terms as the "girlfriend" of a male gang member. The other as "tomboys"—rough women or girls displaying unfeminine characteristics who are seldom accepted by other women.

Yet, in a recent study of African American gangs by John Hagedorn, researchers found the same traditional relationship between female and male gangs. The female gangs, with related names, existed only because of male gangs.[6] Professor C. Ron Huff, found several female gangs during a late 1980s study of Cleveland and Columbus, Ohio. These female gangs, however, were similar to what Hagedorn found from his work in Milwaukee. These females actually were similar to groupies whose identity was closely tied to that of their male gang allies.[7]

The 1927 classic study of Chicago gangs by researcher Frederick Thrasher underlined these gender roles in his text, *The Gang*.[8] The underlying assertion of Thrasher's study was that female gangs existed only in association with some type of male gang. In 1943, another researcher, W.F. Whyte, supported Thrasher's findings, suggesting that the formation of female adjuncts/gangs was based solely on the notion of females as sex objects.[9] It should be noted however that both Thrasher's and Whyte's findings were derived almost exclusively from the male gang members' points of view. This kind of approach has given the research community limited and often erroneous data.[10] The structure of female gangs aside from an auxiliary relationship with male gangs has rarely been observed directly. The defining characteristics of female African American gangs are often blurred when interwoven with those of the more visible male gangs.

In response, some female researchers have presented arguments for a more comprehensive perspective on female gang research. Anne Campbell presented a balanced study of female gang life in her 1984 work *The Girls in the Gang: A Report from New York City*. Campbell showed that there is a great need for future research in the area of female gang study. As far back as the 1800s, Campbell points out serious flaws in the historical perspective of female gang evolution and in the preconceived notions of females and females in gangs.[11]

According to Agnes Baro, a criminal justice professor at Grand Valley State University,

> *We know very little about African American female gangs or about female criminality in general . . . much of what we do know comes from a suspect knowledge base not just because it was developed with considerable male bias but also because so much of it lacks reference to the actual feelings, socioeconomic circumstances, or daily lives of the women who were studied. The task then is one of gleaning as much as we can from older and mainly ethnographic studies before we construct a new and, hopefully, more accurate perspective.*

Criminologist Georgette Bennett, in her book *Crime Warps,* addresses the issue of females and crime. In the chapter "Women Alone," Bennett focuses on what she calls the "feminization of poverty," and the fact is that women, in particular African American women, will head single-parent families in the 1990s at alarming rates.[12] Detroit is one of the cities in America that has an extremely high number of families that are not only headed by females but are also living below the poverty line. The national median income for all female-headed families is between one-third and one-half of the income for all other family arrangements. For African American and Hispanic female-headed families alone, the median income is $2,000 below the poverty line.[13] By 1980, more than 80 percent of the African American families in Detroit, with incomes below $4,000, were headed by single women.[14] The economic realities of Detroit are representative of other rustbelt cities in the Midwest.

Deborah Prothrow-Stith, in her provocative book, *Deadly Consequence,* explains how violence is plaguing the lives of women, men, and youth.[15] While her text addresses young adult violence, it also sheds light on the impact of violence, crime, and drugs. Females, children, and families are suffering severely from these social ills—and this is not unique to Detroit. Her book discusses how violence is intertwined with substance abuse, child abuse, and overall the role of brutality in destroying neighborhoods and communities.

The research thus far on female crime has had mixed results—from theories that support gender as a determinant—to theories that support race as a determinant.[16] One of the more relevant studies pertaining to the study of female gangs was conducted by researcher Darrell J. Steffensmejer. His 1983 work found that the structural and operational properties of crime groups affect the degree and existence of sex-segregated criminal organizations. Some females revealed a traditional, auxiliary relationship with male gangs.[17] One female gang supported recent research, showing females in autonomous gangs involved in organized criminal activities.[18] As our study discloses, a new attitude of female criminal independence is emerging. The male-female gang relationship is also being altered.

Female gang members and non-members are beginning to display attitudes that are diametrically opposed to earlier theories about female participation in gangs.[19] The social structure and economic plight of Detroit and other cities play a significant part in shaping female roles and attitudes presented in this book. As previously discussed, the infrastructure of the inner city has produced many single, female-headed families that are prime candidates for being dysfunctional, largely because of their poverty and isolation.[20] These families are part of a continuous chain of poverty that has produced fourth and fifth generation welfare families.[21]

L.T. Fishman, who studied an African American female gang in Chicago during the 1960s asserted that there were profound changes in the type of female gangs in Chicago and in the crimes that their members committed.[22] Fishman maintained that "black female gangs today have become more entrenched, more violent, and more and more oriented to 'male' crime." Like other criminologists, Fishman rejected the "women's liberation hypothesis" as a satisfactory explanation of the changes she has observed. Instead, Fishman referred to a "forced 'emancipation' that stems from economic crisis within the black community."

Our study of Detroit also includes serious consideration of the deterioration of an inner city's economy and the impact that such a situation can have on the opportunities, circumstances, and values of young African American women. Thus, although there is agreement that much of the earlier research on females and gangs has suffered from a male bias, it is also clear that some of it may have been relevant at the time it was written.

INNER CITY DETROIT

In 1920, Michigan had the largest membership of the Ku Klux Klan in the United States, by 1924, 32,000 were in Detroit.[23] Detroit's growing automobile industry and Henry Ford's five-dollar-a-day wage lured southern whites and blacks northward in droves; the climate was fertile for the Klan. In 1924, the mayor of Detroit was elected with the full support of the KKK.[24] There were countless acts of terrorism during the the twenties, including the burning of crosses and intimidation of blacks, Jews, and Catholics. The Klan as a gang was violent, oppressive, and omnipresent in Detroit. By the 1930s, the infamous Black Legion, another version of the Klan, was responsible for fifty murders in Michigan.[25] Subsequently, the KKK has been implicated in race riots and in fomenting problems between ethnic groups in the central city.[26] The role of women within the Klan structure has never really been researched.[27]

In June 1943, Detroit had the worst race riot in the history of this nation to date. The segregation of Detroit at that time kept blacks in certain areas almost exclusively, while Detroit's other ethnic groups, the Irish, Jews, Italians, Sicilians, and Hungarians, were spread throughout the city. White gangs roamed Detroit; black gangs, on the defensive, fought back. The Detroit Police were slow in restoring peace; and, worse, some blacks felt that the white police (known as confederates of the Klan) were more than accommodating to the white gangs during their offensive into the black neighborhoods.[28] The white gangs were from local neighborhoods and, in some cases, joined their white ethnic rivals to form confederations which attacked the black community at large.[29] Regarding gangs during the race riot, it is unclear if these gangs formed only for the riot; that is, a group of neighborhood residents not usually in any gang that collected themselves to protect the race or neighborhood from the enemy. The distinction between gang and mob is vague. The same is true for female involvement. Definitions hamper any study of clear-cut roles of females in Detroit gangs at this time. Detroit was extremely rough for black females. There is no suggestion that females did not participate in the violence of the black or white gangs during the 1943 Race Riot nor that they did.[30]

In the early 1940s there were African American gangs in the section of town known as Black Bottom, on the Eastside of Detroit. These gangs were formed in much the same way as those Thrasher reported on in Chicago and were divided into compatriot and delinquent gangs. There were no specific commercial or territorial gangs within the black experience at that time.

Segregation kept black gangs in the black ghetto, paralleling other ethnic gangs in the early 1940s.[31] Another factor in shaping the nature of gangs was the presence of a black police officer, Ben Turpin, a detective who ruled Black Bottom. Earl Van Dyke, a renowned Motown musician, grew up in Black Bottom. Van Dyke attested to the power that Turpin demanded and received from the black community.

Everyone in Black Bottom knew Mr. Ben was the man in charge. He simply didn't take nothing off the blacks or whites. You had your young gangs, but these young boys knew how far they could go, and with Mr. Ben that wasn't very far. Girls? Gangs? Naw, the neighborhoods had boys, and some were bad and some were just young boys growing up with their neighborhood buddies. But, you got to remember, the community kept girls under a watchful eye. Unless you were messing with some fast girls, girls had to follow a strict order from families, and the church was right there. Mr. Ben was real sensitive about young girls, he didn't tolerate no messing with young girls, he wouldn't let no pimp or no man ever beat any woman in his neighborhood. Now, don't think some fool wouldn't try it, maybe he was drunk or went crazy for a bit. But, you could rest assured that Mr. Ben would make him real sorry.

Ben Turpin was the law in Black Bottom. He loved kids, you hear all this talk about him being so tough, and he was tough. But this man would let kids come to his house and feed them, pay for their baseball team, his wife would cook a full Sunday dinner of turkey with oyster dressing, every Sunday he would have kids, poor kids eating at his house. There was two sides to Mr. Ben, you wanted to stay on his good side. He took the second floor of his home for young kids, put in a ping pong table. I know because I lived around the block from him, he lived on Jay street.

There was serious drug use by black youth in Black Bottom. Van Dyke spoke of the gangs in the neighborhood prior to the 1943 riot. The Feather Merchants and The Bar Twenties were two Black Bottom gangs.

I can remember young fellas in the neighborhood on heroin as young as 14 years old; when the fellas couldn't get horse [heroin] they would go to the local drug store and purchase paregoric and mix it with benzene and get high. If they couldn't get that they would get a fifth of gin and get high. You had your little gangs that never got in any trouble because they were just buddies, pals, kids that grew up together and did kid things, nothing to it. But, you didn't see no girls in those kinda street gangs, that was just fellas hanging out on Hasting in the early '40s.

Hastings street was a rough place for young kids to play. There were problems, however, youths involved in drugs and delinquency were a minority. For females, as Van Dyke said, it was taboo to be out at night or at spots such as the famed Flame nightclub. It was easy for a young girl to get a bad reputation. The only women in the night life were those dating men in entertainment or illicit professions and party-goers. The position for black females was clearly defined in the 1940s. This does not mean that there were no female gangs; it simply means they were not very important.

A former doorman at one of the nightclubs in downtown Detroit, talked about the women who were fancy-free, and who ran with the Purple Gang.[32]

These gals were having a ball, living high on the hog in those days. You didn't see no women folks driving no big Caddies unless they were married to some doctor, Duke Ellington or Walter Briggs. Women in those days didn't have a lot of choices as to what they could do. The gangster girlfriend could live real good. But they were ladies and they didn't have nothing to do with the crime stuff. Nope, they just spent the money in those days. Ladies were ladies and they didn't talk trashy like women today. Now, mind you, girls who gambled or drank with men, they talked like sailors, but those women were not like regular women, like your wife, or mother. The only women criminals I knew were the ones that worked for pimps, the ones that boosted, sold their bodies for money, or women who worked the flim flam. In the club you see everything, maybe they weren't gangsters but some of them gals were more than just some floozies. The problem is that in those days, you didn't think of women as being able to be tough enough to do business like those boys. The Purples were tough guys, you didn't think about women like that . . . tough women, tough maybe like Mae West, tough and sexy. But, tough like killing people, naw, it never crossed my mind.

Detroit was growing and ethnic diversity began to penetrate the suburbs. There were gangs in most neighborhoods in Detroit. The distinguishing factor was if the gang was criminal or compatriot. Compatriot gangs were not involved in criminal behavior. Good-natured pranks might result in scoldings from those in social control, but these gangs were not considered menaces to the community. Many in the neighborhood did not even regard these compatriot gangs as real gangs. The delinquent gang, however, was considered a problem. There were delinquent gangs in the general Detroit area by the 1980s. In fact, there were problems with black delinquent gangs in the 1940s before the riot of 1943.[33] Young white gangs were on the offensive during the race riot of 1943. Delinquent gangs made their presence felt in the late 1940s; in the 1950s there were Italian, Hispanic, Polish, and other ethnic gangs, but they stayed in their territorial neighborhoods. While there were problems with the various gangs, the police and other social controls dealt with them.

The historical role of female gangs in Detroit is identical to other cities in large urban centers. The first visible signs of females in gangs could be seen in the 1950s. Women and girls were involved from the very outset in the early days of boomtown Detroit. In the 1950s, the infamous African American male gang, the Shakers, had the traditional auxiliary female gang found by Campbell in her research on early New York. Without The Shakers, there were no Shakerettes. Francine Norton, a former Shakerette, shared her views:

Girls were the sister gang. Without the boys there wasn't anything. Our lives were involved with these bad boys. We got reputations in the neighborhood 'cause we were fast girls. Lots of girls were so scared to get a reputation in those days because it was so easy to become a bad girl or boy. If you kept the wrong company, you were labeled real quick. The fast girls would skip school, smoke cigarettes, curse like the Shakers and have sex. The good girls didn't skip school, curse, and they went to Cass [High School] if they could. Me and most of the girls in the gang lived in the projects. If you were with the boys, bad boys, it was just the thing to do on my street. Being with the Shakers was big time. Today, the Shakers would probably be into selling dope like everybody else. My sons are in the streets and it's really hard. I have three girls and the only thing they talk 'bout is the boys who got money. In my day it was pimps, but today it's these dope boys who get all the attention.

The Shakers had a fierce reputation for fighting. Their reputation, like that of other Eastside gangs, was city-wide. Linda J. Folmar, a public relations executive, spoke of her memories growing up as a young woman on the Westside of Detroit in the 1950s.

Everybody knew about the Shakers, and their sister gang, the Shakerettes. As a student at Central High, I can recall how they had been known to invade the school grounds to fight . . . football games were a favorite of theirs to show up at and beat up someone. Even the tough girls at our school didn't want any part of the Shakerettes. This gang was definitely from the lower class of the city. The middle class kids had their own gangs, they called them clubs, or organizations. But the reality was we had the Gamma Petites, and lower class kids had the Shakers. We didn't fight, because we had nothing to fight about. Middle class and upper middle class kids were happy with the things they had in Detroit. Our gangs were giving dances, and entering into debutante balls. Our parents were teaching us about society, going to college and those sorta things.

The class distinction that Folmar mentions is important. Women in gangs would fight over boys, or to support their brother gang. The activities of female gangs in Detroit in the 1950s were not much different than gang activities in earlier days and other cities. Laura Thaks, 48, and Mary Thaks, 44, former members of the Shakerettes, addressed their gang days.

Well, it's really lots different today, you can't compare our gangs with these young jits today. In the Shakerettes we knew the gang boys as brothers, boyfriends, cousins, friends, before the gang. Were we sexually active? Yeah, some girls were with the boys in the gangs, others had boyfriends outside of the Shakers. See, girls in a way belong to the gang, we all hung out together or knew everybody from your street. The gang, as far as the girls, was our own thing under the boys. We carry things for 'em . . . things like cigarettes, weapons, wine, or when they stole something and we had to walk or go a long way and they think they might get caught, we would carry or hide their things. We just help anyway the boys would need us.

Now, sometimes girls would fight each other over boyfriends, that happened a lot. Me and Mary would always stick together, no matter what. My first child was by one of the Shakers, he never gave me shit for the little crumb snatcher. But, back then I was in love, so I got pregnant by this bum. Lots of us got messed over by the Shakers, lots of fights with our gang were over Shakers. When the boys would fight, we usually go for the hell of it, we find somebody to scare, we didn't care if they was a boy or girl. I couldn't fight a lot 'cause I was expecting my first child. Once you had a baby your whole life changed in a way. My mother was mad as hell at me for getting pregnant. But girls in the gang was my real family. Me and Mary would just love to skip school and hang out.

Do I think we were paid much attention as a gang? Not like the boys, we would do all kinds of shit and the boys would get all the blame. Shakerettes could beat lots of boys' ass, but all you really ever heard about was the Shakers. The police didn't bother with us like they did the boys. When they thought the Shakers did something you'd know 'cause they come looking for us first. Now, we would be laughing 'bout how dumb the cops would be asking us shit 'bout the boys, like we would tell 'em. We be doing lots of the same shit as the Shakers, nobody even thought we could do the same shit, [laughing, they both agreed that they at least tried to do the same things that the Shakers did, maybe after no one was around] . . . but, now, the boys in the Shakers would get real mad if they saw us getting all the attention. We were the same as the Shakers, we got drunk, smoked, had sex, and would kick your ass if needed and that's the truth . . . but nobody paid us no mind. Girls would sometimes kick the shit out of another girl and maybe somebody like their momma or something would call the police. That would get taken care of, but it wasn't the same as the Shakers. But the main reason I joined the Shakerettes was 'cause my cousins, it was five boys, they was all Shakers. That's who we were with all the time, they was our boys and we was their girls. That's the way most of the gangs I remember used to be, if you live in the neighborhood, went to school and grew up with those people, then you usually stay with 'em. If you jumped one, you had better get ready, 'cause we all was gonna jump you . . . we stuck together, no matter what.

Dennis Payne, a criminal justice professor at Michigan State University, remembers his Detroit childhood in a neighborhood where youth gangs prevailed. Females in the area were considered the property of the territorial gang. "The guys in those neighborhoods didn't want outsiders dating or socializing with their girls . . . the girls were their property, even if they didn't personally have any relationship with the young women."

The Shakers were in the scavenger gang mode; simply a group of young toughs on the Eastside of Detroit. The role and name of their female counterpart gang is similar to those seen in other urban environments. Anne Campbell points out that female gangs in early New York carried names complimentary to the names of their male counterpart gang.[34]

If a male gang had street notoriety, more than likely there would be a sister gang. One consequence of this was the labeling of young females within the black community. Traditionally there were the good girls and the bad girls. These labels were considered serious; and because of segregation, the black middle class had emerged as the powerful class within the black community. The black church was the cornerstone of socialization for black residents. Mary Smith, 80, moved to Detroit at the age of ten. Ms. Smith spoke of how black females were labeled in the 1950s.

Just a different time, folks knew everyone, and everyone went to church. If you didn't go to church on Sunday, well you were labeled as a worthless kinda person. The church was where all the children went to have fun, besides learning 'bout God. There were always picnics, social programs, the choir, you just stayed in church all day . . . girls that didn't go to church, I don't remember that many. The same was true for boys, children that didn't go to church, I don't remember seeing that many, if any, really. But if you talking 'bout bad girls, fast girls and boys, well, er, if you got known as a bad boy or, it was worse for girls, it meant you was not with the other folks, regular folks. Bad girls were treated different from other girls, folks. There were certain things bad girls would wear, say, or just do and that would make them different, and that was bad. Now don't get me wrong, childrens would be with fast kids, I would when I was a child, and my children would also. But, you better not get caught, specially on Sunday you stayed away from those folks 'cause you knew they was trouble. Especially for girls, if you got pregnant back then it was the end. Girls just went away. If you got yourself pregnant back then you had better get married. If you didn't get married you were known as that fast hussy; yes, it was different in those days. I can't say I remember no girl gangs in our neighborhood, but you sure knew the bad girls and boys.

Good paying jobs in the auto industry provided a certain economic power base for the segregated black community. The middle class that emerged was a direct result of black professionals providing services to blacks who had money that segregated white Detroit would not accept. It was this middle class that shaped its social image into a proud, bourgeois, elitist, caste system. Ted Smith, a lifelong resident, spoke of the elitism.

Without any question there was a caste system. Blacks were very aware of their own presence and worth. Doctors, lawyers, store owners, some were elitist thinking, yet they were connected to the community. A strong community sense of order regulated the members in those days. It was how one went about life in those days. Whites would frequent our night spots with no problems. The upper class blacks, the elites, would frequent the same clubs also. During the day, people were very conscious of where they went and who they did it with . . . without question there were night life people who didn't see the world in the daytime. There was mutual understanding between people in the fast lane and everyday citizens. The church people controlled the community in the day. The sporting life, the fast lane, controlled the night life in the city. Somewhere in between good girls knew where not to be on Friday and Saturday nights. Young men in the fast lane, young gangs of toughs had their female companions. Now, if they were calling themselves anything particular, like a gang or name, I don't know. But, you knew the girls that hung out with the guys in the fast life. They definitely were not church girls. Any young, or old, woman, for that matter, that smoked, drank, or cursed was considered and labeled as being something of a Jezebel. . . .

Detroit was growing fast in the 1940s and 1950s. Blacks fresh from the south were greeted with inferior and limited housing. Everyone coming north was after a good job. The fact that a person could get a solid job that paid well and did not require any skills or education made school a secondary concern for many ethnic families. The lure of a good paying job in the auto industry was tremendous for many who had never had this opportunity.[35] It encouraged youngsters of all ethnic backgrounds to abandon their education and enter the plants. There were many high school dropouts. Urban cities, the centers of industrialization, shifted their skills to materiel production, and during World War II, Detroit had become the "Arsenal for Democracy." The void left by men leaving the factories to fight the war was filled by women. The image of women in the factory was promoted with popular songs such as "Rosie the Riveter." Women became the backbone of the wartime industry, and Detroit played a significant role in the wartime economy. However, opportunities for African American women were different.

According to Dominic J. Capeci in *Layered Violence*, black women were not part of that "Rosie the Riveter" force.

Actually, black women fared the worst of all workers throughout the war. They remained the last hired, both because white workers insisted on segregated facilities for supposedly unsanitary, diseased females and because federal officials gave their equal treatment a very low priority. They also suffered from the emphasis that both black and white societies placed on male employment, and society's habitual relegating of black females to unskilled, non-industrial jobs . . . . There were few black Rosie the Riveters, however. Black women made only token inroads, mostly as matrons, sweepers, and stock handlers, though a minuscule number did set precedent by advancing to production lines. In January 1943, they comprised merely 1.5 percent or 990 of 66,000 females working in the fifty leading war plants, automobile or otherwise; in fact, black females found work in only nineteen of these factories. By spring, small gains occurred in several area industries, but one month after the riot, 28,000 black women constituted the "largest neglected source of labor" in metropolitan Detroit. Their long history as breadwinners and contributors to the economic survival of Afro-America notwithstanding, black women in the Motor City encountered unyielding race, gender, and class discrimination amid the wartime boom.[36]

In the 1950s female gangs were auxiliaries to male gangs. There were basically two distinct types, scavengers and territorial. Commercial female gangs seemingly did not exist, or if they did, they did nothing significant. The role of auxiliary female gangs seems to follow the traditional history of female gangs. The females were the property of their male "brother" gang; some were rough and physically capable of fighting or willing to fight with other girl gangs or for the "brother" gang and were sexually active with the "brother" gang or with someone. Most of the female gangs during this time were criminally active. Their activity may have been simple petty crime. Female gangs at this time never received equal billing. Compatriot type gangs during this time period were not criminal, and had strong support from the community in some manner.

Black females had few choices outside of the middle class. Gangs represented acceptance in something that was theirs. Meg Stoveall, social worker in the 1950s, explained the plight of girls who were victimized in her opinion,

Poor girls were getting used by boys in the gangs, they weren't bad girls. They needed someone to help them with life. Their mothers were young and some didn't know what was going on in their own lives. I spent lots of time with young girls trying to explain the difference between love and sex. They were no different from the black girls from middle class homes or out in the suburbs. Their little gangs were just girlfriends getting together like school kids would do. Sure, they did things, they fought and got in trouble. But they were always remembered for one thing, getting pregnant, that is what everyone dwelled on, no one ever wanted to look at the reasons of why they got pregnant. Society says they're bad. Forget them, poor and bad, and let's forget them. Their mistake was not knowing, and trusting some older boy with lines like some smooth movie star. Sure, they got into trouble, but it takes two to tangle. Nobody talked about what the boys did and didn't do. Why did no one talk about boys having sex? Blame the girls all the time. Gang boys were not the same as boys from good homes who knew what a shotgun marriage was . . . you had bad boys, you had bad girls, although I always said there are no bad girls.

Delinquent female and male gangs were caught within the distinct class lines within the black community. Lower class youth were left out of the social networks of the organizations dedicated to self-improvement. Even when recruitment efforts were made in the lower class there would be friction that further alienated the lower class from the middle class.

Ronald Roosevelt Lockett, director of Wayne County Youth Services, was socially active in the movement for African American justice during the 1960s. Lockett began his activism in high school on the Eastside of Detroit. Speaking of the role of females, he pinpointed a sense of how the street culture had a certain chemistry with social consciousness.

In our quest to name our school [Eastern High] after Dr. King, it was in the conventional sense a team effort; that team included bright students, both male and female. Sisters pushed for strong brothers in the street culture to support our school spirit from the streets and school. Everybody wanted the change. When I say everybody I mean students . . . even the brothers who didn't necessarily support higher education in the same vein as the college-bound students. My sense of black females and their community involvement became acutely sensitive and more aware because of the kindred spirit forged during that time. The period in which we took up our cause in high school was followed by our protest at Wayne State. There was a great deal of community interest and women played various roles. There were a number of organizations such as the All African People's Union, the Black Panthers, the Shrine, and that doesn't include the traditional organizations like the Urban League, and the NAACP grassroots programs. Females were in all these experiences and the other factors like women's liberation, escalating drugs in our community, Viet Nam, shaped the black community into a constant conduit of action. It certainly would be a mistake to look at females in lieu of those changes and gangs and not look at those facts. When you look at what is taking place today, it's easy to trace where things started over the years.

The 1960s represent a period during which Detroit cultivated Black Power; this dimension was important in relation to other movements in the black community. Gangs were one of several avenues through which people could participate. Political movements such as the Black

Panther party and the All African People's Union, along with the Nation of Islam, provided different levels of activism. In July 1967, the worst civil riot in the history of the United States broke out at the intersection of Clairmont and 12th Street (Rosa Parks).

Escalating black consciousness in Detroit was propelled forward by the 1967 riot. White flight from the city now proceeded at a record pace. Political networks formed and expanded throughout the city. Some females began to cultivate a new way of thinking and joined various organizations which reflected these new views. The common bond was black consciousness; the *lumpenproletariat* were lured by different black political-labor groups. Gangs who had been empowered through criminality were now being challenged to work for the community. This was a time of change. Many of the gangs were in a state of confusion. Gangs were challenged by the rising social and political thinking of the Black Power movement. Black females now had choices beyond the limited ones of the early 1960s. The church was being challenged by the Shrine of the Black Madonna, and Christianity was under siege from the Nation of Islam and their fiery spokesperson, Malcolm X. Female gangs were changing along with male gangs during the 1960s. Women were suddenly thrust into the arena of black consciousness.

Ronald Hunt, a community activist and lifelong native of Detroit, who is today a human services administrator, belonged in the late 1960s to the All African People's Union, a community organization on the Eastside of Detroit. Hunt spoke of the change within the community and in the streets, particularly with troubled youth who were in neighborhood gangs.

There were lots of changes during that period for everyone in the neighborhoods. Some kids were exposed to political issues and became part of the movement and others continued in the criminal activities. The big change was that they had choices they hadn't seen before. I don't think gangs disappeared, it was that they were no longer the only thing to do. The sense of brotherhood and a unified community was spreading and that made doing the old things not as popular. Getting drunk, or high, was challenged and some kids met the challenge. In the late '60s, our streets were losing lots of young boys to Viet Nam, so girls were active in the movement in different roles. Remember that some of the high school students had already taken political stands in the schools. There was an attitude about treating our women as our sisters. It was different for the young boys and girls. Girls were taking leadership roles and demanding to be heard within our organization. Sisters were growing Afros, identifying with positive things like tutoring younger kids, helping set up food co-ops and protesting against racism. There were lots of young and older sisters and brothers in the grassroots movement against the injustice of police brutality, sisters were out there against things like STRESS.[37] People were participating in helping the community. Times were changing in both good and bad ways for neighborhood gangs. The good was that young people were becoming responsible in the community. The bad was that the drug problem was taking off. We started experiencing junkies, heroin, that was the ugly change, the heroin junkies started to escalate in our neighborhoods. The dope thing was hard to take, people, men and women you knew, suddenly became strung out and some of the gang kids fell into that slavery. Then the problems just went crazy, stealing from the neighborhoods, people stealing to keep up their habits. After the riot in 1967, heroin was the new enemy.

Eleanor, 45, mother of five, talks about her life in a gang:

I got pregnant when I was thirteen. This counselor at school, a Mrs. Jenkins, tried to steer me right, but it was useless. She told me that William was too old and experienced for me. But I wouldn't listen and just said she was stupid. Me, my sisters and cousins, were the Jackie Girls. We called ourselves that after Jackie Wilson . . . he was so fine, the man was like nothing else, we loved us some Jackie Wilson. Mrs. Jenkins tried to tell me that Willie had babies all over town, but I was in love My momma couldn't do shit with me. Now, my grandmother was strict, but I just used my momma to overrule her. If my grand had been in charge, well, things would have been different. I really thought that William was in love with me, we was gonna get married, right, married. That fool left me the day I told him that I was pregnant. I cried and my girls cried, I listen to "Lonely Tear Drops" by Jackie and would cry more.

It was ten of us in the Jackies, we would kick girls ass who lived across Linwood, or who looked cute and acted like they were scared or acted better than us. My brothers and his boys were in their gang and they would just hang out on Linwood all day. The boys would be beating up other boys from 'round Northwestern or trying to screw all the girls from the other schools. My mother was taking care my little boy, until she got mad or if she had a new boyfriend. My dad was in prison until I was sixteen, we get along real good, and that makes my momma mad 'cause she hates him. When I turned seventeen I had stopped going to school. We were still the Jackies and lots of kids from school and the neighborhood knew 'bout us, we had our reputation, I liked that.

Today, it's different with these young kids. My girls is tough, and my boys are gangsters. I don't like it, but what can you do? My daughters would never take the shit I took off men. These girls are more ready to get what they want. You ask if I am proud of my girls and their posse? Yeah, it's nice to see 'em so sure of themselves, and it's nice to know that they ain't gonna make the same mistakes. They don't smoke, drink, and they ain't on no drugs. My girls don't want no welfare, they just like the boy gangsters.

They're ready to make it on their own terms, they know what welfare and white people got waiting for them . . . Nothing but shit and grief, that's all.

Black females had a choice of three lifestyles. They could follow the path of the good girl which consisted of school, church, and the American Dream in the traditional sense. The bad girl's path was the antithesis of the traditional girl. The Shakerettes were a symbol of the time, bad girls with bad boys, with the ending certain to be bad; this was the life of living young on the wrong side of the street. Or as a third alternative, there was street life; prostitution, gambling, drinking, and whatever else the fast life offered in the 1960s.

The mid-1960s brought change. The Shakerettes grew up and got married; the Shakers, as a group, disappeared—some went into the military, some were incarcerated, and some found employment in the auto industry. The Black Power movement brought the street culture into Black Nationalism. The social structure of the black community was ripe for change. Organizations such as the Cotillion Club, the National Urban League, the National Association for the Advancement of Colored People, the black Greek organizations, the Masons, the Elks, and strong black political action caucuses in unions like the United Auto Workers contributed, along with the black Christian church, in creating social networks for youth. There were numerous activities in the city in which everyone, including youth, could participate.

In many neighborhoods, street gangs became part of the recruits educated in the new order of thinking. Middle class youths were targeted by the various social controls in the community. The lower class youth population had the YMCA, Boys Club, Westside Cubs, Brewster Center, and other recreational centers. Yet, there was no attempt to bring lower class youth into the mainstream cultural events like the Cotillion Ball or the Nellie Watts concerts.

In June 1971 however, the city had its first gangland-style mass killing on the Westside. The Hazelwood Massacre (which was not gang-related) marked the beginning of an era of murder and drug-related crime.[38] Seven people were murdered over heroin business. This event also marked the resurgence of territorial gangs. Eastside gangs, like the Errol Flynns and the BKs, became infamous in the early 1970s. The Errol Flynns, who at times called themselves the Earl Flynns, originated on the east side of the city, but their power and reputation reached far beyond. The BKs, also known as the Black Killers, were no less famous, but their territory was exclusively the Eastside and membership never matched that of the Flynns.

The presence of hard drugs was being felt for the first time in many Detroit lives. Roy James, 46, an auto worker on the Westside, recalls the changing times.

My brother was involved in the streets, belonged to a small gang called the Richton Boys, they did everything. Don't know where they are today. My brother died from drinking and living in the streets in 1976. They wasn't nothing like those Shakers when we lived over on the Eastside. These here boys would get high and do all kinds of crazy things back then. I remember when they was, in 1966, they all was chewing gum with Robitussin cough syrup on a stick of gum. They sniff glue, drink Wild Irish Rose with lemon juice or (laughing) they would get Thunderbird wine and mix it with Kool Aid. I went to the army, got lucky, didn't go to Nam. I came back in 1970, my brother and all his friends were strung out on heroin. All I can say is that when I left, dope was no problem in Detroit and when I got back we had junkies everywhere. Things just got bad when the riot hit, when I got back the plants weren't in good shape and that blew my mind. When my brother wasn't getting high on the smack, he was drinking hisself to death. Girls in gangs? Don't remember nothing but lots of girls on junk, junkies everywhere on the Eastside. It seemed like the Westside didn't have the same type of problems before I went into the army. All of the rough customers lived on the Eastside. Today, it's everywhere, the Westside is messed up and so is the east, south, north, wherever you go, it's the same.

The Eastside gangs were ruling the underground. Illegal commerce involving gambling, property crimes, car theft and other criminal activities included gang members both individually and collectively. The BKs and Flynns were well known, and in the early 1970s they teetered between commercial and territorial status. These gangs were similar in several ways. Like traditional African American gangs in the city, they began along friendship and family lines in their respective neighborhoods. In both of these gangs there were brothers and cousins; their leadership varied. They did not have the capital to invest in narcotics, so drug-selling was minor. Willie Jackson, 33, a former Flynn and chief enforcer for the gang, addressed their status in the 1970s:

There was no gang as big or bad as us. The BKs weren't near us . . . we were the kings of the 'hood, the Flynns, the first ones was in charge. Later, you started getting little Flynns, younger guys from our streets would call themselves Flynns, I mean they was, but they wasn't the ones calling the shots, we was . . . you had the Dirty Flynns, and lots of niggahs from other streets who was down with us, but they still wasn't the Flynns for real to me.

Girls, girls, what are you saying, girls was in the Flynns? (laughing) Well, now, that's, ummm, ummm, that's a hard one . . . we had friends, you know, girls who were friends or were sisters, cousins, or girls you knew all your life. Girls from the 'hood, girls that hung out with us. Some say they was, they was the Flynn Girls, me, I didn't pay that kinda shit much attention. If you went to war with us, girls or guys, it would be better if your ass was on the Flynns' side.

Mike Jones, 28, a member of the Black Gloves, discussed the farm team under the Flynns and the Flynn Girls.

We was the younger fellas on the block or from the 'hood, and the Flynns was the shit. I remember being proud of the Flynns, we called ourselves the Black Gloves, and we all knew that the little fellas had the blessings of the Flynns. The Black Gloves was some fighting fools (laughing) and we knew that the Flynns had our backs. We would look out for the big fellas, the Flynns, tell 'em if there was anything that wasn't straight or if they was getting watched by the hook. We was in elementary and middle school, we learned how to fight from the Flynns. The Flynn Girls were in there, they were some of the sisters, cousins or friends of the Flynns. The girls were serious and they would beat you down. They was always beating other girls down, they could get crazy just like the fellas. Trust me, the girls would make you sorry real quick if you thought they was some little soft hos.

During this period, these gangs were delinquent, scavenger, commercial, and territorial. The emergence of females at this time demonstrates the change in attitude by males and females toward female abilities in relation to gangs. This period is also a time when compatriot gangs existed, but were, as usual, not controversial. The evolution of the Flynns during this time is comparable to what is described in Thrasher's study.

It does not become a gang . . . until it begins to excite disapproval and opposition. It discovers a rival or an enemy in the gang in the next block; its baseball or football team is pitted against some other team; parents or neighbors look upon it with suspicion or hostility . . . the storekeeper or the cops begin to give it shags [chase it]; or some representative of the community steps in and tries to break it up. This is the real beginning of the gang, for now it starts to draw itself more closely together. It becomes a conflict group.[39]

The Flynn Girls testify to the existence of female gangs in the 1970s. Their relationship to the Flynns is not the simple female extension of a male gang witnessed in earlier decades. Yes, they did exist because of

and were born of the infamous Errol Flynns, but their actual incuba-
tion had glimmers of autonomy. Female gangs were, in fact, in the
scavenger-territorial-commercial stages in the 1970s. The historical
quandary for female gangs in Detroit was their invisible status; there
was no focus on them and they were discernible to only a few.

Teresa Boner, 26, is a former Flynn Girl. While reluctant to talk
about her specific involvement, she agreed to explain their general
presence as a gang in the city.

*Yes, there were Flynn Girls, we were gangsters [smiling]. People just don't
respect girls, they think we're playthings. Me and the girls would be into lots
of things, most of us was kicking it with somebody in the Flynns or we grew
up with the fellas in the Flynns. It was the same with the girls in the BK-
ettes, they was all from their 'hood, and we would beef with them. Today,
the girls is wilder in a way. Now I knew girls in our crew that were just as
wild as today, just as cold and ready to throw. But, most of us was down [in
a gang] before the Flynns even was down. I used to belong to this gang
called the Mack-Babies, we were just 'round thirteen, we hung out, did
things girls wasn't suppose to be doing, [laughing] sometimes we just jump
on somebody, just to see them run, and then we start something else and
get the fellas in the 'hood in the shit. We was known, and even today, people see me that went to school with me and they look, 'cause they remember, specially people from school or the 'hood. They know we was the girls
. . . yeah, the girls was in there . . . . Now, today I am straight, got bigger
things to do, like my boy here, Mike, he knows lots of fellas and girls knew I
was a star, me and the girls was doing it, we didn't need the boys like everybody always think.*

Field Investigator Clyde Sherrod has lived on the Eastside all his life.
Sherrod, 35, spoke of the changing attitudes of women in the 1970s
as typified by the Flynn Girls and the BK-ettes.

*The girls have been overlooked to a large degree within the historical
overview. The girls in the big gangs were certainly more than groupies, they
were the first wave of what we're looking at in 1991. My memory of the
Flynn Girls going up to Southeastern High School and robbing some females
in the lavatory is very vivid because it hit the street so fast and spread like
wildfire. You should remember, this act was separate from the male gang.
This had nothing to do with the Flynns, this was their own independent act,
no males involved in any manner. It was a big statement at that time.
Those girls were raw, hardcore, just like their male cohorts. We have interviewed several young women who were Flynn Girls. Some have disavowed
any membership as of now; a few will talk in the general sense. Some are
the parents of the new wave girl gangs and boy gangs. It's scary in relation*

to what is taking place out in the street; the girls are just as capable and deadly, regardless of age.

The 1970s were pivotal to female gang development; during this decade, females began participating in different types of gangs. Organizational structures differed, but generally they were still in the embryonic stages. Other groups, networks, and compatriot gangs were in existence; but, only the criminal and delinquent gangs attracted public attention. Women were not considered in conjunction with gangs and gang activities, simply because of gender prejudices, although there has been some limited research on Hispanic female gangs.[40] However, in Detroit in the 1970s black female gangs did exist. In some ways, they were typical of traditional female gangs of the time; yet, they were beginning to set their own tone, establish their own goals, and make their own decisions. While our understanding of their organization and structure is still ambiguous, they did exist.

The 1980s marked a new era in the evolution of African American gangs in Detroit. The rise of the notorious corporate gang Young Boys, Inc. initiated the merger of juveniles and an illegal narcotics trade. *The* corporate gang of the 1920s and 1930s in Detroit was comprised of young Jewish gangsters and was known as the Purple Gang. Some sixty years later, the corporate criminal enterprise evolved and black gangsters are firmly in control in Detroit. As illegal alcohol empowered the Purples, so heroin empowered YBI. The 1980s also marked a change in thinking about juveniles and serious crime. Prior to YBI, the Eastside gangs such as the BKs and Errol Flynns worked commercial operations at times, but rarely if ever on any large scale that would have included the entire gang membership. The YBI model was the first of its kind. This highly organized youth gang grossed $7.5 million weekly and $400 million annually in 1982, according to two federal indictments.[41] Following on the coatails of YBI's success, in 1988 the Chamber Brothers controlled half of the crack houses in Detroit. They ran their organization like a Fortune 500 company, grossing up to $3 million a day.[42]

Some females were impressed, as were some males, with the fruits of these successful corporate gangs. The introduction of illegal dope and its acceptance as a valuable commodity, along with organized gangs beginning a commercial practice, launched a new day for Detroit. Although females were invisible, as usual, this era was crucial in the evolving development of a female persona. Black women, while not identifying in the same way with white feminist "women's liberation," had grown up in the 1970s with the kind of strong black women symbolized by activist Angela Davis. In the 1980s, black females played a different role in gangs than in the 1970s. The 1980s brought about radical change for females in Detroit.

Nothwithstanding the dramatic successes of corporate gangs, scavenger gangs continued in the 1980s with no distinct change in structure or motivation. The status of females in gangs was still territorial and still attached to male gangs and hence, not detected by authorities in the criminal justice system. What was unprecedented was the involvement and integration of females into corporate gangs, beginning with the YBI. Initially, the roles of females in corporate gangs appeared to be the traditional ones of girlfriend, friend, or relative of the gang. There was no media coverage nor did anything suggest to the police, the school or other community officials that something out of the ordinary was occurring regarding girls and their relationships to gangs.

While females were not actually members of corporate gangs, they carried weapons, participated in transporting drugs, and learned the chemistry necessary to process dope. They were educated through affiliation with corporate drug gangs. There were field observations that females were in scavenger gangs and territorial gangs, both integrated and all-female. Yet, none of these gangs proved unusual or outstanding. The turning point for traditional black female gangs came with the creation of YBI. Corporate gangs are willing to focus on members and the merits of their work. This may not be women's liberation in the fullest sense, but it is pivotal. The mixture of gender, youth, and high technology introduced a different corporate methodology than the Purple Gang employed six decades previously. Females did not become high profile members of YBI, in reality they were more like secondary employees or freelancers. However, they became students of the criminal corporate enterprise of selling and distributing illegal narcotics in Detroit.

Melinda Jay, 24, is currently working in a legitimate job. She agreed to explain her role while working for a corporate gang in the 1980s and into the 1990s. She is concerned that her identity be kept entirely secret.

I grew up on the Westside near the X neighborhood. The fellas in X were my neighbors and my brother's friends. I was impressed with the fellas when I was as young as ten years old. Me and my girls were always trying to be around Tyrone and his boys. You didn't really know what they did, but it looked large, it looked like they were stars, they were stars in our 'hood. All I remember is that my brothers were scared and wanted to be like them.

Tyrone always had money and he acted like he was important. We weren't a gang, we were just the girls in the neighborhood. It's hard to explain what you feel when you see the fellas driving their new cars, wearing the booming clothes. And the paper is wacked, it's what moves ya, it's the paper, the money, that makes little kids, yo momma, yo older sisters and brothers look at 'em, the paper says it all. They were large, and you just want to be down with 'em. Tyrone is the one that got my brother into working for 'em. My brother worked just long enough to get a little paper and he joined the army to get away when his friend got wacked, he wasn't made for their thang, he was kinda soft. See, people don't know it's hard being down in that dope thang. I always liked school, me and my girls, it's four of us, we all kinda liked school. I was too young to be going with Will, and my father was drugged about me running around, but he didn't know what to say to Will, he was really scared in a way. My mother was upset at my brother until he went into the army, he lives out west now, got a nice job and says he ain't coming back, it's too wacked, he says. My sister is in one of those college sororities and she won't even say hello to a dope boy. Tyrone and his friends used to laugh at her friends when they come over in their little college clothes. That was in 1983; Tyrone got killed in '87, and lots of the fellas are still in the game, but it's their own little crews.

I was working for X in 1982, the year they got popped and I was only 'bout fifteen, I didn't know shit, I just counted the bundles of dope. There are girls like me that got their own crew separate from X, or whatever the big crew is called. We worked for the crew, we weren't a part of their gang, we just worked for them, provided them with our services. Me and the girls would make 'bout $500 a week doing little counting things. But all of us was seeing some dope boy and your allowance could be as much as you could spend if you was with the money crew, or one of the fellas that was rolling hard. It was twelve girls and everybody at school called us the X Girls, we were their girls and we called ourselves the Getting Paid Bitches. There were some real hard girls who worked in the crews after the X bust. These babes were real hard and they worked just like the fellas. That's what's happening today, girls is in their own crews or they work with a big crew. I knew how to run dope thangs, 'cause my man taught me, and I had been 'round the shit since I was little. I thought it was straight until 1990 and Pappie and three fellas I knew got slayed and that made me think how close I was playing it. Then my girls got beat down like dogs by some other fellas 'cause they thought that they had the paper. They was kidnapping the girls who were with certain fellas or crews, they was getting it on. Then I came to this house right after some fellas had taken this fella out, blood was everywhere. I got sick, something scared me to get out, I mean I knew this fella, it was real fucked up, this was too close. I went back to school and started community college. This counselor helped me get my head right, and my aunt got me this real good job, it pay $11.28 a hour and has bene-fits. I got a little cute fella, he's in community college like me, and he ain't near that rolling madness. I know this female crew right now, they getting it *on, they is out there. These girls is making paper and living large. They use to be down in the Eastside, they was with some of the people in the Chambers Brothers. The Chambers wasn't all that shit they hyped in the papers. These girls is down with the right connects, and they ain't showing off, but they getting kinda large and that's bad, that's what made it bad for the fellas in X. There are crews and some is making it and others are talking about making it. Like, I got out, lots of girls stay in, it's just business. Girls can make it if they want to take the chance. Me, I got out when I saw the killing shit happen too close to me. One of my girls, who is still down with her crew, check me, and said you might get taken out just going out to the store, and she's right.*

In the 1980s commercial and corporate gangs were established as the dominant forces in the city. Commercial dope gangs were formed from smaller gangs, some of which were integrated. There were females like Melinda working in lower status positions that required little knowledge of the gang's operation. In the crack houses, younger females were assembly line workers, packaging and making cocaine into crack for organizations like the Chambers Brothers. This practice of using juveniles and females was part of the YBI model from the early 1980s. The dismantling of YBI by law enforcement forced commercial gangs to redefine their method of operation. So, females who had been restricted to lower positions within the drug gangs moved on to the next stage.

The new stage was ideal for young women. The covert nature of commercial gangs demanded smaller groups of members or supporters. The term Covert Entrepreneur Organization is used to distinguish them from past commercial gangs. The success in attacking corporate gangs in Detroit was made possible partially because of their visibility. Like the more famous Los Angeles gangs, with their colors, it was easier for law enforcers to identify the hundreds of members in YBI because of their known moniker, dress, and lifestyle. Reflecting on how quickly their demise came about, Mickey Franklin, 31, spoke of how the community at large knew his gang, YBI.

Everybody knew us, if you messed with us they knew it would be real trouble. Little kids, stores, car salespeople, Burger King, White Castle, girlies, police, everybody knew us and that was just the way it was . . . in the end that's what caused us problems, we was too well known. It was easy for the police to stay up on us.

In the 1990s, there is another dimension to female gangs besides that of commercial and corporate. Women's independence means taking power and territory and that means fighting over what is deemed important. This is similar to what Anne Campbell described in her studies of female gangs. There were battles over boys, and yet the focus was not primarily boyfriends but the issue of respect.

Police reports and school records in the early 1990s give little indication of female gangs or females in male gangs. Territorial battles, at times by younger crews, have gone unnoticed. This ignorance of female activity sometimes simply means that authorities are following the practice of traditional ignorance of female gangs. At other times the media has been misled, creating gangs of females when, in essence, there is simply female criminal behavior. One classic example is that of a young woman from a troubled background who, at seventeen, was the leader of a group of three young black males who were convicted of the first degree murder of seven people in the worst massacre in the city since the Hazelwood Massacre in 1971. The St. Aubin Street Massacre, like the one at Hazelwood, was drug-related. There was no gang; while the young woman was the instigator of these murders, the events were not gang-related; they were no different than drug robberies. The young woman had some personal contact with some of those murdered; but allegations of jealousy have no relevance to any gang theory. This case is a reminder of women's changing roles in major crime in America. In the 1990s it was revealed that Detroit had African American females in many disparate gang types. Women in the city were involved in non-gang activity that supported the nationalism of African Americans in both social and political advocacy networks. The gangs in which females participated ranged from compatriots to corporate. Territorial gangs were conducting on-going battles in different parts of the city. The 1990s disclosed varied experiences for African American females.

There are female criminal and non-criminal gangs in Detroit in the 1990s. Theorist Walter Miller named three ways in which females appear in relation to gangs. These are as independently functioning units, coed gangs, and female auxiliaries to male gangs.[43] This only begins to define the current status of female gangs in Detroit in the 1990s. The common denominator for commercial and corporate gangs is money. Within the sphere of commerce women either function or falter. In the gangs that have become competent it is apparent that gender is irrelevant. There may not be equal opportunity all the time, but the opportunity for women is there. Where women have entered the corporate arena and proven their worth, the gang generally does not differentiate between the sexes. They may not have the same level of participation, but females are included in the sub-culture of crime.

Black female gangs are part of the new era of commercial gangs. They are participants within the various gang types. The scavenger, delinquent, criminal, compatriot, territorial, and corporate types are all part of the transfamilial social organizations in Detroit. Gang types are not limited to particular parameters because they are constantly redefining themselves. It is necessary to include females in the history of Detroit gangs because the city has not acknowledged that female gangs exist nor that they are a problem. This study does not claim that they are dominant or growing. This study declares their presence both in the past and at present. [44]

The complex issues involved in defining how girls were part of the gang culture in Detroit is displayed in the contrast between the 1960s and the 1990s. The evolution of a young female engaging in delinquent acts, and, eventually, criminal acts as an adult, is summarized by a paroled, 40-year-old, African American woman, Johnnie Gladstone:

> *I was in trouble in grade school. I knew I was gonna stay in trouble because I got kicked out of school all the time. Me and my girlfriend Delores would smoke in the girls' bathroom on purpose.*
>
> *We called our gang the Dexter Girls. The boys didn't have no name. They didn't need one. Everyone at school knew they were the baddest in our school, the neighborhood. We all wanted to be with these young niggahs. They were all out of school and most of 'em was older, like sixteen or seventeen, and we was twelve or thirteen at best. I lost my cherry when I was in the sixth grade. Most of the girls I knew were screwing by the time they were in the sixth grade. I remember we all had Angel blouses and black tight skirts. I had to sneak my blouse 'cause my girlfriend Delores' grandmother was watching us, or trying to. By the time I was sixteen, I had my first child. The gang shit stopped in one way, but it just kept going on 'cause we got knocked up at the same time. So you just talked to your girls, 'cause they were the only ones you could talk with. You would just stay in the house. In those days people would just act like you was a tramp if you got knocked up. My momma kept me in the house and my life was just messed up from that day on. I got mixed up with some pimping niggahs and later learned how to steal real good. I was boosting real strong by the time I was twenty one. This niggah named James tried to get me to ho for him, but boosting was easier, and I looked real good so if I got caught the police would always let me go most of the time.*
>
> *Our gang was real small. After we all had babies it just meant you had to change your way of getting action with the men. Today, it's different in the street. Girls can make it without men, and my boys are making money in the streets. It's just different for women today. I wish I was young and fine as I was. I would have had me anything I wanted. In the '60s, girls had to do what the man said or get her ass kicked, but today, it's different, these young girls ain't taking no shit.*

Notes

1. J. Hagan, A.R. Gillis, and J. Simpson, "The Class Structure of Gender and Delinquency: Toward a Power-Control Theory of Common Delinquent Behavior," *American Journal of Sociology* 90, no.6 (1985): 1151-78.

2. Anne Campbell, *Girls in the Gang* (New York: Basil Blackwell, 1984).

3. J. Hagan, J. Simpson, and A. R. Gillis, "The Sexual Stratification of Social Control: A Gender-Based Perspective on Crime and Delinquency," *British Journal of Sociology* 30 (1979): 25-28.

4. M. Chesney-Lind, "Girls' Crime and A Woman's Place: Toward a Feminist Model," *Crime and Delinquency* 35 (1989): 5-29.

5. W.K. Brown, "Black Female Gangs in Philadelphia," *International Journal of Offender Therapy and Comparative Criminology* 21 (1977): 221-28.

6. J.M. Hagendorn, *People and Folks: Gangs, Crimes and the Underclass in a Rustbelt City* (Chicago: Lakeview Press, 1988).

7. Ibid.

8. Frederick Thrasher, *The Gang: A Study of 1,313 Gangs in Chicago* (Chicago: University of Chicago Press, 1927).

9. W.F. Whyte, *Street Corner Society: The Social Structure of an Italian Slum* (Chicago: University of Chicago Press, 1943).

10. Campbell, *The Girls in the Gang.*

11. Ibid.

12. Georgette Benett, *Crime Warps*

13. Ibid.

14. *Report of the Detroit Strategic Planning Project,* November 1987, 79.

15. Deborah Prothrow-Stith with Michaele Weissman, *Deadly Consequences* (New York: Harper Collins, 1991).

16. Laub McDermott, "Analysis of Serious Crime By Young Black Women," *Criminology* 23 (1985): 81-98.

17. Darrell J. Steffensmejer, "Organization Properties and Sex-Segregation in the Underworld: Building a Sociological Theory of Sex Differences in Crime," *Social Forces* 61, no. 4 (1983): 1010-32.

18. Carl S. Taylor, *Dangerous Society* (East Lansing: Michigan State University Press, 1990).

19. A.K. Cohen, *Delinquent Boys: The Culture of the Gang* (Glencoe: Free Press, 1955).

20. W.J. Wilson, *The Truly Disadvantaged: The Inner City, The Underclass and Public Policy* (Chicago: University of Chicago Press, 1987).

21. Campbell *The Girls in the Gang;* J.W. Moore, "Changing Chicano Gangs: Acculturation, Generational Changes, Evolution of Deviance or Emerging Underclass?" In *Proceedings of the Conference on Comparitive Ethnicity,* eds. J.H. Johnson, Jr. and M.L. Oliver (Los Angeles: Institute for Social Science Research, UCLA, 1988); Taylor, *Dangerous Society.*

22. L.T. Fishman, *The Vice Queens: An Ethnographic Study of Black Female Gang Behavior* (Paper presented at the annual meeting of the American Society of Criminology, Chicago).

23. *The Report of the Detroit Stategic Planning Committee,* Detrioit, Michigan, 1988; Nora Faires, "Transition and Turmoil: Social and Political Development in Michigan," in *Michigan: Visions of Our Past,* ed. Richard Hathaway (East Lansing: Michigan State University Press, 1989), 205.

24. Leonard Dinnerstein and Kenneth T. Jackson, *American Vistas* (New York: Oxford University Press, 1987).

25. Dan Georgakas, *Detroit, I Do Mind Dying: A Study in Urban Revolution* (NewYork: St. Martin's Press, 1975).

26. Dominic J. Capeci, *Layered Violence: The Detroit Rioters of 1943* (Jackson: University of Mississippi, 1991).

27. Dinnerstein and Jackson, *American Vistas.*

28. Capeci, *Layered Violence.*

29. Ibid.

30. Ibid.

31. Taylor, *Dangerous Society.*

32. Carl Sifakis, *The Mafia Encyclopedia* (New York: Facts on File, 1987).

33. Dominic J. Capeci, *Race Relations in Wartime Detroit: The Sojourner Truth Housing Controversy of 1942* (Philadelphia: Temple University Press, 1984).

34. Ronald C. Huff, *Gangs in America* (Newbury Park: Sage Publications, Inc., 1990).

35. Capeci, *Layered Violence.*

36. Ibid.

37. STRESS (Stop The Robberies Enjoy Safe Streets) is a decoy unit of the Detroit Police.

38. Arnold P. Goldstein, *Delinquent Gangs* (Champaign: Research Press, 1991).

39. Taylor, *Dangerous Society.*

40. Campbell *The Girls in the Gang*; J.M. Hagedorn and J.W. Moore, Milwaukee and Los Angeles Gangs Compared (Paper presented at the annual meeting of the American Anthropological Society, Oaxaca, Mexico, 1987).

41. Tim Belknap, "Young Boys Inc. Ring—20 Plead Guilty in Dope Trial," *Detroit Free Press,* 3 April 1983.

42. Isabel Wilkerson, "Detroit Crack Empire Shows All Earmarks of Big Business," *New York Times,* 18 December 1988.

43. Walter Miller "The Molls," *Society* 11 (1973): 32-35.

43. Campbell, *The Girls in the Gang.*

3

Case Studies

In this chapter, I present interviews with three different women who are, or have been, involved, to varying degrees, with gangs and illegal drug sales. These interviews, conducted during a four-year period, provide a detailed picture of "the life" in urban Detroit—the gangs, drugs, and violence.

DEWANA

Dewana is a twenty-year-old African American woman. She dropped out of high school in the tenth grade. She is single with no children and currently lives with two other women. She comes from a family of six. Her mother is still living; her father is unknown. During her childhood she lived in several foster homes and had extensive contact with juvenile authorities. Her present occupation is unknown, but she participates in a scavenger-type organization, in this case, a small, gender-integrated group who carries out narcotic sales at the lower level of a crack cocaine organization.

What was your childhood like?

Well, it's like this . . . . I was always getting fucked around when I was little, like everybody used to fuck me over. My sister would do it, my brothers, anybody on our street could just kick my ass when I was little. Being little ain't fun, 'cause all I remember is getting dissed and my momma just didn't give a shit, she was always trying to get a man. I never knew my father, my brothers showed me some ugly motherfucka and said that he was my father, but they always fucking with me 'cause we ain't got the same father. What I remember the most is having my grandmother beating my ass 'cause she said I stole some money from her purse; it wasn't me, it was my no good brother Bobby. But my grandmother never liked me anyway and she always liked the boys, so fuck it, it's just some more bullshit. Childhood was full of shit for me, it was just fucked up and what else is it in life when you little?

That's why the kid ain't having no babies, 'cause it's just bullshit for little kids. When I was real little my momma had this boyfriend and he used to tell all kinda lies on me. I still hate his ass to this day. If I would see that motherfucka, I pay one of the real crazy boys I know to set his ass on fire, and then smoke his ass. He would be calling me ugly and saying I was fucking all the boys in our apartment building. You could always feel his nasty old breath on your back, he never try anything, but you knew he wanted some ass, especially from a young girl. But you know how men be? Y'all want some ass, and that is something I learned real early, men and boys want some ass all the time. Men will try and act like they don't, but I know they want your stuff anywhere, and anytime. I remember that from early in school . . . anyway, my brothers is trying to fuck little girls in our 'hood all the time. If you little, get the fuck away from big people, 'cause they will fuck a little kid real quick. I know.

Let's kick it 'bout something else, 'cause my childhood was just shitty, nothing I wanna really 'member, it was fucked up. I had nobody that really was down with me except my brother Jimmy, and he got killed when he was fifteen. He was my friend, but nobody liked him 'cause he was a fag. But he cared 'bout me and tried to stop all the bullshit from getting outta control. He used to stop my brothers from eating all the food from me, and he was the one that took care of all of us in the winter. That's why I like fags, they know how to treat people better than dog ass men. My Jimmy had some tramp ass, faggot friends but they are still better than my dirty ass brothers. A fag out here is catching it from everywhere. The hook is down on 'em, street fellas wanna fuck'em or kill'em or both [laughing]. Shit, they catch hell from everybody . . . anyway, my Jimmy was the one that watch out for us, even when we went to some foster home, it was Jimmy who taught me how to get in touch with my momma, grand, and him . . . . I miss him, he was the only person that cared 'bout me when I was little.

How does crime in the neighborhood affect children?

Crime is just part of everything around you, I mean what is crime, it's just the way things are in your 'hood. When you see it all the time it's just there, so what? Ain't shit to get stupid 'bout, crime is going on all the time unless you live in some big rich place. Crime was always in my 'hood, I mean, that is where we live, so what you gonna do? Like I told ya, little kids ain't got a chance out in the world, 'cause big people like to fuck little kids, that's the way it's always been.

I always hated school, 'cause that's where I felt like shit more than any other place in the world. The teachers always treated me and my brothers and sister like we was nothing but shit. The kids used to tease us 'bout our momma and I hated the school 'cause they sent me to the principal office for anything. We never had straight clothes when I was little and I got called all *kinda shit like black skillet bitch and real fucked up shit 'bout where our house or apartment was, like dirty and full of roaches, smelled real nasty. I hated where we lived, it was like the worst shit in the world. The neighborhoods we lived in was fucked up, if you looked at the houses you think someone should tear the fucked-up house down. We used to move all the time, like every year we lived in some other house or apartment. If my momma didn't move we was getting picked up at school or by some social worker would be fucking with us, asking me and my sister if we knew where our mother was, or why wasn't we in school. Like, my momma only knew where the liquor store was, she didn't give a fuck about nothing but her Budweiser . . . . My brothers would kick a muthafucka's ass if they said some of that shit to them, but me and my sister, we didn't count like the fellas.*

In elementary school I got called names and I would cry and Jimmy would tell me not to cry. All school meant to me was the place where I was going to get dogged and laugh at . . . school is not where I would go to for nothing, 'cause it's the place I hated the most when I grew up. Some teachers are nice, but most of the muthafuckas treat you like you dumb, and they talk real fucked-up at you. Like you is some dumb ass ho, or like they think you smell. Women teachers used to diss me the most, they always pick the girls with the nice clothes, like you got a choice when you little. My clothes used to be so dirty and smelly. I wanted nice clothes, but my momma used to spend our money from welfare on liquor, trade the stamps with somebody for Budweiser or whatever she could get her lips around, long as it was a bottle of liquor. My momma always had plenty time for men and whiskey. My brother Jimmy would look out for our momma, he said she needed somebody to watch her back. My grandmother was mean and she liked her Budweiser more than me, too . . . I like all kinds of get high thangs, especially a little 'caine, that's why I like this crew, they got the big connect and you get the best 'caine in the city.

Selling dope is the best way to make it in the streets in this city. Dope is what everybody want today, it's the shit in the street for making it. Bunches of girls is trying to get busy with this dope thang. Some tried to get a dope man, but you learn real fast that dope men are just bigger dogs than other men. They know everybody will fuck and suck to get next to them. The dope man is the king in our 'hood. If you want something like a television or a car, maybe you want somebody to get their ass waxed, or maybe you want to get your car stolen for the insurance money, the dope man is the one that can make it happen. The dope man is bigger than anybody in the 'hood.

I've been using dope since I was little. First, I was drinking my momma's Buds and grand's homemade wine when I was real little, like maybe nine or ten years old. My momma would beat our asses if we fucked with her drinking things, but I did it anyway. By the time I was eleven I was smoking weed with the fellas in the 'hood. My brothers used to get me to fuck this man named Fat Larry, who ran the dope house around the corner. I hated that muthafucka, he was fat and didn't have no teeth. I hated my brothers for making me give up my ass for this no dick muthafucka. I got to like his dope, he had the best dope and it made me feel real good. My brother Jimmy got beat up by my brothers Phil and Ty for telling me not to fuck Fat Larry. Fat Larry would fuck anybody, boy or girl, I think he would fuck a dog if the dog would let him. Fat Larry treated me like I was his woman, I mean this was real fucked up, I wasn't even thirteen, but he would give me money and he would give me dope for having another girl come over and fuck him. He couldn't even fuck, but he always wanted to get young girls, said they had the best pussy; he was fucked up, fat and ugly but he could get anything in our 'hood, 'cause he was the dope man.

I sometimes sell dope for Fat Larry, but I rip his fat ass off anytime I can, he is so nasty, he stop counting his money long time ago. He wouldn't count his paper 'cause he trusts me, I bring him young girls and he gits off on that. . .he being talking 'bout I am his main ho, right [laughing]. I tell the young ho's how to pretend he's so good, that his dick is so big. They be laughing like I used to, everybody in the 'hood knows he can't fuck, he jist a fat, nasty freak. I've been fucking him for the past eight years. If I wasn't smoking up this dope I could done had a def car, but I likes this 'caine and it cost cash money.

My girlfriend, she started out with the big fellas, working after school, she was just mixing jive in the basement of the big fella's place. She hates dope, she ain't using nothing, it was a job. Now, she is real smart in school and she wanted to get her own thang. She started going with this fella who was rolling real big. He was real large, had stupid money, she was kicking it real hard. Got the big Bemmer, plenty of clothes, and they go to all the big concerts, season tickets to the Pistons. She done learned how to cut dope, got clever in how to meet the right people and she ain't forgot 'bout her homegirl. She bought her sister a little Geo car, and she always giving me big bags of dope. I wish I had got smart like her, she will be making paper when I'm still smoking all of Fat Larry dope up. I'm just making a little money, but my girl is like lots of young girls out here. Some people think it's just men getting paid. But girls is making cash money, like in the big money, they will be getting bigger in a minute.

To me, selling dope is the best thing a young girl can do in trying to make it in the streets. The money is large and if you're smart you can get paid and even help out some of your friends, if you get large like my girl I told ya 'bout. Girls is making it, fuck the fellas, if I want it then I got to make it, just like the fellas. If we can work for some man selling dope, why can't we sell for ourselves? I don't need some man telling me shit, and I sure don't need some man making cash off my ass . . . . Call us a gang or whatever you want, you got the book over there with you. What we is, is getting paid. Is this going to be in one of those books 'bout niggahs rolling? I didn't finish no school, and who gonna hire me? This here is good as it's gonna be for me. Let's look at my chances of doing anything else. Some caseworker told me something I'll never forget. . .she said that I was just like my momma, and that if I didn't go to school I would be nothing, probably have lots of babies and stay on assistance the rest of life. Fuck that bitch with her know-it-all ass. Well I'm doing ok, and I ain't got no damn babies. The way I see it, slinging dope is the best thing in this life for me.

Now, my friend that's getting it on big, she goes to Wayne County Community College. She's the girl, wish I could be like her. Girl is in college, and she says she is gonna go to some big college up in Ann Arbor next year. She is getting it on, and you know all the fellas in our 'hood love the girl. All of the dope fellas talk 'bout how she is dope. One day she's gonna be in charge of something real big, watch what I say, she is the one.

Are you afraid of violence?

Violence is part of life out here, in our 'hood you see violence all the time and that's what time it is. When I was real little I was scared 'bout everything round me. But, it's just happening 'cause that's the way things are. I've seen all kinda shit jump off in the 'hood and it's scary to you and your crew, looking at it, but it's just life out here. My grandmother use to tell me and my brothers that the street was gonna get us dead. Shit, Jimmy used to laugh and say it was gonna get you anyway if you didn't do shit, the street can get you anytime. I knew this real nice girl at our school, and she was minding her own business one day after school and some of my brothers' dog friends beat her down for nothing. They just kicked her ass real good 'cause they want to beat somebody down and it was not her fault. That's just the way the street is, either you stay ready or it's gonna get you. The street don't give a fuck 'bout if you is nice or whatever. I done seen people killed out in the street and other people just keep on walking like it wasn't shit. . .the street is just cold. I saw this man beating his girlfriend down and Jimmy told me that wasn't our business. But, it's fucked up to see people just watching somebody get fucked over. But, that's the way it is out in the street. I hate to see little kids get fucked over, 'cause it reminds me of when I was little and everybody was kicking me around. When I was in the juvenile home my first time I remember being real scared, the judge told me that the home would help me . . . right, they showed me how many people could kick your ass and nobody would give a damn. Violence is what makes people take you serious, the way I see it.

Is selling dope dangerous or risky?

Man, these are some fucked up questions. Everything is violent. If you out slinging dope and somebody is trying to get your shit, what you gonna do? Call the hook? Fuck naw, it's time to take care your own shit. If a bitch fucks with my shit, well somebody got to bleed, and it's better your ass than mine *[laughing]. Why do they have guards and the hook watching those armored cars at banks? Is that violent? Naw, that's just the way things are, got to protect the shit you own. Anyway, the police is the biggest dogs in the world, they take people shit and act just like a crew. I hate the police, that's why I like that song "Fuck the Police," and that other song by Public Enemy 'bout 911 is real, too! Selling dope is serious and you and your crew got to be ready to protect your shit, if people see you soft and you out here in business they will take your shit and just laugh in your face. Just like dog ass men, they'll take your pussy and laugh if you let'em. Now, me, I'm ready and can shoot me some niggahs. Learn from this crazy niggah at the dope house. Can shoot a forty-five, a three fifty-seven, and will fuck you up with a nine millimeter. If you let niggahs know that you don't think shit 'bout popping their asses, they think twice before they start dissing a girl, trust me, I know.*

What does the future hold for you?

The future is far away, who says I'll be round in the future? I ain't worried 'bout nothing far off. Right now I'm worried 'bout getting it on, I mean it's getting tight out here. There was a big bust out in Southfield and me and this house need our dope and these crackheads need their crack. I need lots of money for the winter and I want to get me a fur and some new clothes. My sister is pregnant with her third child and two of my brothers is up in Jackson [prison]. My momma is begging me for money and I'm tired of catching taxi cabs, so I'm looking at getting me some wheels. Got to stop packing my nose with this 'caine. If I could get serious I might make some serious money.

My girl Sherrie just bought her mom a new house, but her mom is cool, not like my drunk ass momma. But Sherrie is getting it on, and she is running her own little thang. She bought a brand new 'vette. Girlfriend is getting real strong, her paper is stupid, she got lucky 'cause her people is from out in Farmington Hills, ain't no dumb shit out there. All she got to do is drop off a few kilos and she is straight. That would be sweet in the future, if I didn't have to get out in the street and deal with all the crazy shit. Sherrie is fine, she don't look like me and she is hooked up with her brothers, they real young but they some cold-hearted little niggahs, they take business real straight and people know they will cap a fool in a minute. The future is now and I bet it's gonna be fucked up with lots of problems like it's always been. . . but, the kid is ready and I likes the way I can buy whatever I want. This here dope thang is like having a big gun and be able to shoot anybody whenever you get ready.

Look at the houses and look at the kids round here and you can see the future and it ain't looking good to me . . . life is fucked up 'round this 'hood. What do you think big fella, you're smart, is this future looking good to you?

Probably is good for your shit, 'cause you're getting paid writing books 'bout our fucked lives, huh? Caseworkers, the police, prison people, the social workers, all them muthafuckas get paid when things is all fucked up out here. I used to think 'bout teachers and this principal at my elementary school, they loved to make you feel like you wasn't shit. Wearing their expensive suits and driving what they thought was a smoking ride. Now, young girls is smoking them with their clothes, their hair is laid, the jewelry is def, and the young boys got more paper than all them fake ass principals could ever think 'bout. The future is tight for all them fake people who used to love to see me and my brothers with no clothes or no food. The social worker ain't talking all that shit 'bout you ain't ever going be nothing. How you like me now? When you're looking at them, wish they could have some of that gold. . .[laughing real hard]. The future is gonna be hard on all those people who was dogging people like me. The real big fellas is looking so good it makes some of the rollers (rollers here means police) wish they could get with the getting paid boys and girls. That's the future for me and this crew is to get some of that real big paper. Now, I'm living in a smooth apartment and got some paper, but it ain't stupid and these boys here want to get stupid paper . . . that's the future for me, get paid and get large. Ain't gonna be on no welfare and ain't going to jail, and sure in the fuck ain't getting married to no dog ass man. The future ain't shit down here, what's the future mean if you can't remember the shit from yesterday ? [laughing hard again]. When I get enough paper to buy me some fine ass boys and make them do whatever I say do, is when the future will mean something real.

ERICA

Erica, 23, is the mother of five children, four boys and one girl. She is currently living with her boyfriend, who is selling crack out of the house. Erica has worked for the past three years in several dope houses in different positions, working for the dealers who are cousins or friends of hers. She has agreed to the interviews on the condition that the interviewer help her leave Detroit. Erica is tired of her relationship with the young man who has taken over her house, yet she is afraid for her family. She refused to allow interviewers to come inside her house, or even come on her block during the interviews.

Life is hard over here in this neighborhood. Now my mother and father lived on the Westside and their block is real nice, it still has real nice, clean folks on that street. My kids see all kind of bad things over here, and now this bastard selling dope out my house. I'm scared and my mother told me to call the police; this niggah would kill my kids and me. I hate his mean ass, but he gives me money and if I try to leave he'll just find me and beat my ass or kill me. That's why I want to leave Detroit and start all over, I need somewhere I can get a new start for me and my kids. I got pregnant when I was fourteen, it was my fault, I was one of those fast kinda girls, my folks is old and they couldn't do shit with me. My mother had me when she was almost fifty, and said she was too old. It ain't their fault, they just couldn't make me leave all those no good niggahs alone. The more my mother and father said no, the more I screwed 'em. Now, my life is all messed up and I got nobody to blame but my own damn self.

I got three grown brothers who got good jobs and have tried to help, but I'm not like them. They're smart and they got their own families. Anyway, I've made some good money working for my cousin, he got a small crew, and I mix jive for him, and sometimes I used to deliver dope for him in Ohio. I was kissing that pipe a little last year and did some real bad shit. Shit I ain't telling ya'll 'bout it so don't even ask, 'cause it's something I don't want to remember. I guess I've always been kinda messed up and I just would fuck things up. I gave my folks hell. My folks are good and I just fucked them over, having babies five years in a row was just fucking dumb. I love my kids, but look what I'm doing, raising them in a damn dope house. You can bet my brothers would never do no shit like that, I know that.

How does this impact children?

I'm not the best mother, that's for sure, nothing like my mother . . . I'm just weak I guess, this niggah I'm living with tricked me, telling me how fine my eyes and all that shit men tell you when they trying to get next to you . . . I just trust the wrong men, hope the big fella ain't lying 'bout helping me and my kids get out of Detroit. I like money and big cars, but this niggah is lowlife and I'm scared of him and his lowlife friends and family. My oldest is my son Tyrell and he hates John, I know it and if he was a little older I think he would do something to protect me from John. My kids love me, and I guess I love them, but I've been one lousy bitch with 'em. Sometimes I feel like I should have had my tubes tied, I can't believe that I'm not having babies now . . . John got children, and as he sure ain't no father and my kids hate him, they just put up with him 'cause they can't change shit. My mother is getting older and my father died last year. I didn't go to the funeral 'cause I was too busy kissing that pipe. I'm worried about AIDS from that time in my life and I would have lost my kids if my mother hadn't took over. Hell, I had money, it was that pipe that had me all fucked up, that's when I let the devil in my house with this niggah John. It was because he had crack and money, I gave up my family at that time for some crack.

I'm still doing cocaine and smoking fifty ones, but getting high ain't gonna change nothing for me and these kids. My mother wants to move down south and leave Detroit. I'm concerned about this street, that's why I couldn't let y'all come down 'cause if somebody knew I was talking 'bout the life, well it could get crazy. John is real low with his shit, I mean he does all kinda dirty ass shit with crackheads [laughing]. I mean it takes one to know one, right? They get girls on crack, sometimes they get boys and just make them do all kinds of fucked-up shit. Niggahs be doing strange things that you wouldn't believe, but crack make you so crazy that you'll do any-thing, and I mean real embarassing shit that you wouldn't never do if you weren't kissing that pipe. I'm not a crackhead, but I sure wish I didn't have these kids sometimes when I'm wanting to just get high and not remember how fucked up the world is for me.

What about your children being in a dope house?

Working in the dope house is just business and taking my kids is no big deal. Shit, they ain't gonna get hurt in the dope house, not with the doorman, and the police ain't doing no shit to the kids, now they might try and take them from you . . . but they ain't in no danger in the dope house. The dope house is just where the business is at, my house now is getting lots of dumb shit happening because John is trying to get slick, but I'm not happy with my kids being there and I want to get out, but that's me, and anyway, I know lots of folks that got little babies in the dope houses. If you use one of them daycare places they might call the man on your ass, and anyway, who wants to mess with kids, dope fiends is after dope and crack, they ain't after kids and babies.

My kids is in school so I don't take them to the dope house, my mother used to keep them but now it's getting stupid at my own house 'cause John is always trying to scam the crackheads by getting pussy for his boys or his own freak ass. He beat my ass when I caught him in the bed with two young girls at my house, ain't that fucked-up? It's so bad that I rather work at the dope house than see that snakeass motherfucker in my house. Now, there are some bad niggahs at the house who would kill John if I asked them, they work for whoever got the juice. But, these some real bad, scary niggahs and they might decide they want my little ass or it could get crazier than John. So, I just decided that I'm getting the hell out of Dodge, I got some money saved that, thank God, my mother didn't let me get hold of when I was pip-ing. I need to get my life straight and it ain't gonna happen here, not as long as I got John and his crew around. Look, I learned how to mix dope real good and there are plenty of dope houses that need folks who can do what I do, so I could learn how to do something that's honest if I got a new start. My mother is a Christian lady, maybe some church, a good one, could help me in another city, huh?

Are women in the drug business?

Girls are making paper and everybody knows it, if girls ain't getting paid one way they getting the other. If I didn't have these kids I probably have me a Benzo or maybe a big house. Oh, trust me, the paper is out here. Now some of these sack chasing bitches is out here making it hard for lots of girls with their trampish ways, but if you got the time there is plenty of money for girls . . . . Look, I work everyday in a big dope house and girls are working like me, and you learn the ways of making it work. Some girls just go and fuck the dope man, but some just learn and then get their own shit, the fellas that know 'bout it don't like it, but fuck them. It's done real quiet and most time men don't even know their girls are kicking on the side. You see all these little beauty salons 'round the streets, well some is real and others is just dope money. Girls is getting rich. Look at me, if I hadn't got on that pipe it would be big money for me and my kids.

Do you know how much money I can spend on my kids or me and you better have some stupid money, or it's just no way in hell you can get anything without a man, make that a dope man, to make it. I know sack chasers and I know the big time bitches and they all getting paid. Shit, look at some of the rides these boys driving and the girls getting their rides too. When this shit first happened my cousin was trying to get him some wheels, any old car, right. That was five years ago, now he's large. Pete got a brand new 560 Benzo, a Pathfinder, a Saab, and bought his momma a new Lincoln, his sister a Fiero and I'm working for his sister in her own house. I fucked up some money last year and she loaned me the paper so I wouldn't get wacked. 'Cause, even if you somebody's cousin, that wouldn't stop Pete boys from wacking me. Sandra was my lifesaver, I didn't care 'bout shit, I was in love with that pipe and it had me all cracked up. Sandra ain't but twenty, and she got her six girls and four boys in her own crew. I probably blew my shit acting like a silly ass crackhead, but there are plenty of girls out here making up for bitches like me.

MONA

Mona is twenty-five years old, a veteran of the streets since early childhood. She graduated from high school in Detroit and says her occupation is a "business woman." The principal investigator has known Mona since 1980. Her cousins were involved with a large scavenger gang from the Eastside of Detroit. Her father died in 1988; her mother died in the summer of 1989. She is the guardian of several nieces and nephews. There are two siblings suffering from AIDS; she has never told the investigator exactly how many sisters and brothers she has. She is also responsible for her grandmother and three older aunts. Mona has agreed to this interview only on the condition that she is not referred to as a drug dealer. Her actual connection is considered to be in a major circle of the illegal narcotics trade. The first interview is stopped before it takes place when Mona decides she wants no females at the meeting, and no tape recorders.

I don't need no bitches or tapes out on me, so send that bitch somewhere . . . this ain't "Soul Train," I'm not here to profile or entertain some bitch! This gotta be with quickness, I got business in the world . . . and this costs me monay. So what you want to talk 'bout?

You seem to be extremely irritable today? Is there something wrong?

Y'all out here asking for information, and y'all ain't giving up no paper, so whatever I am, y'all gonna take it . . . this weather is cold one day, and today it's hot as hell. Crackheads will be out doing all kinda fucked up shit when it's hot. They got this here crackhouse over on East Street and it's called the Hall of Fame. Them rock stars over there will be at the Hall of Fame. Lots of fucking and sucking and lots of freak shit will take place . . . see it's scary out here in this new shit, these young foolish boys is making stupid dope monay!

Is this new place different from what we have been seeing all summer out here? Are these new crews and are girls in these crews or posses?

Yeah, it's new crews all the time, and lots of young girls is getting large out here. I done told ya, it's different out in the streets. All that old time shit is over, it's new and girls is out here. Let's just say I have known some young girls and they are making monay and it's big monay. See, girls learned from boys, and some were in crews with boys and were doing little thangs for the crew. Plenty of girls were working in kitchens cooking rocks or packing crack packs. I used to do thangs for my cousins when I was little and still in middle school. You learn, boys learn, but they so busy buying gold or fighting, getting neat. If you get with the game early and just learn and chill, it can be straight.

This Hall of Fame is scandalous, it's got nasty ass people, all kinds of people coming and buying crack. These dirty motherfuckers ain't using the crack, they give it to the crack bitches or punks. It's a freak scene, it's like going to the zoo, and watching people feeding the monkeys. The rock stars just want that crack, and they will do anythang, I mean anythang, for that hit . . . now, boys, you know, fellas are the ones that like shit like this Hall of Fame, my people don't like that freak thang cause it's bad for business. It's trouble and people get real crazy when it comes to fucking in these joints. The ho's in these joints make me real mad, they just out here doing freak shit for some damn dope. Some'em got kids and they have the kids with them in the house . . . it's tight, I won't let my people git into that kinda shit, that ain't business to me. Some of these lowlife ho's will do anything, even do freak shit with their kids, it's fucked up out here . . . . That's it for today, I got business.

Several days later, Mona is discussing a rash of shootings in various parts of the city.

Business is tight, it's business and somebody got greedy and other boys is taking care of the competition, that's the way it is out here. The problem is that some of these people, including girls, like this shooting and killing. See, some girls want the big earrings, gold chains, the Gucci's, gitting their hair done everytime it sweats, want the cars, and they want the fine ass boys. But some boys and a few girls is gitting this other way. They want to be in charge in a big way! Now, that's when you start gitting crazy out here. I know some little tramp ho's that set up fellas for other killing niggahs. The kind of niggahs that kill everythang they touch. Trust me, it's some real deep, sick mothafuckas just loving what they do, they like to fuck people up. They enjoy killing . . . better not try interviewing them [laughing], oh, they illing, they the kind that will talk little bullshit and you be thinking they kinda quiet, and they be done popped your interviewing ass! It's just the way thangs regulate in the streets and it's tight for everybody. The shooting and killing is part of the life. If you can't take the killing you had better stay away from this game, 'cause it's always gonna be regulators out here, and the hook, or nobody can change that, it's just business gitting regulated."

Do you have respect for authority such as the police, teachers, politicians?

The police? All them suckas is fake, they be perpetrating, they ain't shit . . . . I hate the police, okay, git that straight. Fuck the police. Teachers and all them ho's you named like politicians, right, they is the biggest gangsters I know, the teachers don't do shit but come to school and git paid, for what? I graduated from high school, so I ain't one of them dumb ho's . . . teachers be smoking dope, fucking young girls and boys. Teachers be in the mix with some scandalous shit all over the city. Look here, the Hall of Fame is full of your authority kinda people. They the main ones at the crack house buying freak sex, gitting their dicks sucked and talking 'bout street life. They're the ones who want girls to kiss each other, and they're the ones that want to see other people have orgies, fuck boys, and run trains on tramp ass crack bitches. All those mothafuckas are the ones that love for the fucked up crazy boys that run the Hall of Fame to git dogs and video the shit for their freak ass. I know all 'bout authority . . . like the dog ass hook, break a bitch down in a minute and make'em do all kinda freak shit. Please, git the fuck out of here with that authority bullshit. I respect one thang and that's monay, George Washington and his crew. Monay is what I respect. If you got monay, you got respect. I done seen it in the street . . . no matter what you do, monay can work shit out and if you ain't got no monay, it's gonna be fucked up, trust me, it's gonna be real fucked up. That's why I'm a business woman, people respect me when I go places . . . y'all love me, cause y'all know I'm gitting it on.

Do you plan on becoming a mother in the future?

Mona looks surprised at this question. She is driving a new 560 Mercedes Benz; with the sticker still on the window. She is accompanied by two younger women and two younger children. Mona explains that these are her sister's kids. The investigators ask if they can go shopping with her in a particular mall. She replies, no, because she doesn't want her sister's kids around our surveillance or inquiries. She also explains that the car is her friend's; she also has a Mercedes Benz, but prefers to drive her new Geo convertible in daily life. She laughs about her grandmother teasing her about buying a convertible as if, with her dark brown complexion, she needs any sun or tanning. Again, Mona tells the investigator that her family is off limits and that is the end of the subject.

> *I don't need no kids, I got all my sister's kids and they need all kind of things. Three of them is in private school, can't go to the public school with all the shooting and foolishness these days. I can't see having children in this city, or in this world . . . I know some tramps that I would like to beat down, and take their kids cause the kids didn't ask to be in this shit. My mother was always trying to keep us straight but it was too much in the street. I look at all the perpetrating bitches on television crying and protesting 'bout right to life, but you never see them bullshit holy bitches when you see them crack babies! I am just business, no kids for the girl, let somebody else do all that work, plus, kids is gitting out of control these days, kids is talking smart shit, and these kids know when you is fake, they can tell if it's bullshit . . . why bring something into what you know is fucked up from the very day it takes off?*

How do you feel about drugs in Detroit?

This meeting takes place in a McDonald's restaurant downtown. Mona is accompanied by four young men and three young women. The young men are traveling in a Black 1990 Nissan Pathfinder; Mona is being driven by the young women in a gun metal grey 1990 Pontiac SSE. The young men wait outside in front. There are very few people in the restaurant at 4:30 p.m. on this rainy, August day. The principal investigator asks her who the young men are, are they in the narcotics trade?

> *Everytime you see some young boys you think they rolling? These boys are friends of mine, cousins, and they own a small store on the Eastside . . . . You think everything is dope, dope, dope . . . . Drugs in Detroit? Well, what*

*I think is that people want drugs and that's what, people who got it, sell it.
What sells, sells, that's the way things suppose to be . . . . Selling dope is
business, it's like everythang in the world. Dope is business, and if you think
'bout it, its just business in the streets. Detroit is just another place for selling dope. Dope has always been round, and that's why y'all can't stop it,
dope is something people want. Like the rich people in the suburbs, they
come into the city and buy the shit, and then talk shit bout how bad things
is in Detroit. Right, they buy more dope than the poor ass junkies and nasty
crack bitches be doing that sex thang.*

*There's so much dope in this city it's stupid. But dope is in all the cities,
the little ones, and the big ones got dope (laughing). Those authority people
you always talking 'bout, they git with the dope, they tell lies and say NO,
right, well where is the dope, is it gone? Hell it's right here and you got
crackheads talking 'bout beam me up Scotty! All kinds of people be gitting
high, and if it's the pipe, well, it's like freak city. Detroit has lots of people
selling dope, it's the way to make it large in the street.*

At this moment a shiny, new, red convertible Corvette drives up in
front of McDonald's. Two young men, who look no older than nineteen or twenty exit the car. They are carrying what looks like a green,
reptile skin briefcase, and one is talking on a portable phone. Their
hair is cut short with designs in the back and side of their heads. Their
attire is almost identical. They have light blue and grey striped shorts
with matching white tennis shirts and shoes and are wearing large
gold chains with name plates written in diamonds.

Mona laughs and shakes her head in amazement.

*Now, these here boys is out of control. They may as well have a sign on say-
ing I am rolling and living large. See, that's what girls won't do, shit like this
here . . . these niggahs is showing the world. The hook, gonna be all over
them, look at that Vette. Drugs in Detroit means that somebody is making
monay off this kinda niggah. Look at their Vette, it's got spoilers, the hub-
caps cost more than some poor peoples pay for their whole damn car . . .
this car done cost some coin!*

*I'll tell you this, there are lots of people that don't think monay is gitting
made out here, or that most boys ain't making it large. First, it's so many
fellas and some girls, too, gitting paid I don't think they could catch 'em if
they really tried. Then, what makes a stupid muthafucka think we gonna
talk 'bout what we make or how we git it on? Your shit is special and you
know you better not talk 'bout some shit. I done seen some of them silly
looking hook kinda dickheads asking shit 'bout whatever. They just like the
other dickbitches trying to git you to talk 'bout shit that they gonna use to
fuck yo thing up . . . . I don't know, not this girl. We ain't saying shit to no*

newspaper or nobody else. They trying to trick us, we know that. Look, some boys don't like yo big ass and they say all kinda ill shit 'bout you, it's some people asking us what you gonna do. But, I know you straight, your crew is straight . . . when you write those books or be on the set talking 'bout us you don't try and make fun of us or try and say it's like this, it's like we tell you. Now, that tape shit, I can't work with that shit, but you won't fuck us around and say it's the news, right? Sometimes you hear shit or see some illing fakeass on the set talking shit and you just laugh, um, it's sometimes a niggah talking 'bout us and you know he lying or done got tricked.

Now, sometimes somebody might git a fiend to tell 'em shit like that Chinese television reporter, this muthafucka paid a crackhead to smoke in front of the camera . . . but a dope fiend can't be trusted. When people come 'round the 'hood, we know what's up. If they black don't mean shit, you working for the man, and that done cancelled yo own shit, you just another invader. Sometimes they have a black cameraman, or have the black guy asking questions, right? Kick that ho bitch ass, too! Like the black police right? Either you with us or you 'gainst us, ain't no two ways 'bout the shit, okay! People should be real careful 'bout asking shit that don't concern them . . . lots of times you can tell that the bitch is scared and want to leave but they keep on dissing you and asking questions. Tell you what, this is for all the mothafuckas out there that's talking shit 'bout us. Tell them that go and study and ask those pussy buying white men why they do what they do? Ask those niggahs that help sell us out, why? And tell'em that they the ones done made us monay, and we ain't dumb or little bitches. We gitting it on, lots of us is out here! Before they know it, we gonna be so large they won't know what hit'em, and we ain't going nowhere, trust me . . .they don't know nothing 'bout us!

Mona is defensive when asked about what she thinks about innocent people getting killed in the ongoing drug battles in the United States.

Well, it's kinda tight when it's little kids gitting popped. But, uh, it's like something you can't stop, it just happens . . . peoples git shot all the time, hey, look at car accidents and airplane crashes. I hate it when some little kid git taken out, but it's always happening with lots of crews, especially fellas . . . but there are some ho's that's out there and they make shit crazy too!

What kind of movies do you like?

Joining this conversation with Mona is Angela, 19, Felicia, 18, Randy, 19, and Howard, 20. Mona, laughing, says that some of the males that are in the "life" love to watch porno and snuff movies. Arguing with Howard she reminds him how inferior she feels men are for watching these types of films.

Y'all perverts, huh, huh, just perverts watching somebody killing a babe while they been getting laid . . . it's strange shit, it's real fucked up . . . . Boy, you got problems if you watch that kinda shit, and your whole crew is into that kinda shit. That's why I just use men for whatever I need, but men or boys want to git freak shit going, anything that's got to do with getting freaked is okay. I ain't with it, you just don't want my boys here to write how freaky shit is with fellas, well, it's not just these fellas, it's all fellas, they just freaks, men love pussy, they love watching or talking about screwing, fucking, call it whatever, they freaking all the time, and that's the kind of movies they like or it's some gangster thang like Scarface, *or any movie with gangsters, and lots of knocking off people.*

The interviewer asks if she is suggesting that females don't watch the same kinds of movies. Angela and Felicia chimed into the conversation.

Angela:

Nasty fellas always watching fucked up, scary shit like Freddy Kruger, or big sex thing movies, that's it! They got one thang on their minds, and it's getting sexed.

Mona interrupts with great intensity,

Ain't suggesting shit, these fellas is bona fide freaks, and all men is freaks. Some just don't, uh, . . . let it show like others. Some ho's will not only watch, but want to do all that nasty, freak shit . . . what's up with ya, you ain't never seen no freaks, I mean it's ya, too! Me and my girls like good movies with fine ass men like Denzel Washington, and that boy on "L.A. Law" (Blair Underwood), or that cutie on the stories, Rodney, what's his name on the stories on channel four, he is one fine black man . . . the boy on the Bill Cosby show is fine, but I don't watch that shit much, it's fake . . . that little cute Spike Lee is bad, his shit is stupid crazy! I liked that picture he had, when they burned down that pizza place, I hate pizza, these ho's eat it all the time. Anyway, it ain't lots of blacks in movies, so in a way you like whatever they show and it got blacks in it. Silly ass boys be watching gangster shit trying to learn how to git tough. Girls know that shit is silly; boys be looking for themselves up on the screen. If it ain't shooting somebody, these boys can't git to it. Like that Scarface *shit was silly as hell, that bitch in there should have smoked his crazy ass. Just like boys in some crews, they just got to control everything and try to regulate the pussy. I mean how you tell somebody who they gonna git it on with? That crazy Tony Montana kills his sisters, man, 'cause they was gitting it on! I mean, how fucked can you git? Ain't nobody telling me who I can git it on with! Movies is straight, if they show something like Spike Lee's shit that's what I want . . . .*

I like fine ass Rocky [Sylvester Stallone] and Mel Gibson, Whoopi is cool, niggahs be dissing her but she's straight and she'll git a bitch straight, she ain't perpetrating like some bitches, like that Robin Givens stank ho.

Disputing with the females, Randy comments,

That's cold, Robin is fine, y'all dissing her 'cause y'all crazy stupid over that little ugly mug Mike Tyson. Me and Howard like all kinds of movies, but the real bad babes in the nasty movies is straight, what's wrong with seeing some love movies, that don't make me no freak?

Felicia counters,

Who you calling ugly? Mike is cute as he wanna be, and you like watch shit you and your boy wanna do, but can't even do unless you git some crackhead bitch. A bitch gotta be on dope to let some of that freak shit git done to her. Your punk ass is jealous, Mike would beat your ass into the ground . . . and y'all is freaks waiting on some young silly bitch to fuck like a dog and let y'all have y'all way, I am not gonna talk with these ignorant ass bitches . . . . Mona like Spike Lee, but he must hate bitches 'cause they always gitting fucked over in his movies. Like that one called She Gotta Have It, *fuck him with his little funny looking ass, shit, men the ones always trying to git it! Men, or nasty dogs like Howard and Randy always want to fuck any girls . . . huh, what 'bout his other movies, they always fucking over girls. That one with the college boys (School Daze) , and I know some college boys, they freaks like street boys. The one with that real dark dude playing Shadow (Wesley Snipes) playing the horn in Denzel's band. They fucked all over my girl, and she was fine, but she was gitting dicked. Denzel was dogging all the bitches in the movie. Bitches should make movies and then they wouldn't git dogged. Men can be skeezers too, they just don't think so, or nobody gits on men when they fuck everybody!*

4

Drugs and Females

Crack cocaine first became apparent to the media in the later part of 1985. Few at that time realized the epedimic abuse rates that it would reach. The immediate popularity of the drug is relatively simple to understand—a very intense, instantaneous "high" at a very low cost. Crack cocaine "rocks" can be easily purchased for $3, $5, or $10. While the high cost of cocaine is prohibitive to some, the low cost of crack makes it readily attainable to everyone.

Unfortunately, most of the attention given to this issue of abuse has ignored women within the context of their own lives and focused primarily on the impact of addiction on pregnancy. The public outrage toward "crack babies" has devoted the majority of concern to the drug/pregnancy issue rather than to drug treatment and prevention issues among women who are not pregnant. In the following interviews women describe their lives as crack addicts.

MARY

Mary, 29, had been addicted to crack cocaine and cocaine for seven years. A single mother, she has recently been promoted to a new job, out of the state. She talks about her ordeal and how she broke away from drug addiction and welfare.

My life was messed up from the word go. My parents divorced early and both of them are substance abusers. Things just went to hell for us. My father was very successful in business and left my mother for the better life, the fast lane. My mother was crushed and fell out and just started drinking and stayed drunk. I took to boys and got pregnant at fifteen. I was upset about my parents and all the other things that normal teens endure were happening too. I started smoking weed, drinking hard liquor, and next it was cocaine and then that damn pipe took over.

Hanging out with concert people and going to the television dance show was my life. My younger sister started to get real out of control. But she had no one to help, 'cause my mother and father were caught up in their own drug and alcohol problems. We went to school, I graduated and I don't know how. Got on welfare and just hung out in the street. I wasn't much of a mother; I had all kinds of men around, young ones and old ones . . . I was going nowhere real fast. My mother was acting like she was my child. My father had got with the real fast people and lost his business. That's when I found out how bad that pipe was. He had this young girl, younger than my sister. He lost everything, smoked it up like it was nothing . . . the pipe got him, me, and my younger sister. My mother was living with me and she stayed drunk. So here we are, a drunk and a crackhead. It was hell for my baby, he was in elementary school and his mother and grandmother are supposed to raise him; we couldn't raise ourselves, it was messed up!

Then one day, I don't know what it was, something just sent me to this church. This little lady open the door, and just smile at me and said, baby, it's gonna be alright, 'cause God loves you. It was like some dream, I still, 'til this day don't know how I got there, it just happen. I would go back to church and sometimes I would be high from the pipe, but that little lady just won't give up on me, and it just got to be the place I went no matter what. Next thing I knew I wasn't thinking 'bout that pipe. She just won't give up on me. Then I dropped all the people that kept me back, all the people that gave me dope. I wasn't one of those crazy Jesus girls, I just found myself with that little lady, Mrs. Jones, helping me. Next thing, I was in school and I wanted to do better, and I was doing much better.

The church helped me, and then one morning I just woke up and said I am not going to depend on welfare no more. I remember I was in bed and just decided it was time to get off, and do for myself! I started to cry and thank God for making me alive and feeling like I was better than waiting for some welfare check. I finished trade school with skills and got a job, a good job. In less than two years I got another chance to move out of Detroit, out of Michigan, for a real big job. That pipe is still on my daddy's back, and my momma is still drinking; I realize they got to do it themselves. My son has a chance now, and I am still working to better myself. All I can say is that crack made me a slave, bless that little church lady for saving me. I got off, but I got lots of girlfriends on that pipe. My daddy used to own his own business and now he's sleeping in his car. That pipe has taken lots of good people to the dogs . . . once you get on that pipe, it's hell, and the only thing that can save you is God.

THE WALKING DEAD

Cherry, 25, and Wanda, 22, are on crack; they are living on the street on the east side of the city. This interview is one of several over the summers of 1990 and 1991. Their residence is an abandoned house which serves as a meeting place for several other crack addicts.

Cherry had been interviewed for the book *Dangerous Society,* as a girl-friend of one of the members of the Chambers Brothers narcotics gang. Today, she is in poor physical and mental health. She is asking for money in return for sex. The interviewer has talked with Cherry for the past seven years; yet she has no recollection of those conversations on this warm summer evening.

Cherry is asking the interviwer why he can't give her money for sex:

You don't want to get with me? Are you funny, or do you want more than one freak? I'll make it worth your time, big fella. [Interviewer answers that he only wants to talk about her life] Well, what's to talk 'bout? I was on full, getting tore off, and then my boy got popped on the Boulevard, boom boom and it was over. I didn't have no big paper saved, and his family took every dime in the house, left me out cold. I got fucked around by some other fellas in his crew but what can you do? I started getting high, and next thing I knew it was on the streets for me and my girls. Are we a crew? Do you mean are we some sort of crew like the fellas? Naw, we ain't got shit, how can we survive without paper or somebody to take care of us? I was with Nate since I was eighteen, and then he gets wacked! See that babe over there, well, she used to be so fine the girls would be jocking to just talk to her, she was the queen of the dope girls. Now look at the ho, she is out here giving her ass away to whoever she can. I knew I had it made, me and Nate was kick-ing it and planning to get married. My family was real proud, 'cause Nate was gonna buy me my own salon. My momma and my aunts were gonna work for me, everythang was going straight, then he gets wacked by some snake muthafuckers. . .back then I got all the 'caine I wanted and when I want it I just get my little stash, and I had my own paper . . . boom!

Could you get off crack if you wanted?

Oh yeah, just like that! Get the fuck outta here! This pipe is kicking my ass, I love that little pipe. It's like the only thing I do, and I am gonna keep hitting it, 'til I die . . . see, the high is better than fucking, naw, . . . it is fucking, [laughing] it's like fucking yourself, like having a dick and a pussy and all you gotta do is just stick yourself into yourself and come! And you ain't got no man or woman to beg like I been begging your stingy ass for some paper to get me some rocks.

Are there others in the house that were once in good shape but now are homeless?

Cherry screams,

I am not homeless, I can live with my family whenever I want! This is where the action is. If you want fish go to the fish market . . . this is the crack market, that's why we live here. It's the action, the dope, it's all we want, so why go any place else? All we want is to get high, why not live in this house?

Wanda shakes her head in disagreement; she says,

Cherry's people and my family won't let us near their houses. We is crack ho's, and that's worse than a crackhead, we is the lowest hos on the planet [laughing].

My father told the police to just shoot me, 'cause he was tired of coming down to the jail to get me out; my kids hate me. They should, I ain't shit. I tried to sell my daughter, who is fine, she is just beautiful, and I was trying to sell her for some rocks three years ago. My children was taken from me, and they was right, the judge said I was evil; well I don't know 'bout all that, but I know I am a dope fiend. My parents was good to me, and my father was the kind of Christian man you be proud of . . . . I am gonna give you their phone number, go see my family, they straight. I chose this shit, but my family is good, write that down. But don't go to my kids' school 'cause I don't want other kids saying their momma is some crack ho, 'cause kids will make up bad shit 'bout your momma or anybody if they can, 'cause kids is mean. Wait a minute, if you write 'bout us, I don't want my kids hurt or my family, my daddy is a big church man in Detroit . . . they should just say hos like us is just dead, you know, the living dead, forget about us. Who else would live like this? Look at this house, ain't nothing here but rats . . . ain't no water, no heat, and no windows. This is the crew of crack fiends, the boys in here is tramps just like the ho's. The boys with us is part of our set, and they sucking and fucking too!

Aren't you afraid of catching AIDS or some other disease?

Cherry cooly replies,

Humm, well it's like what else could I catch? I don't go to the doctor, and my eyes is yellow all the time, but who cares? The fellas getting with me don't mind, and AIDS is something I don't think 'bout, I just don't think 'bout it. You hear all the talk 'bout rubbers. But most of the white boys have 'em but they don't use 'em. And they live outside the city and want some strange shit, like pissing on 'em, or letting them do silly shit. But they got the paper, so let's party. They will buy the rocks and still give me monay . . . now, you get some young black fellas and you better watch out 'cause it's serious shit, like beating you down or making you do some fucked-up, wacked things like kissing dogs or sucking the whole crew, yuck, yick . . . it's live sometimes.

Wanda replies rather lifeless,

> *AIDS, fiending, beatings, fuckings, shootings, whatever . . . I am already dead, even sometimes it's hard to remember when things were so bad. The dope just takes over, it's wild, kinda strange . . . you got to live it, it's too hard to talk about.*

USED TO HAVE A JOB . . . A GOOD JOB, CRACK TOOK IT AWAY

Kari, 28, George, 27, Kyle, 33, and Nancy, 24, are all crack addicts. The interviewer meets them in Cass Corridor near downtown Detroit in a motel that is frequented by addicts, prostitutes, and others in the underground. Nancy is from Flint, she is the only white person in the group and she talks about her becoming a crack addict. Looking thin and talking very low, she sighs and offers:

> *I worked in the plant and got laid off and that's when I got to messing with this damn pipe. I had it made, I was going to Mott [Community College] and taking classes for business, because me and my sister was gonna open up a restaurant, a truck stop on I-75 exit. My mother cooks real good German and Polish food. Her father used to cook in the army; he was German and his wife was Polish. My whole family worked in the shop. My husband, he worked there for eighteen years, right out of high school. Then the shit started to go bad and my father got laid off. He went back to another plant, but hell, he's been with GM for almost all his life. Next me and my husband started to fight about his money and his girlfriend, and I stopped just drinking and smoked more bud.*
>
> *Anyway it was my friend over there Kyle, he took me to this party. Hell, everybody at this party worked in the shop. You know that movie, Roger and Me, well it was like that at the party, we was all laid off. We fired and we just got higher and higher. My marriage was messed up and everything was wrong. I knew I had a problem 'cause I just kept drinking and smoking when I was scared or depressed. Glad I didn't have no kids, our marriage was down the drain. My father hates black people, calls them monkeys . . . . Well, my ex, Dawson caught me with Kyle at the 7-11 and went crazy. He made sure my family knew I was with the monkey boy. My father told me I was a monkey loving nigger lover. My mother was mad and my family pissed me off so I just hung out with Kyle.*
>
> *We went to Detroit to party, now you can get crack in Flint, but I wanted to leave Flint. So, we stay in Detroit, first Kyle had a cousin and we had money, so the partying was fun. Then it got crazy, I really wanted help, you know treatment at the hospital and I wanted to stop because I could not see*

what I was doing anymore. Well, that was six years ago, I ain't been home since my father told me one Thanksgiving that if he saw me with the monkey people, he would shoot me on sight. That hurt, so I stay out here and crack has captured me . . . . I am sick and so is Kyle. I know I am sick, serious sick, but where can we go? So you get high, and do whatever it takes. I heard that my ex is living with this Mexican woman, and he tells everybody he caught me fucking Kyle and left me . . . lies, lies, but what the hell? I want to say one thing, okay, there are lots of women like me, women who got nothing and we just get fucked over out here and then we give up. My father says I am a nigger, I am not white anymore. Well, that's okay, 'cause there are lots of women and young girls out here and all of them ain't black. Fuck it, all of us is gonna die and all I can say is I used to make General Motors [laughing].

Kari tells how she used to make it:

I was a model and crack was not my thing at all, I am the one that keeps these children off the street. Now, sir, you might think our home is run down, well I am not in the street. My mother and sisters are assisting me in getting back on my feet. I am friends with George, he used to be a photographer and worked at Burroughs. My work in the modeling field was on the side, I graduated from Catholic school and went to business school. My mistake, and it was mine, was trusting and getting in the fast lane. I had a car and a great job in the post office. I guess you could say I had a real good job, crack came and took away everything because I let it, but crack did it.

My supervisor who was real smart got me to try it. Seriously, I didn't do drugs, if I got caught up anyone could. My supervisor lost everything—his wife, job, and his sense. He got killed last year, nobody knows nothing. I heard about it from my sister. They never said how it happen, but he was in Viet Nam, and he could take care himself, nice guy, but he loved dope. See he was my friend, and then crack ate him [eyes tearing]. My mother is trying to help and so is my sister. If it wasn't for George, I wouldn't be around, he saved me from some scary people down on the river last summer when I was out there crazy doing shit I never want to remember. So I rent this room and they kinda protect me, and I try to get them to stop getting high. It's hell out here, people talk about dope, kids saying no, man, it's unreal, this crack could destroy a whole world . . . . I am getting off, and I pray that they get off, it's sad that I had to get caught up in the fast life and find out the hard way. This is a hard life, this is hell, I know people like my father think that we deserve this, but no one deserves the way we have to live, I wouldn't wish this on my worst enemy. This is the worst way to learn about life. One more chance and I promise you, I wouldn't even drink a beer . . . . No more dope, alcohol or anything, I am moving out of Detroit, starting all over, it ain't Detroit, I just want a new place, a new chance with no memories of the hell down here.

JANINE

Janine is 30 years old and comes from a small, predominantly white town. Her family was one of the most prestigious black families in the community. She went to very good schools. During this interview, Janine often becomes erratic—her life with hard drugs has had an emotional toll, leaving lasting scars. While she has recovered and is pursuing a more tranquil and productive life, readers should bear in mind her experience of violence, street life and illegal drugs have caused a great deal of mental and physical anguish.

Did you feel loved at home? How did you get off track?

Ya, oh ya, I was surrounded by love. Like I said, my great uncle was a preacher. How, why? I'm not gonna put the blame on no one. But I was introduced to a fella that, we'll call him Tom. Tom was a con artist by profession, he was a professional con artist, a professional thief. His con game was women and rich white men.

And you met him here in Detroit?

Yes, I met him here in Detroit.

You were just visiting?

No, I wasn't visiting because at this time I had started, just started. He had started introducing me to smoking crack cocaine. Like I said, I started using cocaine at the age of twenty-one but I started as a blower. And it was, I told you through a Cuban guy that was here, coming to Ypsilanti, that was making a lot of money. See what happened was, the Cuban guy was an illegal alien.

We all had built up his confidence that we had a cousin here in Detroit, Albert, that had been doing this all his life. So he listened to how we had built up this, that this guy is a Cuban and illegal alien. He know he has no ties here and that this was a good pigeon. Because there was nothing that the guy could do to him. So through us he beat the man out of a lot of cocaine. So after he got through with this man, beating his money out of cocaine, I'm not trying to be bad, I'm not trying to say that I'm cute or whatever. I'm not into that bag, because beauty is only skin deep. That's what I was taught. Like I said, when we came home we worked in the fields. We didn't prance in front of the mirror, you know what I'm saying, we had to get down with the books. And I bless my grandmother and her efforts.

So you came from a strong work ethic?

Right, right, we wasn't into this beauty thing. So, after we beat this Cuban guy out of all this money and I was dating the Cuban guy. He introduced me to one of his friends. Like I told you, that taught me the con game and gave me books, I read books on it, I seen videos on it. And this guy was a heavy smoker. That's when I started smoking heavy.

Had you experienced or experimented with drugs prior to meeting him?

Well, ya.

In high school?

I was a depressed teenager, it was because of my home, the parental guidance was gone at an early age and as I came up in high school I missed that. That all the other students' Mom and Dads was there. And I was a depressed teenager.

So when you say they was gone, what happened to them?

My mother and father split up, I guess when I was about five to, no, maybe about eight. Because my baby brother was about three years old. And that's the one that is in the hospital now. So, when father was gone there was a lot of pressure on me as being the oldest child and to help mother with the kids. A lot of that depressed me too, so I started, you could call be a cross addicter, that's what I was. I started out with marijuana and I went on to chemicals because I went to a predominantly white school. Where I am from, the white folks out there pay good taxes, for kids to get the best education and they were doctor's and lawyer's children but they were the ones who had access to these chemicals. And selling them in school that we were using. So I was a chemical user . . . . When I was introduced to crack cocaine it was like the gates of hell opened. That's when it was, it was a whole new world. And I was about to walk into.

I have talked to other people who do drugs, crack, is it true that you do it one time, you get addicted, it doesn't take long?

No, no I didn't get my first hit the first time, it took me awhile before I really got, what you can call yourself 'addicted.' When crack cocaine becomes God.

How long?

It's like, Ok, like when Moses came down, this was something, this was a idol thing. Thats what this addiction is, this thing is taking control of you like completely. It took me, before I really got addicted, I would say it was like about a month.

But you know why, because it was so available to me, I was smoking like three or four ounces and maybe I just psychologically thought I wasn't getting high but I was getting high.

We were all smoking and talking and Tom said "Do this." Like I said, I was like a dog. If I wanted to get my reward I did what Tom said to. You fuck, whatever it was, excuse the language. That's what I had to do. I was a German shepherd and Tom was the obedience school. He was preparing me for what he had in store for me further down the line.

So he got you smoking crack cocaine?

Right, but when I started it was like, like I said, like a dog goes to obedience school, I had one master. And that's what I had, one master. And a dog learns to love this one master, I learned to love this one master and do as he told me to do . . . . This is my master, the dog learns to love the master because he is constantly rewarded, right.

And your reward was always drugs?

Drugs, cocaine. It was the thing that I wanted most in my life.

What happened, you had no one else around to stop the cocaine?

Ya, a lot of people did.

Anyone here?

The fellow that just walked out the door, he did. My aunt did. My aunt said, why do you want to mess with him, he's using you. This guy is where he had been all of his life. I think he was thirty something, thirty-eight, thirty-nine . . . . He was about the same to most women. He had women, like I said, if I slept with him I didn't sleep alone. You know, in the beginning I did, but if it came down to it, I had to sleep with other women with him . . . if that's what he told me to do, if I wanted my reward. I had to. Now, let me explain something to you, OK. At this time I didn't have no mind, no mind of my own. Had I had, had a mind, and my confidence in myself was broken.

And your self-esteem?

Right, and you can say there was brain-washing too. I look at it, like I told you in the car. It's like cocaine is like a tool of the devil. That's what he used, it's a tool. You know what I'm saying. Just like you take a wrench to tighten a bolt, he took this pipe to make money, for pleasure, even just for pleasure, to entertain his friends. You know, maybe I was his little entertainment thing, just a play thing to him.

Did that happen to the other women that you were with?

Ya, I seen a lot of it, even his ex-wife.

Really?

He got her tanked up . . . . There was one time she, him and I was on the set together.

On a set? What's that?

On a set, it means like, we were at a place together, this home, and we were smoking. This was when I had broke down and really realized what I had stepped into, I was too far gone then. He made me have oral sex on him while him and his wife smoked.

I was gone, by the time I was twenty-four I didn't care if I had my child, I didn't care about my feminine hygiene, it would be a week sometimes before I would go somewhere to take a shower. But after I took a shower and put those clean clothes on I was right back out there.

Do you have any regrets?

Ya, I cried. You know cocaine is, if you have ever done a study on it, I read a little bit about it during the time of my youth. At the time I wasn't using, you know, let me see what I got myself into. I was diagnosed once, I tried to commit suicide because of the use of crack cocaine. I was diagnosed as a manic depressive. Cocaine is a depressant, a drug. The come down off of cocaine is depressing. And I did, I had regrets all through it, I had regrets.

Do you see yourself as being very different or do you see other young women being in the same shape as you?

But see, these women that I was around, they flashed it up. It was something that they was used to doing, it meant nothing, it meant nothing to them, these women were fine women with jewelry, professional lives, you know.

Professional, you mean?

Hair dressers, you know, some were women professional boosters, you know what I'm saying. Something that they had been doing all their life, in high school, it was like picking up a glass and drinking water, a child learns to do that. It was something that they had learned, sixteen, do you know their whole family was into this.

Did you idolize them?

I did, I idolized them too. I wanted to be like them.

You seem to be independent.

Not independent from the drug.

OK, but independent from men?

No, not all of this, and the men always had three or four or five women.

The man would be the oppressor?

Right.

Do you see crews or guys all the time?

Right.

Do you see any female crews or girls that work for male crews?

Well most them was like bartend, barmaid in that level. When my supplier went to jail, I had to find another supplier, so at that time I was low. I was on a level where I was dealing with young people and a level where I did anything. The cocaine that I was getting, wasn't what I was used to.

You lose weight?

A lot of weight, I used to wear a size one.

One!

One is a size, is a size one and zero, and I was an alcohol abuser too you know.

So you were a substance abuser, cross abuser?

That's a street slang, cross abuser, addicted.

In the square world they call it substance abuse.

Cross addictive.

Now, Tom went to prison?

Right.

If he showed up today would you get back with him?

No.

How do you know?

Because of the medication that I am taking and the after effects that I am experiencing, I'm too scared to go through this all over again. But, like, I said, like I told you in the car, I feel I'm telling myself I can do all things through Christ and strengthen me. Because I am still, you know, you worry about slipping back. But I know that if I fell away from this person, 'cause I know if I get with this person it's going to be the same thing over again, no doubt in my mind. Unless he had changed and I don't know.

What about church, do you go to church?

No I haven't been to church but, I talk to a preacher on a regular basis. I met him at the birth of my third son. I was using crack then, I had back slide, but he was born with a breathing problem. His lungs were immature, so he was on oxygen. Luckily, he only stayed for a week, I thought I was going to go through this thing again. You know with my oldest child, I wasn't using drugs when he was born. But I was with the last two. And that's what I think contributed to the breathing, that his lungs were not. Because of the smoke, the constant smoking I was doing. So, anyway he was born. What were we talking about now? Anyway, he was born like that. You were asking me but would I go back? No, I wouldn't, because of all this that I went through. This, I have been through a mental thing, a mind thing, I have drove a physical thing, using my body, you know what I'm saying. Like I told you I felt like the gates of hell had just open and I could feel the fire.

So what do you plan on doing now?

Now, right now I'm spending a lot of time with my children. I am going with a guy, not because I have an attitude towards black men, I did pick up because of the men I have dealt with when I was on crack cocaine and the things that I did, which weren't, wasn't their fault, it was my fault like I told you, I had turned completely, my constitution had been turned around. My whole way of thinking, the foundation, what I was brought up and raised and believed that was through. My moral standards was through, my self respect, that was through. So now I'm seeing a guy, that, a Chaldean guy. He's younger than me and we can talk and discuss putting my kids in private schools. You know, bettering my life and bettering their life. Because the most important thing is that my mother had came back to me. And that was God given. I know that, I have been through an experience with God, knowing that, that right there, you know that right there, knowing that is motive baiting me to keep on doing right. And eventually I think I'm feeling that I'm going to come into the spirit as a whole. You know what I'm saying. Settle down and get a good marriage and be happy, be happy and be raising my children. Instead be happy because I have a drug. You know I'm going to find all that happiness that I lost. So it's like I'm really a baby again.

Being re-born?

Right, that I already knew that were within me, but I'm learning how to do them again now. That's why I told you in the car, I said, I love to talk about the end because the ending is the most beautiful part.

Happy ending?

That's right, so far. But I tell you I'm still saying to myself I can do all things through Christ who strengthens me.

Have you been tempted to go back?

You know what? No, I haven't been tempted because I have been around it and still walked away from it. But I couldn't, I'm not gonna say that I could sit in a room with a group of people, you know, and not want to.

Really?

That would be telling a lie. And I am just like an alcoholic stands up and says I'm a alcoholic, he still is an alcoholic even though he stopped drinking. The need, he wants to do this, you know what I'm saying. Like I still want to smoke, but I'm saying "no" to myself because this is not good for Jane, this is what destroyed her. This is what destroyed her, that's the only thing that's making me not. I have dated a guy that blows, you know. I won't even blow it because I know that that want is still in me. That crazy, is still there because I could be at home and I could lay and my child and one of my child had bed with a cross right up above it, just look there and wonder and just look at Jesus and wonder, you know, why must I crucify myself? Well, who was I sacrificing? When Jesus crucified himself and sacrificed, it was for the other people, but when I was doing it, it was for my selfish reasons. For myself, it was for dope.

What about the kids?

I told you, I didn't care. I lost custody of the oldest one, I told you. Remember, I had came to my family about a beating that one of my child took from a boyfriend I had, that was a cross addicter. From morphine to heroin and crack cocaine. He was getting better, but he wasn't, he was addicted to it. And alcoholism.

And he beat your kid?

He beat him. He whupped him.

You did have him arrested?

You know what? After, after I got like, I experienced a nervous thing behind that . . . because of the need, of the drug, he was a drug dealer. The forgiveness was never there. I always hated him for that but I needed that drug. You know what I'm saying, I never, when we had sex it wasn't because I loved him. It was because I knew again that I was going to be rewarded.

So you never really got over what Tom trained you?

I still haven't, right. Tom's training stuck with me, Tom's training was what got me the drugs that I needed. I learned from him, how to get these drugs. And the things that I had to do, to get these drugs. I had alienated my family, the good people. I stopped going around, refused to be around them. Because I know that I was going to come here, and hear, you know like here is this beautiful home and this beautiful family and all the things I want and burst into tears. I knew that I was going to hear this lecture about take it to Christ, take it to Christ. You know and I already knew because I had been right in this house, I had been, it had been dictated into my head. Constantly, the first day, that a person was saying to me when I walked into the door was "Have you gone to Christ yet?" Or "have you tooked him yet?" And then he would get a book out and I would read it. And at that point in my life I started to like that life. Because of the reward, you know what I'm saying, because of the refreshment afterwards. So I alienated those who loved and cared and tried to, you know, tried to help me along the way. I didn't want help, because like I said, I thought cocaine was god.

Is there any truth to "You cannot be helped until you're ready?"

Ya, you know what, when you get down on your hands and knees, you look, like I said, in the end I said, "what have I got?" I have lost my child, I'm getting ready to have another baby, two more responsibilities. I don't have a house to put them in, I don't have nothing. And these men that I am fucking and sucking, getting this cocaine. They're not going to help me. I had one good man that helped me, that took me off the streets, took me out of prostitution. I used to come to his dope joint and I would, like I told you, excuse me, but I would fuck his whole crew before the night was over with.

Just to have enough for one day and then I would be back the next day at the same time and do the whole thing over again . . . my aunt took me in. She ran a dope house.

What do you think about young girls and young boys in this city?

You know what, that drug, I have feelings, I didn't even know how to love anymore. I lost custody of my child and didn't care. I had no feelings.

You were dead?

Right. The spiritual part.

The living dead, a zombie?

Right, I was a zombie; no mind, no feelings, no concern, no care, filled with hatred.

You had hate?

Yes, I had hate.

Who did you hate?

I hated myself mostly. Then I hated the man that was doing this. The most hatred I had was the hatred I had for myself. I hated myself for what I was doing. That's why I tried to kill myself.

What about the young girls in this city, right now. And what's happening to them? Do you see them being oppressed?

You know what? Ok, I'm gonna tell you this. You're saying "the young girls now." You know the young girls now, I think that they're like, they have looked and they have seen how the young, the older women, like me have been treated, so a lot of them are getting more involved with the sales of drugs. Not the use of drugs. Because there is more respect to a woman who's selling. You get more respect out of a black man, that way, than the use of it. That's how I feel.

We have had a couple of interviews with girls who are dealing.

They are selling it, my brother has a lot of women that he deals with. A lot of women that go on trips for him, a lot of women that go and get the stuff and bring, a lot of women that pick up money for him.

Are they better at handling business than the guys?

Well, yes. You know, a black man is gonna kill a black man before a woman. I learned that that night, the night that my brother was shot. The guy held the gun on me and my nephew, but he never shot me. I ran out the side door with my nephew, thinking he was gonna try to take my brother's son for extortion. Because the guy that was shot in my home was not giving up the drugs. He felt this way, "you're not gonna take my life and my money and my drugs too." And my brother thought the same way. That's the attitude. This is the attitude that young men have. I'm telling you, I living it, that the life of it now.

What would you have done?

I had gave him the dope and the money, there was kids in that house and if they tortured my brother and shot him seven times, excuse me, do you think they'd care about snatching my nephew and taking him, but to get. They were there for $60,000 and two keys of dope. If they didn't care about holding a gun on me, do you think they care about snatching my nephew and taking him for extortion? If it came down to it, they'd a took one of those kids. The only thing that saved us was God, they ran out of bullets and my brother shot one. And they jumped into a car that they had already took the license plates off of and left.

When you say that, I talked about the addiction to money.

I called my cousin; I told him, I said, "I really got a lot to tell ya, Fred, don't I, after my brother was shot." That night we didn't know if he was ever gonna walk again. But, his leg, the left leg has came back but the foot is still dead and they have it in a brace. He's got six to eight more weeks for the right leg to be in traction.

The kids were in the house when this took place?

Yes, my kids, my nephew and my baby son. He was the seven-month-old son and a nine-month-old, an eight-month-old baby and my nine-month-old nephew was in my arms. He was the one we were afraid he was gonna, they was gonna take first.

We've had reports of that.

Kidnapping, they don't care. They don't care. And that's why I ran four houses down and hid and I said if he shoots me I know I still can be, he hits me one time I'm still gonna have a stretch to run. Because I felt like this. We had no damn business having those kids involved in that. They just got here, God gave us those kids. It was my motherly instinct that I had, you see what I'm saying. It came back. I had to protect this child and whatever it took. If he shot me I know I still could of made it at least next door or the next house or hide him, you know what I'm saying. We hid in the basement four houses down and I called 911.

Are there a lot of women in similar situations like yourself?

There are a lot of women, just like you hear on the news now, that are in situations. I have a cousin that is in that situation and I think she just don't give a damn. Her mother is deathly ill and she leaves. She just had another baby, her boyfriend, both of them were on crack cocaine. She thinks she's gonna take this baby and open up another crack house for her and her boyfriend.

So you feel good about yourself today?

I feel good about my motherhood coming back to me. I feel very good about that, that part. That's the part of gaining back self respect also.

Did you go see Farrakan?

No I missed him, I would of loved to have seen him, though, 'cause as far as what he says about the black man and the black woman and telling us that this is the white society, just like I said, you have to live a ghetto life, a slum life and let the gates of hell open on you. That's what they did to me before I realized that maybe it was because I had no worldly knowledge, you gotta remember when I was turned on I was still a baby. I didn't know nothing about living here in Detroit. I was married and divorced and I had a good husband, a good provider, and I let that go to crack cocaine.

Tell me how do you feel, about two weeks ago a young man was at the Broadway downtown and he was murdered?

Ya ya, his step-daughter is related to a cousin of ours. Her father was just killed, in a drug house, shot in the ear?

Why are young men so cold?

The money. Look what they did, right. The guy that my brother shot, they drove around for two hours and let him die before they dumped his body in Ann Arbor Park. It's the money. It's the white man's world money. With money comes power, with money comes respect. You are a big dope man, you know what I'm saying, one of the best. And you had to kill a few people to get there, you had to rob a few people to get there. That even gives you more respect out there. It's the lack of intelligence, that's what I'm saying, brother. When the gates of hell opened on me, I was done. I had no worldly knowledge, we're talking about kids, right. Okay, so that's what's happen, it's the intelligence. That lack of, you know, I don't know. To me it was the lack of, you don't know. You think this is what life is about but it's not.

What about your neighborhood where you live now? I drove down there and I saw, the alleys and the street look pretty rough.

You know what though, the neighborhood that I live in now, is for me, a step up. A big step up. I was staying in west Detroit in this place really looked like a back alley, or the homes did. I mean this street looked like a back alley. All the homes up and down, they'd remodeled them now, if I took you down there now you'd see but. One man had squatters' rights. He lived right next to the church? And he was living, and the police came and got him, 'cause he has squatted there and he was selling dope out of the house.

That's the business for a lot of people.

That's right, that's their way of living. That's why they are fighting and killing everybody. This is my money, this is my bread. You know, don't butter my bread, I'll butter it. That's what it is, it's living, it's a way of life.

What do you think is going to happen if things don't change? Is the black community in danger of blowing itself up?

We are in danger of becoming an extinct, and you know an endangered species. You know just like the eagle, the bald-headed eagle, we are, we are starting to kill ourselves. And we are killing ourselves. General warfare like I said. You know they killed the Jews, but we're doing it to ourselves, but they're giving it. They're giving us the materials to do it.

On the record now, are you against legalization?

Do I think it will work! If you gonna legalize cocaine you might as well legalize robbery 'cause that's what's gonna happen. Everything, they're gonna be selling it right out of the store. That black man is going to be coming into the store and robbing ya, not for your money, but your cocaine, that's you selling. Just like in probation days, that's what's gonna happen. This is gonna be Al Capone all over again.

There has been some talk recently with some Muslim brothers who were telling me that if the police would look the other way they could

clean up the drug problem in thirty days. That means they are gonna take military action.

You know when I was sixteen years old I got my ex to be a Muslim, I studied with XXX, but I was talked out of it by my grandfather, who is dead now, God rest his soul. Uncle, he told me, he said, he sat me down he said you've been raised as a Christian all your life, now you're turning. He made me think, he said, don't you know that Ala Muhamed is preaching hatred, he's telling you to hate the white man for what he's done to you. But what are you doing to yourself you, you're at school using drugs. And the white man not telling you to do that, you're doing that because you want to. And I thought about what he said.

So family is important?

Yes, yes, like I said, the time I came here and sat and cried, if they shut the door in my face I might of killed myself then. But I knew that they care, even though I was destroying myself and if they, what they made me feel was that I was even hurting them, not just myself. Because of the love and more. You know what, they even allowed their children to sit at the table and said, I want, he even told them I want you to listen to this. To see what's happening here and they listened, you know they listened.

Cocaine is devastating, it's devastating, do you understand, like I told you, you lose your sanity. And it is dangerous for a person, with no mind, like cocaine is like having a gun in your hand, a person running around with no mind. Smoking that and hand guns are free, you know, available to you.

Do you think you will overcome the guilt?

No, you never overcome the guilt. Well, I haven't, I'm still living with the guilt, that for seven. I haven't had my child from seven, now he's eleven, that four years of his life. And his grandmother still doesn't really trust him, yet really, being with me, he was here for the summer, he was allowed to come and spend summer vacation with me. He will be here Christmas.

Would you tell another woman not to go down that same road that you went down?

You can't tell a woman, no, a woman talking to another woman, you know there is already rivalry between two women. You can't stay in the same house together, there is rivalry. You can't tell a woman. Like the girl that is sitting with my kids now, we talk openly because we have been through the same things. But I can't tell her not to because I know how the drug is. People couldn't tell me nothing. People who loved me. How can a friend tell you not to? You're gonna do it if that's what you want and that's what your body craves. They say that cocaine is not an addictive drug, a physical addictive drug. I'm going through changes where I shake and I feel, you know, like I want to smell the scent of cocaine. Cocaine is a mind addictive drug, cocaine is a physical addictive drug, cocaine will destroy, it is devastating. It will destroy you, in every definition of the word.

Do you want me to talk about the Neo-natal unit? OK, we were saying as a black unity, as a black family as a whole, that we are becoming extinct, endangered species. But the neo-natal, when the birth of my young baby, was born, there was so many crack-addicted babies there. There was a little baby about this big, he was one pound, and the baby literally had the shakes. And they had to leave it on a water bed and laid on its stomach, so, excuse me I forget sometimes and that from the drug too. To make it breathe.

Tell me something, how did your neighborhood respond to the shooting on your street, with your brother?

I was so upset you know, the first thing I did when I seen my brother. I told him how to tie the tie, he was bleeding to death, literally, he had been beat in the head with the gun, plus with a beer bottle. And he was bleeding from the head, blood, he was losing it, he had lost so much blood that he turned yellow. Pale, yellow, like the door yellow. So we had to stop the bleeding. I called my aunt because she's a nurse and I knew she would, if EMS, it seemed like it was taking them awhile to get there. I had called two times.

How long did it take?

Well, to me it was a long time because of the bleeding, but it was like five or ten minutes. His son called the police. Because my brother was talking to my cousin that is incarcerated. He was talking to my cousin that was incarcerated on the phone when the shooting occurred and he heard the shots. And my brother's girlfriend picked up the phone and was crying and says Jim got shot and dropped the phone, so he called here to Louis, to tell him to call the police and the police got there before EMS did.

How were the police?

There were two car loads, they made us stay out of the house, they weren't concerned with the condition of my brother, they were concerned with what happened. Why it happened. What, well it's their job. You know and what happened to him, where did they go? They tied rags around him, I told them to tie them, 'cause I worked as a nurse's assistant. I had got myself together a little bit but they turned into being a job just for crack cocaine too.

What did the neighbors think about it?

We was all standing out there looking. They were saying "I haven't heard anything."

They didn't say anything to you?

No, but they say the FBI. Well, ya, one neighbor mother said that she didn't want her kids in my house anymore. That hurt my feelings. 'Cause they always used to come over after school and I got a VCR, and they watch like, I might with the kiddy play or the kid's Ninja Turtles. She, the little girl, call her grandmother, left her home and came to my house. To get the baby. She told her to come on out of there. But, see, her grandmother works downtown for the FBI. And the FBI is saying that they are going to start questioning people in the neighborhood. I guess it didn't go over too well with them.

I'm sure it didn't. Now what were the young guys like? How old were they?

Twenty, and twenty-one. And one of the guys had just shot a boy down at the Dancery here in Detroit. So he's wanted for that. Ok, he was wanted and they used to come down. I always had a feeling about him because he came from the worse areas of Ypsilanti which is Willow Run and suburban areas, where it is predominantly black. And where, just like Inkster, cocaine is taking over. And one of them was very big. Had a Mercedes you know and all this. So I always had my doubts about them.

What was the place you said that you were in Ypsilanti and you were in a really bad area and you were at some apartment complex, Lexington, Liberty?

Liberty Square.

Liberty Square, OK.

What did I tell about that?

Well, you were saying how bad it was.

A girlfriend of mine got killed in there. And me and her, there was a big argument. Before she got killed and another girlfriend said "Let's go." Just leave them alone. And about a half an hour later they shot at each other.

One of them got her head cut off.

Chopped off, ya. Well you know, when women are basing with men, how men mistreat women basing. They call them crack heads or whatever have you. Dope fiend bitch, they don't have too much respect for women that on drugs. The women is there for one purpose and that's for the fuck or whatever. And you know when it get down to the point where they tired of the women they don't want to give them drugs no more. But after you have been using this drug your body is so geeked up you steal if you have to. And she stoled, that's what happened with her, why they killed her. But she had a big suit come in, law suit, so she was getting a lot of drugs on that too. You know, messing around with the wrong people, I never really found out actually the whole story what happened, but I knew that she was found dead. And my girlfriend that I told you that I use to work on Eight Mile with, she was in a fire bombing 'cause the dope. To escape burning to death, I guess you can call it the fires of hell, she crawled into a refrigerator and suffocated.

You talked also about being in a house where guys hit the house?

Ya a guy, I was with a guy and I was smoking, he wasn't a smoker, just a provider. And I was smoking there with, he had his shirt off. We were in the process of having sex, what have you. And some guys came in and they asked me to leave. Well, what could I do?

Because they would of went ahead and killed you too, right?

Ya, right. So I left. But as I was leaving out I heard the gun shots. But I left when I heard the gun shots. I went to Lima, Ohio. I left there and left my child and went to Lima, Ohio for two weeks.

To hide out?

Because I thought they were gonna blame it on me. Because I was the last person he was with, they took his jewelry, his money, his drugs, everything. You know, it was a robbery. I left and stayed gone, and they thought I was dead. I drove all the way to Lima, Ohio, in a car with no brakes. I was that scared. And this happened over on Van Dyke, off of Van Dyke, closer to the Eastside, that's the worse area.

I stay away from over there now 'cause I don't want to be recognized or you know. 'Cause, I don't know. I don't know what they think, you know, I don't know if it was investigated. Because a lot of those murders they never really find out who done it. Just like what happened to my brother. They, one of the guys turned himself in because we wanted to plea bargain. The other guy died and the other one is, they say he is in California or Texas but he got away. You know what I'm saying. These murders, and then they never. My boyfriend, the guy who got me off of the streets, his best friend was murdered. It's been almost a year now and they never found out who killed him.

Do you think there is something to that?

I don't think the detectives really investigate drug-related murders.

Do you think there is police corruption?

I know there is. I turned tricks with officers.

In uniform or in plain clothes?

Plain clothes, and one of them took me in before. And he had to drop the charges. It worse off to me than soliciting. I was four months pregnant with my son, and I had, turned a date with a detective and he turned me in. And it was because it was a disputed argument over the money that he owed me. He felt like he didn't have to give me nothing. But I wanted some dope, he had to give me something.

Are you afraid in the streets?

I'm not worried about no one. I'm not in that type of life. I have been, that's part my own sickness, the paranoia. Because of the freaks that I use to run into, you scared of what a person might do.

What kind of freak have you ran into?

One time a guy followed me around, you know, everytime I turned around, I looked up. You know, how I used to walk late at night and I would go over there, over on that street, and everytime I looked up he was around, I was scared for my little cousin even.

Was he black or white?

He was black. Everytime I looked up. And he paid me good money, but everytime I looked up I started getting, I actually started getting afraid of him. Because when we were having sex he was calling my name. He was obsessed. And I left again and stayed in Ypsilanti for a long time. You meet all kinds of people. And he give me anything, dope, whatever I wanted, but he was getting obsessed. And he was a married man, too. Prestigious, you know, good, married man. And he picked me up on Eight Mile late at night. So that, it told me that he was a freak, not no man with no good job or wife, don't go up and down Eight Mile for a prostitute unless they're sick. Right, am I right? But at that time I didn't care.

5

The Life

The following interviews were collected over a four-year time period. The conclusions drawn are open ended; many of the individuals have communicated with the field team since 1985. The following interviews are with women and girls in gangs who discuss their daily lives in urban Detroit.

ARE GIRLS IN GANGS IN DETROIT?

This interview takes place on the Westside of Detroit. The neighborhood is filled with abandoned houses and poorly kept apartments. This gang consists of three females and nine males; they are considered small, yet successful, since they are making money. They are leaving scavenger status and now entering entrepreneur organization status. The gang is working out of what appears to be a two-family flat. The upstairs unit is empty and the downstairs is occupied by the gang. There is no running water and the house smells like urine. The lights are very dim and the windows are covered by newspapers. The door is opened by a young man looking very aggressive. The person taking the investigator into the house is related to the gang members and tells the doorman, "it's ok, it's business." The females are Renay, 17; Diane, 17; and Tracie, 15. The males are Julius, 16; Rafial, 19; Benny, 22; and Junius, 20. After introductions, the investigator asks if women are involved in gangs in the city? The group laugh hysterically at the question. Tracie replies,

Girls is in crews, gangs, money, shooting . . . they in it all! What makes you ask that question, is you from somewhere where the girls don't count?

Rafial says,

Babes just like fellas, I know babes that are killing niggahs like the fellas . . . it's cold with lots of these babes today. Girls like to get paid and some of

95

these babes are so out they just want to get paid and they don't care what it takes.

Renay is shaking her head in agreement and adds,

Look here, it's noon and in a second the crackheads will be here, and you'll see bitches out there, the rock stars ready to sell their ass fo this crack. That's what made me into a business wo-man, them is the bitches that make girls git into the life. Who wants to be some stank ho? The three of us is tight, we ain't no gang like fellas, these guys is our partners, they help us git our shit to sell to the crackheads. Now, Raf is right and we ain't like them ho's he's talking 'bout. 'Cause we ain't down fo some of the silly shit some niggahs do, and we ain't out here doing crazy shit like killing babies. We know some bitches like that, but that ain't us.

Benny and Junius explain what they feel is the reason girls are in gangs, while sitting on a ragged couch, drinking a quart of beer. Benny begins his female gang rationale,

It's always been girls in the mix, girls always got into shit. It's just now peo- ple start noticing babes. I got some gangster cousins. Every last one of them is gangsters, the momma, daddy, the boys, and the girls. But it's the boys that got the note, the girls would beat niggahs down all day. And that's the way it is with people and that include the hook, they don't treat girls the same. People think girls only do things 'cause they soft, but girls is smart and some are muthafuckas, like these here girls ready for prime time . . . girls is out here. Now, some are sack chasing and some are rolling and some is just out here being knuckleheads. But you best know that girls is busy in this town and others. I've been in Cleveland, Los Angeles, Atlanta, Chicago, all over, girls is getting some of that rock like everybody else in America.

Junius,

Girls, they just tired of getting hand outs. That's why these babes is down with us and that is why we work young girls, 'cause they know how to trick the hook. Girls been involved since time began, we just didn't know that girls were valuable to making everything easy. . . . Some babes make more money and less noise than some of these boys in our crew. Girls are in the life just like the fellas . . . it's just business with these girls. There are some dumb fellas and there are some dumb babes. Some people want to get paid and some don't care 'bout nothing but crying 'bout give me something. Girls want to get paid like everybody else, sure they're out here, and any- body that believes in getting over in Detroit is out here . . . you be surprised who's out here.

ARE WOMEN MAKING MONEY
OUT IN THE STREETS?

This is one of several meetings during the month with this all-female group. They are members of the Red Gucci Girls: Gail, 18; Patricia, 16; Harriet, 23; Natrina, 19; and Vellicia, 19.

Harriet responds matter of factly,

> It's like life and some are and some ain't. It's like fellas in some ways, lots of fellas out in the street and they starving. Everybody can't get paid, lots of girls are just waiting for somebody to drop that paper on them. Some girls want some guy to take care of them, they just lazy and they think some man is just gonna give them money . . . that's what makes it tight out here. Girls who will do anything for paper make it bad for all us smart babes. There are starving girls and girls getting stupid monay. The monay is out here. Benzos, Beemers, Jeeps, you name it, and I've seen it right here in the city.
>
> Now you ain't seeing that kinda shit off no ho monay. The babes out in the life are getting paid, lots of monay out here and girls is getting it . . . I'm getting it on, this crew ain't on welfare! [The girls laugh and give each other high-fives.] Girls that are making it large ain't like fellas. Now, we get our little jewelry, but we ain't wearing no street signs in diamonds like fellas, guys like to show off too much, guys do shit that's unnecessary. Girls like to save their money; now you got ho's that fuck up their monay, but more girls save and do smart shit rather than buy six, seven cars and go to Vegas and just blow big monay trying to impress their boys. Now, skeezers will try to impress you, they will go and fuck up monay and try to open a hair salon every time! But skeezers fuck their way everywhere, so it's tight for them, they don't know nothing but giving up that ass. When fellas get tired of your pussy, it's good-bye girl, naw, it's get the fuck out of my life bitch! Next bitch! So, a girl got to get her own if she is on the know, me and my jammies got our own, and it is stupid dope when you do it this way . . . no wonder fellas do it this way . . . it's straight this way. Fuck being a ho!

Vellicia smiles and adds,

> Anybody that says girls ain't getting it on either don't know or is just full of shit. This city got so many girls getting paid it's crazy stupid. The fellas is making it real large and girls is making it too! Look here, we ain't saying nothing 'bout who it is, that ain't happening, not with us. But, all you got to do is look 'round you. How much does it cost to go out to the clubs and to drive the rides, dress that way? Monay is large and just because some sucka from out there don't know, don't mean shit to us. Everythang is 'bout monay . . . we all out here getting it on, making that manay, that's what

it's all about and that's what everybody is doing . . . . It's 'bout getting that monay. Some do, and some want to do it, but it's still 'bout the monay!

Natrina appears to be somewhat shy. She has never said much during interviews in the past. She quietly suggested,

Girls is getting paid and it's getting worse out here for girls who ain't in the life. If you can't keep up with the girls in the life, I feel sorry for you, 'cause fellas only want you for one thang and that's the wild thang. That's why I got into the life, it's better than having to skeeze out there and get messed over. I seen my mother and sisters let niggahs fuck them over 'cause they didn't have no say, and they had to take all the bullshit. Girls like having shit without asking or fucking for some dog ass man to get it. Getting stupid monay is for real, and lots of girls we know is getting it on . . . .

Vellicia and Hunetta respond when the question is asked if there really are that many girls or boys involved in the illegal narcotics business in Detroit.

That question is easy, there are so many players out here it is impossible to tell the fake ones from the real. But, like we been telling you, the monay is large out here. If it wasn't, you wouldn't see all the girls trying to get it on. Look, if a girl can't get it on 'cause she ain't a cutie, they now got a out . . . they can sell the shit and make their own monay. The cuties get taken by the fellas, but for how long? Until they tired of them, and they kick 'em to the curb. Now, girls can say, fuck a niggah, a girl can make her own connects and that way it's straight. And when you got monay, you gets real fine to everybody. The boys, the car salesman, the shitty bitches out in the big stores kiss yo ass, everybody loves ya when ya getting paid. Look here, there are girls working good jobs, going to college, and they getting on. If they ain't in the life, they hanging with somebody that is getting stupid dope monay. You be fucked up if you knew all the people that is out here making that monay!

VIOLENCE AND WOMEN

Our research found a number of women, and even young girls, absorbed in violence. Many of the youngsters in this city are carrying guns, often for protection. Both women and girls have revealed attitudes that show a willingness to use and condone violence. The following four distinct groups were interviewed to discern the different attitudes between the various gang types and gang members and non-gang members.

Group 1 consisted of former corporate gang members who are now covert entrepreneurs. There are four members in this group.

WHY ARE FEMALES CARRYING WEAPONS?

Group 1: Pamela, 24, describes herself as an independent business woman. She owns a small party store in the inner city and strongly denies her alleged connections with a former corporate gang. Her claim is that she dated a young man who was allegedly a member of this corporate gang. As do others, she willingly speaks of knowledge of "the life," from living in and knowing those who are in "the life."

She is riding in a white and red Volvo with a custom convertible top. There are two younger girls riding with her and they look as if they are probably in their mid-teens. The interview is taking place at a corner store, with the interviewers sitting at a picnic table on the side. Pamela answers,

> It's crazy out here, a woman don't stand a chance against what is happening out here. That ain't got nothing to do with the life, it's just better to have a gun. The police can't be everywhere, and some of them is crazy too! I got business, and I got children and when I'm driving in my car I need all the protection I can get . . . if a girl is out in the streets in any city, she should have a gun! There are plenty reasons to carry a gun, and I don't need nobody permission to carry my piece, I'm gonna have my shit with me, later for that call the police. If you in the life, it's simple, you had better have a gun, and be ready to use it. Now, lots of men don't like women to have guns, but they the ones fucking up. Lots of men be kicking girls' ass, and a gun make 'em think before they start whipping on your little ass. You carry a piece? Asking all the shit y'all be asking, all of you guys should have a piece, talking might make some niggahs nervous, if y'all know what I mean?

Lisa, 22, and Sherrie, 19, explain why they have guns.

> It's not that I'm going for bad, it's just safer if you got your gun. I was dating this guy in this big crew, he was one of the beastmasters you know? Anyway, he beat my ass one night for some crazy shit, said I was fucking his boy. Right, his boy was hitting on me and sending me presents all the time. Anyway, this crazy niggah hit me in the stomach and he is big as hell . . . my momma got her gun and went looking for his ass. My momma shot up his apartment, and his boys were looking for us, me and my whole family! That's when I started carrying a gun. I'm scared of getting beat up or shot. I used to work at a dope house on the Eastside when I was younger, and they be practicing in the basement or in the garage. I stayed away from

guns and all that shooting stuff, but after getting beat down, my momma said "girl, you gotta have a gun, or these niggahs gonna kill your little ass." Now, me and Lisa got our own place and you can rest for sure that if anybody starts acting out of control, they gonna get popped . . . no questions ask, just bang, bang. That's the only thing these kinda people respect. You call it violence, we call it surviving . . . it's just the way it is in the city.

Carolyn, 19, offers another viewpoint,

Look, it's easy for somebody that lives in some quiet place to talk 'bout violence. But, come and live with us and you'll be carrying a gun or two yourself. I had to shoot a niggah's tire out on the expressway one night. This fool was running right into my rear end. It was scary and I got my gun out and when he wouldn't chill, I just push my window button and shot at his car, and his tires. That was one scared motherfucker, he was chilling when boom, boom and his tire went "pop"! He had followed me from a party, got on the expressway and was calling me something . . . I think he was saying, "fat bitch," anyway, I was scared, and my girls were cussing at him, I even pulled over and tried to let this asshole pass me, but fuck that, this fucker was flashing his lights, and he was driving some big ugly ass Cadillac. Blowing his horn, finally my girls got out their shit, and somebody gave me my shit out of my purse. This fucker just kept on dissing us, and when he got up on my side, I just let him have it. I didn't want to hit him, just scare his sick ass away . . . he had almost stopped when we slowed down. I just knew he had seen our guns, but he just kept on getting up on us . . . Now, what would have happen if we didn't have our shit? We would have been some fucked up cuties, that's what!

Pamela:

Call it violence if you want, but I say it's just taking care of yourself. If everybody else is packing, you be dumb as fuck to not have some kinda protection. When all the gangsters, rapists, killers, crazy babes, boys, and little kids wouldn't have their heaters maybe that's when I will stop having my gun . . . that ain't violence, that's just straight and staying alive.

Group 2 is a scavenger gang; they are referred to in the streets as skeezers. The women in this group are scavenging for any means of survival on the streets. Two of the nine women in this group were homeless at the time of the interview. This group has splintered from three different posses. They are not organized in any long range sense. All of these women are high school dropouts and are on, or have been on, some type of government assistance. All have been on some type of illicit drug, and six indicate that they are, or have been, multi-drug users. Nine women; Gloria, 28; Wanda, 23; Sharon, 26; Gail, 22; Jackie, 23; Nadine 27, Malika, 20; Sheridan, 18; and Irene, 19.

Gloria, Wanda, and Malika respond to the question of violence.

> It's just cold out here, it's kill or get killed, life is shitty and it's always been that way . . . bitches are going to get kicked around, it's what men think we're for . . . . Fucking and beasting, that's what a woman can expect from this world.

Sheridan seems to be in some sort of daze; looking at the investigator she offers,

> Death is life, and I know this for sure . . . I'm out here living in the streets [raising her voice very loudly] and you see people getting beat down all day and night. In the shelters it's dangerous for anybody, 'cause it's maniacs just slaying people. I live in the streets or wherever I can stay. Shit, life is dangerous, who is gonna take care of me? I'll tell ya, not a fucking person I know. The shelter got maniacs letting people in and out, the muthafucka that is suppose to watch things, make it safe, protect, be the security for the place? Right? I know the slimy, dirty, dope fiend dog, he use to shoot up dope with some more dirty muthafuckas and let me tell ya'll something [raising her voice louder]. This here maniac, low-life dog will fuck his muthar! Hear me, this dope stealing, lying, dog-ass niggah would fuck anythang moving . . . this maniac fucks little boys, and they got him watching the shelter! Right, real safe, right? I carry a gun 'cause it's the only way I can make it in this here world, understand?

The other women in this group seemed to understand and agreed with Sheridan in her view of why females had to carry firearms. This group indicated that it had experienced more violence personally than any other group during these interviews.

Group 3 is a small, all-female group who works as a narcotics distribution organization. They are very secretive about their business activities and have agreed to discuss only the generic segment of their vocation. This group is making a very significant amount of revenue from their illicit enterprise.

This group represented a different dimension from Group 2. These women are deeply involved in the trafficking of cocaine and crack. Their main source is allegedly solid suburbanites who purchase large amounts of cocaine and have for some time. This street intelligence is neither denied nor affirmed when mentioned by the investigators. This group agreed to talk solely on the grounds that they are young women who have associates that are knowledgeable of the streets. When asked how they could afford their very expensive clothing, automobiles, and vacations, they replied in unison that they had wealthy friends.

This group consisted of three young women; DeLores, 24; KiKi, 20; and Frankie, 27. The interview took place in a very expensive apartment in the suburbs of Detroit.

Frankie led the discussion,

> *Violence is for those people [laughing very gingerly], people who think that being physical can solve your problems. We don't get involved with violence, it's just stupid and it's ugly, ugly . . . I only associate with civilized people. In our old neighborhood you would see violence all the time; if you are smart and a lady, you just stay away from violent people. Now, I hate guns, but take KiKi, she owns lots of guns [laughing], and would shoot some poor sucker . . . she has that attitude about defending herself from the bad guys . . . I think females taking guns for protection is really stupid, acting like all the jerk ass boys out in the streets. I don't want no man to take me out for dinner and carrying nothing but his money and charge cards! Guns is asking for trouble, shoot me, and then what?*

KiKi, becomes very sharp in her expression,

> *Girl, you know that's shit, you need a gun 'cause it's lots of ignorant assholes out in the street. Men think 'cause you little, or a woman, they can do whatever pleases them. Girl, you know it's always some tramp ass bitch or some gangster niggah talking trash and girl, y'all know you got to be ready for anything. Hey Dee, who is the first bitch asking 'do y'all have yo shit' when we out at the clubs? Frankie is full of shit, the only reason she ain't packing a piece is 'cause she is scared of guns. But let some punkass ignorant gangster boy front her. She is looking for KiKi and Dee. We might open a hair salon, and you know you got to be ready for ignorant ass bitches and their silly bitch ass fellas in yo place. Me, I will be ready and able. Trust me and Dee is down with the shooting. Who you gonna call? The po-lice ain't shit and they only come after somebody gets shot. Naw, I looks out for the kid, nobody gonna catch the kid without her little friend, no way.*

DeLores is small in size and has a quiet demeanor that reflects a cautious young woman. Looking at the interviewer she simply replies,

> *Girls got guns for the same reasons guys got 'em . . . it's wild out here, you need to protect yourself. Street law is the same, tough and it regulates itself. You have to regulate niggahs, especially if you're in business. It don't matter*

if it's selling crack, weed, or any kinda dope, business is business. Guns protect you and your business, right?

Group 4 consisted of females not in any particular gang type or associated group. They agreed to discuss how they felt about carrying weapons only on the condition of absolute anonimity. Two of the three attend parochial school, the other attends public school.

Lorene, 16, Juli, 17, and Maxie, 15, discuss carrying weapons in the city.

Juli offers,

I guess it's just what you gotta do, we go to a real nice school, mostly everybody is straight . . . but you never know when somebody is gonna get crazy and it's BOOM. I am real slow on going to house parties, and my people are so worried and they make my brothers take me. My father or mother take me to school and always to the malls. My brothers will stop everything or one of my sister-in-laws will drive me. I got my license, but with all the car jackings, I'm too scared. We got this friend from school and he wasn't with the G-boys and he got killed, well any of us could, he wasn't in a gang or ran with some crew, he was just a regular guy . . . I got a uncle who is a police and he tells me and my family to watch where I go . . . . I would carry some kinda weapon, maybe a gun [laughing] but you know I am just scared. I'm not 'bout fighting and cussing. I just wanna be left alone, just go to school, it would be so straight to not have to worry 'bout getting blown up in something that ain't got nothing to do with us. Everbody that carries a gun is ready to use it, I guess that's why I don't. . . .

Lorene agrees with Juli in her quest for a peaceful life,

It's messed up, it's real hard to go anywhere, lots of girls is scared and some girls is ready to throw. I know we are sorta different from lots of kids in our hood. I go to a Catholic school and lots of people think it's okay, but we get some crazy shit too. I could carry a knife, I use to carry this mace, but I know this girl and she sprayed this niggah, and it didn't do shit but make him madder. Anyway, my dad said to just take my older brothers to the parties, my brother is a gangster, he is always packing a gun and his boys is real ignorant. I tell my brother when his boys try to talk shit to me and my girls, but we just don't like the kinda guys in the hood. The boy I like goes to Catholic school, but it's like a public school, all the boys in the school and lots of the cuties my age are packing. My brother started acting like a gangster in high school, and they put his ass out. He went to community college and then went to Oakland University. But, he is just living off my parents. Now don't get me wrong, my brother is my guy, he takes care of me, but he can relate to the fools in the hood. Me and the girls just speak and keep on moving. No guns, no man, no time, no party, no nothing . . . I don't carry anthing and I hope I don't live in the city after I graduate, my older sister says she likes college, since it keeps her away from the street guys. . .

Maxie smiles,

Well, I understand everybody, but I am on my own, I always got something, and I am not saying shit, but it's wild, wild west. If they grab me, well it's not gonna be like they think. All the young girls in my block carry a knife, mace, gun, something . . . 'cuz, all the crazy shit in the hood or the city. Guess what? If y'all brothers or daddy ain't 'round well y'all is in big trou-ble, not me, I am barely 5'2" and skinny, if homeboy grabs me, he might not know it, but I got something to make me a heavyweight. My momma, my grand, and my aunts all carry something. We all live in the same house, and if you come messing 'round the front, you better be straight 'cuz we will show ya . . . when I go to school, I got it, go to skate, I got it, to the mall, got it, any place I go, I got it . . . crack head, gangster, rapist, or just some silly boy messing with me, I got it, and if you run up on me, you'll get it

A RAP CONCERT INCIDENT

The following interview was taken after rap and movie star Ice Cube performed at Joe Louis Arena in Detroit. Women were asked if they had enjoyed the concert. We categorized the women we asked into three groups:

Group 1—Females who identified themseves as sets or posses (Gang type, organized for some purpose) ranging from ages 13-23.

Was this concert fun?

Linda, 18, Jan, 17, Mellisa, 22, Venus, 20, Jackie, 21, appear to be dressed in casual, but expensive outfits and are very hyper and boistrous as they recall the evening. Jackie and Venus address the question first,

The concert was straight, it was in there, but the hook was all over the place, you know the po-lice was all over the place, looking like they want to bite yo ass. Why all the rap concerts have so many PO-LICE? Fun? Po-lice everywhere I hate 'em . . . the shit started on the main floor and there were fights everywhere and then BOOM, somebody said some girls got stabbed and it was wacked. Me and the girls wanted to meet Ice Cube that's why we got us a room at the hotel. Got back to the hotel and the muthafucking security was illing 'bout did we have a key for the hotel. Niggahs every-

where, it's dope, it's so many niggahs that the hotel got 'em standing in the front and the back, some fellas in the groups is mad as hell 'cause they can't get into the hotel and they the rappers.

The concert was gonna be straight until some ho's started talking shit, and the next thing I knew it was fighting all over the place . . . the security boys at Joe Louis is gonna git popped if they keep trying to regulate like they some kinda of Robocop. Fuck 'em, they ain't paid my way in the concert. Some punk niggahs calling themselves the "Niggahs From Linwood" [NFL] started some shit and me and some girls was laughing at 'em . . . they were wearing these shirts with NFL on 'em like they some big crew . . . we had more fun at the hotel. The hook beat them down like they was ho's, they wasn't shit . . . . The hook ain't nothing but a gang; kick them niggahs ass real bad, snatched them NFL shirts off their fake ho asses. I like that shit, but if they try that shit with me or the girls, well, we got something they'll remember with their Robocop shit . . . . Now that was dope, niggahs was everywhere, me and the girls just hung out all night. The hotel security came up on our floor asking us to quiet down, I told them to kiss my ass, I paid plenty of change for the room and we was partying. You could tell he was worried that we might pop his ass, so we just party all night. The concert was too short, but the hotel had plenty of fellas from the concert, so it was like the concert all over again.

Linda and Jackie cursed the police presence.

The police came out and just gangster everybody. They did the same shit at the NWA concert. They just some dogs, that's why I hate 'em, fuck the police . . . Did you see 'em with all those helmets and horses, now why you gonna bring horses out on us? Police was all over the place, in cars, in helicopters, in the parking lot, I saw police everywhere I looked. They was pushing and talking 'bout beating you down. They should leave us alone. Same shit out at Belle Isle and on Jefferson with the police gangstering everybody, all the police do is fuck with us. Anytime I see 'em, especially the bitches in uniform, I just laugh and leave cuz you know the bitches will start fucking with ya . . . "where's your ID?," "who you with?," "how old are you?," "it's curfew" . . . and they talk to ya like ya ain't shit.

Me and Jackie was in the restroom and this ugly little black bitch come up to this fella outside the restroom and hung his phone call. Now, that was wrong, that man was using a public phone and this bitch, 'cause she the police and got her boys with her, just dissed my boy . . . then this big, ugly, white police said to us "move on, you better git moving." We cussed his ugly ass out. They always fucking with ya, they talk all that shit 'bout they the law but they just some more suckers out here . . . concerts would be straight if they would stay away, we can take care our own shit, we don't need the silly ass police.

Group 2—Females who identified themselves as individuals who attended the concert as patrons of rap solely (Non-gang type) age group 13-23.

This group of women were asked if they were with any crew, set, posse, etc. All answered no; they were just attending as individuals. Answering the same question about their reaction to the concert,

Elaine, 18, Greta, 17, and Hillary, 18, responded,

> It was scary when all the police showed up. We didn't have any trouble, but they were fighting all on the main floor. Some girls had knives and were cursing some other girls. The concert was fine until the fighting started, this is my last concert in Joe Louis. Lots of crazy people and lots of fools illing if you ask me. The crowd got out of control and we just left, it was getting so crazy. I was glad the police came 'cause some people had started talking 'bout bum rushing anybody . . . that's why we just stay home, because you never know out here when it just jumps off and somebody ends up shot.

Group 3—Refused to be identified, but would comment on the event. Age group 13-23, this group was evasive about any identification including age or any personal information.

LaLa, 21, and Nona, 20, address the ordeal of concerts in the city. While they are dressed in very expensive sportswear, accented with jewelry, and driving a foreign car, they were very quick to dismiss the interviewers' questions about their profession, career, or status. When ask if they were in a crew the following conversation developed.

LaLa, in a very sharp tone,

> Now how come you ask us some shit like that? You got on some Nike's, and you look clever, is you rolling? How come everybody think if a girl looks good, its dope. It's gotta be dope money! Why can't we just look good and it's nobody's business where my paper comes from, okay? Y'all asking people shit and you don't even know us, why you asking all this shit. What's this shit for? The concert was dope, I really like these concerts, wish they had more . . . but everything gets wacked 'cause fools git to fighting and shooting and next thing you know the hook is putting everybody out. Our car is none of y'all business, everybody that drives a Volvo ain't selling drugs . . . do y'all work for the newspaper? We just out here, mind our own business, trying to have some fun in the summertime; well summer is over, but anyway its nothing else to do.

Nona continues. She is also very sharp and acts somewhat resentful of our question regarding her status.

Y'all tripping asking us if we rolling, like somebody would say, "yes, I am rolling and living large!" If me and the girls go to the club or anywhere, its the same old shit, "Are you rolling or do you go with a dope man?" Look leave us alone, we just some young fine babes out having fun . . . maybe we got jobs or maybe we just like to look good and that's our business. Y'all need to chill asking us questions 'bout us and you don't even know us. That's wacked asking shit 'bout us and you don't know us, like La said oh yes we're out here living large talking with some fellas with questions and tape recorders 'bout how we sell dope, right! The concert was live, and Ice Cube, and Yo-Yo was my girl, she got the booty and she knows she is the girl. Look, why don't ya tell the police to buy tickets, and go to the concert like everybody else that comes to the set. Naw, they rather jest show up looking like they want to kill us, and fuck everything up. [laughing and pointing to one of the interviewers] Are ya trying to talk to babes and this is just ya way of getting to know us?

Are girls getting violent, tonight girls or females crews were fighting. Is that unual?

LaLa, looking surprised,

Girls fight, shoot and do things the same as boys. So what, some little bitches got out of control tonight and ya gonna make something out of that? Look, fellas get out all the time, so girls can too! Gitting violent? Look, violent is living everyday and that's why you or anybody git violent. If you go to a concert it's no different than anything else, violent is part of what's out here, it's just life. You don't like violence, it's like smoke, I hate smoke but people smoke, right? Unusual, not for me. I see violence everyday, everyday I see somebody getting it on . . . . I know violence is what girls got to do back, 'cause if they don't they jist gonna git the shit kick out of them, and that's stupid and violent, and I ain't with it.

Nona, continues:

Violence is life, and nobody can change that. Girls today know whether they like it or not, violence is gonna be in your life. If you live in the hood or Southfield it's violent somewhere. People who talk 'bout that Detroit is so violent and they're scared is illing . . . whities go out and kill them at stores and cut them up in malls or take their kids and fuck 'em, or sometimes they kill their mommas and other crazy wacked shit. Niggahs, they ill in the hoods and the television gits to record it, but everywhere I look I see violence. Crews with the girls I know don't do shit like shooting, they too busy getting paid. Fellas like all that shooting and violence. The girls that gitting it on and the fellas that's gitting it on, they ain't into shooting, just counting that money. Now some girls will slam ya for anything, just like a fella, but most tough girls had some fella make'em tough and mean, its like my brothers, they got them fighting dogs . . . the Pit Bulls and they beat them and feed them gunpowder and pepper make 'em crazy wacked and mean. Well, its the same with some girls they git beat down all the time and next thing ya know its them that done turn into the Beastmaster. I know some girls who turned into Super Bitch and just beast on their kids, their man, anybody that gits in their way . . . . Boom!

Vernesta King, an EMT technician attended to several young women at the Ice Cube concert. Numerous fights caused the first aid room to be used frequently. Ms. King spoke of the attitudes and atmosphere that particular evening,

I had several girls injured from knife wounds and other related injuries from fighting. It was surprising and scary to see young women in such a combat-ive mood. We have become accustomed to the young boys, the shootings, and the violence. You don't ever like it or understand it, but it's reality in our line of work. But, the girls are becoming just as serious, and their attitudes are defying battles, acting just as ready to battle as the boys. Worse, some of the parents are supportive of the attitudes to engage in fighting, carrying weapons and seeking revenge. That evening I had parents coming in and condoning hard attitudes of both females and males. It's no wonder things are getting worse. Some parents and their children are joining forces in using violence as a means to their problems. There was definite crews of girls that were engaging in some sort of physical confronting of other crews of females.

VIOLENCE AND AGGRESSION

There was constant discussion about female sexual and physical abuse during the field work. The subject of domestic violence and dys-funtional families were well rooted in many interviews. Background records of female offenders revealed a correlation between sexual and physical abuse and criminal activity.

David Pomeroy, a Youth Group Leader with the State of Michigan, Department of Social Services in Grayling, gave his experience of working with young women,

The sexual abuse factor is real, there is a difference with the inner city popu-lation and the girls from the Upper Peninsula. Both groups have been vic-timized, the physical abuse seemed to usually coincide with sexual abuse cases from the city. The rural communities, especially the communities that are in the northern section have sexual abuse, incest without the blatant physical abuse. I have wourked with females from all over the state. Sexual abuse certainly has damaged many women. It's not just one group of females, the abuse is happening in many communities, it's not a subject that is popular.

The following responses are from sample populations of the female study; the views are from gang females and non-gang females. The investigator asked each subject how she felt about violence and agression in America.

Eleanor, 18, non-gang, responds,

I hate violence and anything associated with it. It's just a matter of waiting until I graduate from high school and I am never gonna live around nothing like this city. My street is violent all the time; it's everybody fighting and shooting and it just ruin our lives. Me and my sisters can't go anywhere because it's so crazy out in the street. You just never know what's gonna happen out there. My school is one of the best in the city. We don't have lots of fighting 'cause most of the kids are like me, they hate the fighting and shooting too. But it's like being in prison. I didn't even want to talk about it with you guys. It's like something that you just wish had never happened.

One thing for sure, if a guy wants to talk to me, you better believe he can't be in none of that gun, gangster thing with me and my friends. Some girls think I am stuck up, you know, I am better than other people, but who wants to get shot or beat up? My father is real strict on me and my sister. He and my mother will take us places rather than let us go alone; first I used to get mad, because when I got my license I wanted to drive myself. But I got caught out one night with my friends and some dope boys started shooting up this party on the Westside; after that I didn't go out by myself or with my friends for almost a year. It scared me to death. They didn't shoot at me, it was just being in the same place as all that shooting, it's nothing like television or movies! My grandmother said Detroit wasn't always like this, but it's all I know and I hate it.

Tanya, 23, scavenger gang member, addressed the question.

It's violence and aggression to y'all 'cause ya from somewhere soft [laughing and mocking the investigators]. What's violent? If you don't take care yo'self ain't nobody else gonna do it for ya. I am aggressive 'cause I learned it the hard way. My peoples beat me into understanding that ya better be hard 'cause life is hard. My brothers used to beat me down everyday at the dinner table, at the bathroom, at the schools; ya gotta be hard, rock hard, or you'll die out here. It's like kill or git kill, that's the way it's always been and that's okay with me. I ain't letting nobody take me out. I'm hard, real hard, been hard and ready since I was eleven years old. I jest kicked this wino ass the other day. My girlfriend and me was drinking and talking when this wino come talking trash to us 'bout give him some monay. We laugh and told him to fuck off; he told us to give him some monay and that we was some ugly fat ho's! [laughing] We kicked his ass right in the street, peo- ple was looking and blowing their car horns, yelling, stop, he's old, and some smart ass young boy come talking 'bout he was homeless and stop beating him down! We told him we kick yo ass college boy, and we would of kicked his ass if he hadn't ran off [laughing] . . . . He was soft and he knew it, ya can't be soft out here.

Shera, 26, former corporate member,

Violence and aggression, I don't like violence. Aggression, well are you talk- ing about getting mad or are you talking about getting something when you want it? Aggression to me is when you make your move real strong, okay? My boyfriend is real aggressive, but he's not into violence or aggres- sion like some of the fellas we know. Now, some fellas is real violent and they are outta control, their aggression is real crazy, you know, stupid vio- lent and I stay away from that type of shit, 'cause it's dangerous for your own good, okay? If it's 'bout monay then violent shit happens; it's part of business. But if it's violence just for the hell of it, well I ain't down with it.

Marva, 16, a high shool student who is not in a gang, lives in an area with male gang problems.

Violence is everywhere you turn, so I stay in the house and read. Television is violent, and so are the movies, and the music is real violent in lots of ways, to me. School is violent and the teachers hate it, but it's just the kids and they just do what they want, teachers, principals can't stop'em. We have this white man principal, he's silly. Always talking 'bout our school is safe; right, it's so safe you can get killed just talking in the hallway. He's a joke. Our school is full of gang boys carrying all kinda guns. There are girl crews that will beast on you worse than any boys. Aggressive is the way these fools think life is, large and aggressive; violence is what these fools love, it's like outta control. My mom says I am right and she rather I skip school some days and just stay home. Our principal is just gonna get popped because he's so stupid talking 'bout what he's gonna do. Lots of kids hate him. I don't like him . . . if he got it, would serve his punk ass good. He's fake.

DRUG VIOLENCE

This interview takes place in an affluent suburb of Detroit. The host is an alleged former narcotics dealer (he has never been accused or arrested by the authorites) who is entertaining a small gang of females and males involved in cocaine distribution. The investigator was visiting with another subject who brought him to this home. This conversation began because of the televised news of a murder in the city that was drug-related.

How does it make you feel, listening to the news of such young men involved in these horrendous murders?
Erica, 19, shrugs her shoulders:

> It's tight, it's killing lots of people out in the life. Dope is real dangerous business, you know, it's bad everywhere.

Rene, 23, says very matter of factly:

> Well, . . . it's dealings in the streets, if they can't take it, then they deserve to die, it's just that way. What you expect? It's, like . . . everybody that gets in the game, know what time it is. Lots of fellas get popped over shit that's weak. They deserve it. Niggahs, they be perpetrating out here, everybody acting like they down. I mean lots of punk niggahs out here talking shit 'bout they down with this person, or they know this crew. All that talking and fronting, some guys just ain't playing and they will take a fake or silly niggah out. You got your skeezing bitches out here, and some girls is down and they getting it on.

Earl, 22, laughs and adds:

> All that talk 'bout brothers killing brothers don't mean shit in the streets. If you out here and you know what time it is, you know to stay away from lots of talking and smiling snake ass niggahs. The bitches is the worst ones out here. That's why I stay low profile. If you out here wearing Armani, driving large, spending large, living large, you can bet some tramp bitch and her crew will target your ass for the kill. Why you think so many fellas go everywhere with a crew? Got to have bodyguards if you out in the street. These little crazy po boys, they ain't down with nuthin' but being po. Them and the skeezing ho's is trouble; if you don't watch it you'll get caught, and next thang you know you'll be with the dirt in the ground.

Rene continues her point:

> Fellas get popped 'cause it's so crazy and fellas don't know when to leave or shut up. Lots of girls just chill. Now there are some bitches who are acting stupid and want to fight and shoot, but boys just make everythang crazy.

Fellas will shoot or fight over anything . . . that's why they get shot all the time. I was going with this fella, and he decided to beat this niggah that worked for him one day, 'cause he was stealing his dope, right? Well, I told him to wait and see who else it was down in the shit 'cause it was lots of dope getting stolen, right? Did he listen to the girl? No, he just popped all the niggahs and now his boys are all trying to kill him. If he had waited like the girl told him, he could have caught the three and save his crew of ten good guys. Now they running all over the place shooting up the city. I dropped his crazy ass, I mean this foolish boy likes to shoot up people, dogs, girls, or his boys, with a quickness . . . He done went stupid!

Erica explains loudly:

Who gives a fuck, it's like, what about me and my girls getting beat down, or who cares when girlfriend gets beat up and shot? Fuck the black man and fuck the white man . . . It's . . . I'm really tired of all this shit 'bout the black man or black males getting popped. What about anybody getting shot? It's tight out there! Selling drugs is dangerous, if you scared get the fuck out. It's dangerous living in this city, it's dangerous everywhere for niggahs. It's dangerous, talking 'bout this shit. It's dangerous living in the world. Look on that TV, right now it's dangerous, looking at everybody is getting fucked up . . . either it's airplanes crashing, some muthafucka raping babes, some bitch done killed her husband, some wife done got fucked over by her ex-husband or what about that snake muthafucka in Boston? . . . Ya'll talk 'bout that violence! Talk 'bout that snake bitch who shot his wife and called 911, put the shit on the black man, and the hook was beasting on every niggah in that Boston city. It just ain't the black man, it's ALL BLACKS. It's the way things is, and it ain't never changing, so we may as well talk 'bout something else!

Larry, 24, speaking very low:

I am scared of everything in the city, if you young and black it's tight. My boys go to the show, I rent videos. They go to see the Pistons, I watch on television. They go to the clubs, I get my cutie and watch VH-1. It's, well, let's just say I know what time it is . . . what's really messed up is that lots of blacks are killing each other. Why? Well, it's hard to say, um, it's kinda crazy . . . but the cuties have more slack out here. The girls is getting rich, 'cause nobody is tight on them, it's like they can walk around and they're invisible. Being a cutie has its advantages.

Rene, screams loudly,

That's shit . . . girls is getting it on 'cause they be smarter, they don't do shit like wave their monay all over niggahs' faces. Yeah, it's like that, right, fellas don't care who did what, they ready to pop you for anything, they kill for anythang, it's just the way niggahs is, and you know it, Larry! Babes is 'bout business, and some dudes hate that shit . . . girls will take care mo business, that's just the way it be.

Kira, 26, lives with a successful drug dealer. She arrives late and waits before she adds her opinion on violence.

Well, let me say this, for all the shooting and killing. What's the big deal? Man, you asking us 'bout violence? Violence is what keeps everything in check. If a woman gets out of control, kick her ass. If somebody working for you gets out of control, kick their ass. I tell my man he's too easy, soft on these people. Kick their ass, fuck what's troubling you, the more ass you bite, the more respect you get. My daddy would kick my ass and my sister's ass just like he kick my brother's ass. My old man used to beat the shit out of us, made us scared just to see him, used to kick my momma's ass and would kick her brothers' ass if they tried anything. Now, one of my younger sisters is crazy; she told my daddy if he ever hit her again she would shoot his old ass. She means it, she told my man if he hit me or any of her sisters she would pop his ass, the girl is 110 percent gangster [laughing]. The only way to control violence is with violence, that's a fact! Violence is what makes the police keep people in check; if the police wasn't using violence do you think they could control niggahs in the street?

SUMMER EVENING AT A NIGHT CLUB

This incident takes place one warm summer night in 1991 outside a downtown night club. The investigative team was meeting with several female gang members who had agreed to an interview. An incident breaks out, and there is gunfire. Directly in front of the club the scene becomes chaotic. A young man is shot. The EMS unit never came; the police arrived after twenty or more minutes. The crowd from the night club was hostile. Many voiced their rage toward the police and the EMS unit. Interesting was the gang's reaction to the fatally wounded young man. Tina, one of the six crew members, announced to the crowd, "We should burn this place down, they ain't called nobody . . . the police don't care, they kill niggahs they don't care and they sure ain't saving none . . . . " Suddenly the young wounded man took his last breath, his friend cradling his head in his lap, screamed not to lose it, don't die. The crowd became more aggravated at the death of the young man. The investigative team was feeling like the interview and everything at this time was futile. Walking over to the gang members they were surprised at the reaction of two members. "Let's go and get something to eat , this shit is making me hungry . . . "

The investigator asked them how could you be hungry after this?

One of the girls answered sharply,

> *Fuck him, he shouldn't been acting like he was so bad, he jumped and they popped his ass, he should of had his shit ready. Lots of niggahs out here fronting trying to be gangsters . . . that's what happens when you ain't ready out here.*

A young woman upset over the incident starts to cry as the crowd disperses. Another gang member continues the conversation.

> *Well, we always go to get something to eat after the club . . . all the clubs have shootings, every week somebody gets shot. If I stopped eating every time somebody got popped I would be a skinny girl. So he got dead, it happens, these ho's crying but they'll be right back out here next week at this club. Getting smoked is your fault, he should have been ready, got to be ready out here. If you're soft it's all over.*

While this attitude was not the entire gang's, it certainly did not stop them from going out to eat after the homicide. Investigators found a great deal of truth in the attitudes and in the club scene in the city. Young women and men from different crews, gangs, groups, and backgrounds spoke openly about violence and the consequences. There appears to be a very desensitizing feeling in the streets regarding serious violence.

SILENCE IN THE STREETS

Sadi, 19, Gredi, 15, and Jaye, 18, discuss the problems of talking about happenings within the drug culture.

Sadi speaking softly,

> *It don't pay to be getting in other peoples business. Especially 'bout dope things, you just keep to your self. My momma told us to just stay out of the way of the dope houses down the street. My girls, they my friends, my people and we got our own little crew from school. But, we aint' down with no real live gangster thing. You know who is doing what . . . but like I told that police guy with y'all, it ain't my business to stick my nose in O.P.P., got it. Y'all should be real careful asking questions in this hood.*

Gredi adds,

Girl knows, if you get them niggahs thinking you is snitching, well you can kiss your ass bye. The dope house ain't what you talk 'bout, later for the boys in the house, but most of the time they too busy selling their little dope. You see shit, and you don't see shit, okay? We're moving and I can't wait, good bye, you see the cars, the people buying the shit all night and all day sometimes, white people. The police don't come until the old man on the corner calls. The dope people know who done called, and trust me it's not like the police gonna protect ya ass. There are dope fiends all over the hood, begging and stealing and talking crazy about getting a hit.

Now, some of the old men, black and white ones, come up on the block and they be going to the freak houses . . . getting all the nasty dope fiend bitches. AIDS, AIDS, AIDS, that's all over them freak houses, but it's part of the shit with dope selling. Jaye, tell 'em 'bout the freak shit in the houses. Girls be getting raped, getting freaked, it's too nasty, and they beat down dope fiends . . . you best not say shit 'bout what goes on with any dope fel-las business if you know what's up.

Jaye explains,

They be fucking boys, you know sissy's, homos on crack be sucking dicks. Girls on shit get dogged real bad, but I know this boy who use to be rolling real hard. Anyway, he got strung out on crack, these boys raped him, turned him out, it was scary, they fucked him 'bout nine of them in this crew. They turned him out, heard he left the city after they busted him out like he was a little bitch . . . it's tight out here. So that's why we ain't saying shit, that old man on the corner, he was talking shit. Some of them dope pople fire bombed his garage one night. Then they threw a brick into his front window, they had this picture of an old man with a long nose drawn, the picture said if he didn't stop dipping he was gonna come up stanking . . . he still calls, and he always got his rifle talking 'bout he will shoot a nig-gah. You best not talk 'bout shit that don't cern you.

SURVIVAL

Vickie, 20, discusses her life on the streets as a member of a gender-integrated gang. She shows investigators several scars over various parts of her body. Vickie seems to be proud of her battle wounds. This interview exposes the hardships that some females face daily in urban life.

Aren't you afraid out in the streets with all the violence?

Fuck naw, jest be able to take care of yo'self, the streets is rough, but it's okay if you take care of yo self. That's why I be with these fellas, if somebody fuck with girlfriend they gotta deal with these boys and trust me, this here crew got the shit fo "anybody." Yo ass will be very dead, with a quickness! So it pays to belong to some kinda crew, it's smart to have somebody out here watching yo back, right?

Are there other girls like you in crews?

Sure, lots of babes is out in the street, me and my girls got put out by our mommas. My bitch ass mammy would take me to juvenile and tell them all kinds of wild shit . . . she say she couldn't handle me 'cause I was too wild and I would kick her ass. The bitch just didn't want me, the juvenile people won't do shit for me, they took the fat bitch word everytime. My momma would always tell me "You going end up like yo no good Daddy, dead in the ground; I hate you, you look just like you ugly ass Daddy . . . . That's the reason I am gonna make it, make 'cause the bitch played me like I ain't shit. I am hard, I ain't soft, I can get it on with fellas or whoever wants to try yo girl, I am ready, ready and gonna do it!

Do you see women besides yourself using or selling drugs?

Who said I used drugs or sold them, you sound like the hook? I know some people who use and some that sell, maybe, okay? Lots of girls is selling drugs but you wouldn't see 'em, 'cause the girls is smarter than the fellas. Now, some girls get caught but they the dumb ho's. Crack got lots of girls fucked up, but sometimes it's long time before crack get 'em bad . . . more girls is selling 'cause their fella is working the streets. Girls want some of that money, got to get some of that paper. Most girls on drugs is like me, they lost, but they ain't lucky like me with this crew, we like family. These fellas would kick my ass if they caught me on that pipe. I ain't gonna lie, I done hit that pipe a few times but it's not like, presto, you is a dope fiend, like they say. The girls that get caught is the ones that got nobody looking out for them. Girls is getting it on, it's just lots of girls is still getting fucked over by anything in the streets. Stank-ho's, the ones that will fuck fo free is the ones that need to get it together. Bobby says if babes would get hard they could get lots of action . . . women is on the set, we just don't get the respect, but trust me, we are here.

BUSINESS

This interview is an argument between several gang members who feel that the females are causing problems in their neighborhood drug sales.

Robert, 19 years of age, is angry with Pat, 24, who is head of her own corporate team of five females and three males. The investigators were waiting in an empty house in the early afternoon to meet some female gang members who are moving up the ladder in terms of economic success. This house is one of eight in what our contact calls Crack City. Three cars arrive, one, a late model Nissan Sentra LX, is carrying three young black males. The other car is a 1988 or 1989 Black Volvo 740, with black windows all around. Four young women leave the car. Another car, a yellow Corvette, pulls up behind the Volvo. An argument between Robert and Pat ensues and the young boys, including Robert, leave in a fury. Asked what the disagreement is about, Pat tells the investigator,

It's just ho shit, crying 'bout monay, typical shit from boys who think they can run things better. Rob always crying 'bout girls can't do shit. He's a little crybaby ho. I am in business, making monay is hard these days. If I listen to people illing all the time I couldn't make monay or do anything. Oh, it's like crazy some days, but they make more monay with me than with their old crew. Rob is mad 'cause it was his cousin and brothers who got popped and went to Jacktown [Jackson Prison]. When I took over, this here clique was making ho paper. Why, 'Cause Rob and his boy Ralph was hitting the pipe, and letting every little skeezer in the 'hood get credit or just giving freebies away. I had worked in this thing since I was fifteen. I was in school working twelve hours everyday. My people didn't know I was working one of the big houses for the X organization. That was like school, they taught me how to cook the shit.

When I was sixteen, my boyfriend started to move up in the X. I just learned more things, this was my education. This is a career. Why go to college for a career? I go to community college to learn other shit, but this here is my livelihood. My boyfriend got shot when I was eighteen. It was fucked up, his own boys set him up and fucked him up, he was lucky, 'cause he lived. We broke up after he got shot 'cause all he wanted was to kill his boys after that hit. I had other things to do, and you know people that will kill for monay, so just get them and forget all that other shit. At twenty I bought my own car; now before, I had got a car from my man, that was sweet, but then he would always talk 'bout he bought this and he did this, fuck being the little toy ho . . . buying your own shit is much better.

Me and this big fella started to kick it when I was twenty-two, he had the juice, big juice. I met all the real players with this fella, it was sweet. Plus, I was getting it on, 'cause my man let me get some of his products directly from his source. Soon, I was crushing and had my own serious crew. When I got my first car it was on, like dick and balls, ha ha ha ha, whoa! My next car was real def; you see, this muthafucka was real shitty when I bought my first car. My brothers and some of his friends cut the deal with the sales guy. He thought he was some smooth dressing pretty boy, but he's a ho, ha ha *ha . . . anyway he dissed me like I was skeezing or some little ho that was getting her first car from a man. So the next time I took the girls, and we talked shit, and dogged his silly ass. When he saw my monay, I thought he was gonna piss on himself. Ever since that he knows I am Ms. Pat, and he gives me much play. Still, I drive a little car at work, and we don't drive our fly shit all over the hood. See, I am running a enter-prise, okay? This is serious shit and I am gonna make all the dope monay I can; why not, it's 'bout time girls get some monay that's real and not for sacking.*

What are some of the problems facing girls in gangs?

Pat continues, along with Vicky, DeAnn, and Malika.

Fellas in crews that ain't getting paid, the dirty po boys that will try anything, the ones that got lots of dope fiends in their crews. If you got a all girls crew, um, they think you're "soft," and in the streets if you soft, it's all over. Fellas think girls is soft, like Rob, he think he got it better in his shit 'cause he's a fella, a man. It's wild, but fellas really hate seeing girls getting off. Now, some fellas respect the powers of girls, but most just want us in the sack.

Deann answers,

When I go to a club, I have my heater all the time. It's either some stank ho, or some fella trying to get next to ya. It's always tight when you out. The girls got to watch it 'cause there are lots of scandalous niggahs trying to get over on ya. Those little crews of begging, scheming bitches in crews with scandalous dudes. Why you think so many girls be getting taken off, you never hear 'bout the robberies and rapes these dogs be pulling. Last month these dogs were at a club and they kept bothering Keisha and Debbie; these girls down with some big fellas that went to school with us. Anyway, one of the fools pull his dick out, talking 'bout "hey bitch git on this stick," to me and them. I pull my heater out of my bag. Before you could say shit my boy had zip his dick up in his pants and was booking.

Later, that same night they got robbed by some dirty niggahs, and Keisha said it was the boy who pulled his dick out. They had followed them all night and waited till they got a drop on them. It's hard for a girl crew to get respect. It's bad enuff for girls in with boys, but all girls makes it harder. Niggahs think they can stick us up and nuthing will happen.

Malika laughs,

Girls just got to hang with it, just pop a silly niggah and they get right. Them crews that rob and rape, they only fuck with girls that's soft. Nobody fucks with girlfriend 'cause I will shoot a bitch without even thinking twice. I will smoke anybody that gets in my face. Men think they can do this and that with a girl, and it's the same way with cliques. . .but the boys, and some done tried, find out that me and the girls here, well, we can get the job done. If we can't we got some help, er let's just say we got the juice, just like men. I told this crazy fella in the club one night that he better not grab my ass 'cause he kept whispering in my ear while we was dancing. You know all that "Your ass is so fine. . .," and how he was going home with me at the end of the night. Well, this maniac was talking 'bout his monay, and he could tell I was a monay bitch and all this bullshit. When I got my coat, he walks over and puts his arm around my waist, and whispers "lets go home and get naked." I snatched his arm away, and said "Step off mother-fucka!" He looked at me and started my way. I dropped back, had my heater, then DeAnn came with Pat and the real fellas. My boy was looking at plenty of heaters, and I just smiled and said "what's up, baby," He got chilled real fast, he was no longer illing . . . that's the only thang these fellas understand in the street. Understand, that you can, and will, die in a quick-ness if you run up on these here girls!

Vicky ,

It's simple, girls is gangsters just like fellas . . . we can do anything the fellas can do, and anybody that think we can't is ignorant and dumb. Ain't no man gonna rock us, we rule our own shit, this is our own thang, only bitches that is getting dogged is the ones that let it happen. We ain't letting it happen to us. This crew is small, but we getting it on, we getting it on!

Pat closes the talk,

The hardest thing for some fellas is taking orders from a babe. Now Rob is mad 'cause I am doing the shit they should have done. But, these fellas is carrying their dicks in their hands all the time. Rob is mad when I gets paid, mad 'cause I won't buy no little 190 Mercedes like those tramp ho's that live off their dope men. Me, it's my thang, no one is in charge but me. I'm not buying no little dope ho car, not the kid, I am a business woman, and everybody going to respect me. I keep my monay, not some shit talking lawyer, it's my thang and you got to understand that I will kill to keep my shit from falling, got it? Okay? Rob and his boys better get it or they can get the fuck out of Dodge, I'm nobodies ho! There's fellas who know what time it is, and they making bank. The silly boys talk 'bout bitches, and they got no bank.

6

Women Speak Out

The interviews in this chapter cover a wide variety of topics. They allow the women in this study to voice their opinions on education, racism, sexisim, current events, movies, and other topics of our modern society.

EDUCATION AND SCHOOL

Our research found that different gang types had very different views on this subject. This variation throughout the study and in a previous study signals a definite class differentiation. We have selected samples from the different gang types regarding their feelings about education and school.

Scavengers Gang

How do you feel about school?

Anette, 19, responds,

Hate it! Hate everybody at that place, never liked it. . .School is full of shit. I never went, even when I was little. School was the one place I hated. My momma never liked school, she said the teachers used to pick on her; same fo me, teachers be illing, they all think they know so much! I skipped all the time, it was the only thing I did like 'bout school, the skipping was fun, 'cause my momma would just laugh and say fuck'em. We had this teacher who would call our worker, the bitch would get in my momma's ass 'bout me and my brothers going to school. We all hated school except my brother Michael, he liked going to school. He was always illing 'bout missing or not having clothes fo school. That fool would do his homework. My other brother would laugh and say he was a little faggot, said his daddy was a fag, that's why he was different from us. None of us have the same daddy, my daddy left the city long time ago, fuck him, I don't need no daddy. Anyway, daddies ain't nothing but another man that's done fuck over ya.

Territorial Gang

ReLana, 19, is the leader of a small, territorial, all-female crew:

School was straight in the projects; I liked school. Some of the teachers were fake but some would help or tried to get real. My cousins used to tear niggahs down for their coats, lunch money, their shoes or anything else they saw and wanted. My cousin Ray said school is where he and his boys did their shopping after other niggahs mommas would shop for their school clothes [laughing]. I like school 'cause that's where we meet new boys, and you could dress up and be real neat.

It was real straight when our crew got busy in the life. My first fella was tearing it off, getting paid real swell, he got taken out in 1989, and then my next fella was living large 'cause his whole family was in there . . . he got popped in 1990, and that's when I got my own crew with my cousins, the ones who never went to school and was tearing and beasting on everythang. For me school means that if I was neat, and the fellas saw how fine I was looking, then it was the place to be . . . that's the way my girls and me like school, it was the only place to be, it's where you got sharp and you knew everybody saw your set.

Corporate/Covert Gang

These women deny any association with selling narcotics. The essence of their success is their friends in the life or their business contacts, who may be involved in some sort of illegal business unknown to them.

Tyra, 24, Erna, 22, Gail, 21, and Florence, 25, talked about school and higher education. Three women are high school graduates and were attending community or four-year institutions in the greater Detroit area.

Tyra gave a very different viewpoint with respect to education,

School is important if you gonna make anything in life, what's up if you out here without no sense. I am a business woman, and I don't know nothing 'bout dope or that other mess. I have associates who have small interests in lots of business things, that's why I go to school, to meet people who are doing business. I like school. I graduated from high school and my friend is helping me into college with paying some of my tuition. I'll graduate next spring and then I am gonna open up my own travel agency. The street tramps don't like school and lots of ignorant dope boys who wouldn't live long be dissing school. But for me, school and college is just what you gotta do if you want to make it today.

Erna continued,

Anyway, most of the dope fellas like educated women [laughing and giving each other pats on the hands]. When you're in school, you know the dumb niggahs, and you don't want to be around them. I am in community college; later, after college, I am going to law school. School has always been fun and I like it when I know things and they can help you later. I had this teacher in middle school—my girl was living large, the babe dressed like she was rolling with the G-money . . . anyway, she was always telling me to be a lady, and don't let niggahs fuck you around. I waited for three years before going to college. I had this guy who was in the Pony crew and he was setting me out. Then my boy got busted and I was out of luck. My next guy was out there and he was the one that really set me out. He wanted me to go back to school; first I was gonna try doing beauty college, but he wanted me to learn business. I got a fresh counselor, she tells me that if I want to, I could get a teaching degree. That sounded cool at first. But, naw, it's too many guns in the school and too many silly boys out in the school acting silly or illing and will kill you . . . naw, I'll just go to school and get paid later . . . school is straight.

Gail talks about why she left school after the tenth grade.

Education? Well it's okay. I just stayed in the street and was babysitting for my older sister. Money is what got me out of school; I mean why go to school when what I wanted was out in the streets? While I was babysitting I met these young dudes who worked for their older brothers selling crack. They would come next door to my sister's place and play cards and gamble. My sister's husband used to say that they were young and on full . . . these boys had big change. One of them was treating me real nice. My brother-in-law was scared that they would mess over me. One of them, named Tony, started to come over to get my brother-in-law to join the gambling party on Tuesday night. Next thing I knew, me and Tony Dog was living together. That was three years ago. Now I am living large. I got things and I know how to save my money, and Tony is out of the life. He now has his own business, his lawyer is helping him get it together. I didn't know if what I heard about him working in the streets, but that his business. Like he always said to me, he's a businessman. I got one baby and I am not on welfare and I don't do drugs. My sisters are trying to be like me. It's straight if school works for you. But me and Tony didn't graduate from school, and we is making it happen, so who needs school?

Erna, becoming rather annoyed, sharply asked,

You got some way for us to get out of this no job city? Everybody talking 'bout these boys or us, the ho's jocking these kinda fellas, well, what's up, big fella? Do you know how to get a Benzo or any kinda car with the bull-shit jobs out here today? It feels good to go to college and be dressed to the bone. I am wearing what my teachers wish they could wear. I driving what the rollers who look all stupid wish they could have. Too many college girls out here in the street and they jocking for some paper just like me and the crew. Why? 'Cause the education ya talking 'bout, they got it! And they still is poor ass and look at us! Who would you rather be, me or them? School is straight, but you got to have that monay, got to have a real job . . . we got the paper and we got the real jobs. Education to me is out in the street and in the classroom, it's both. If you got this degree and no real sense, you just a fool with a degree. . .lots of girls know that school is just another thang to trick you while the white man is counting his paper and laughing at us. . .Minister Farrakan knows that the greedy ass white man is tricking us. You need education, but I am still saying you need some help from your friends and if my friends got big paper, what do I care how they got it?

Florence adds her view on education,

School was lots of good times, and I learn a lot at school. I went to Eastern Michigan University for one year then transfer to Wayne State. All of my sis-ters and brothers are either in college or they been at one time. College is different than high school. Education is important if you white, but for us it's important if you understand that white people gonna dis you even if you do go to college. Degree? Right, white kids hate us at school, and the professors is fake, they try hard to act like they ain't racist but you know what time it is . . . they always talking to you like you from the ghetto, you don't know nothing. At Eastern, the white girls in the dorm would be illing and thinking you don't know they dissing you. I knew more skeezers in the sorority tip than out on the street. And dope heads are everywhere; that's how I got over, I just hooked up the white boys who try act like they down, you know the ones that wear their hats like bloods and listen to all the rap music. They is buying mucho dope on campus, but nobody looks at them 'cause they is the white boys. People need to know that kids, white kids from Bloomfield Hills, Farmington Hills, Warren, Southfield, and all the other places that try to dog us from Detroit are the ones who be illing and doing the same shit as the ones from the city.

Education is okay, but the reason I was going to college was to get paid. I am getting paid, I am not saying how or that I am slinging dope, but just say it's girls just like me, been to college and they want it just like I wanted it . . . you can't get no Benzo on the jobs you get from college. You go into big debt for school and who is gonna give you a job to pay it back? Most of the people I know, and my sister is in school and says now you can't hardly borrow money for school, get jobs that don't pay shit. Soon as you get out, and you looking for the big job, or buy your car, it's the loan people chasing *your poor college ass for their paper. Those professors who lied to you can't answer that question of where's the good job. Nope, it's work and join all the poor suckers who just work and pay bills and still live in the same dirty houses in the ghetto . . . now, get the slammin, whip it fellas and work your own thing and get rich. . .that's the best education, the best school and when you graduate you'll be straight. That's the school for this girl.*

HAIR SALONS

There was a great deal of discussion in the streets about hair salons and drug gangs, dealers in business, and females who own them. Mildred, 52, former owner of several salons in the city, explains the complex connection between the illegal underground and legal overground economy. Mildred, who has been in the hair business for over thirty years, cautions that there are many businesses in this region that profit from the underground economy. It is important not to cast negative, unfounded allegations on innocent and uninvolved successful salons.

Are there dope dealers involved as owners?

Certainly there are some dealers, but it's not like what people think. The established owners like myself have been around a long time and have seen some rough customers in this business. You must understand the business is really very tough and you can't run things like these dope people think things run. We don't have anymore dealers, and probably not half the dope boys that other business people have. I bet there are more white gangsters in legitimate businesses than our business. People think this hair salon is easy and it's not! Sure, we have lots of shops opening up. Everybody thinks they can open a shop, some of those people are dope boys and girls. Look, how long do they stay in business? That's the bottom line. If you look real close, you'll find that it's only a hand full of us. The rest is fly by night people. It's expensive and yes you hear things, and you see people, especially young girls who hang around or have relationships with dope boys opening up these big shops. They pay too much for setting up a salon. The salon equipment people love those fools. But there ain't lots of them, a few, but most of us is legitimate.

But remember the banks ain't setting up too many salons, so the dope boys put up the money, and we know when there is some fool putting up a shop sparing nothing. It's bad for us, the ones who struggle and work for years so they can make it don't appreciate the young superstar, but you do business with these young fools and you'll be sorry. Dope people act like they own you. It's nothing like the old numbers people, they respected us.

*These fools they'll disrespect you and kill you over a quarter. The dope peo-
ple open up some shops, but if you know what's good for you, keep away
and don't know nothing. Now, that city council woman talking bout too
many shops on Livernois is silly. She oughta close all the crackhouses and be
glad if people want their hair done, or we got some business on Livernois.
The shops that have that kinda of business is gonna come into your place,
who wants to live like that? They have killed lots of young boys over the
years and it's always linked to selling dope.*

*First, it's dangerous since you don't know if the dope people want to use
your place for selling dope. They all seem to be ready to kill on a minute's
notice. Now, don't think that our salons haven't been the place for number
running over the years. Barbershops, little party stores all of 'em have did
that, but it's like Lotto you know. Lots of shops don't do anything but hair.
Over the years most shops that are successful do one thing right, that's hair.
The young kids who get in with the dope people don't have established customers like me, my customers are professional women, school teachers,
police, business women, politicians, and they will not tolerate the dope
scene. . .some dope dealers are involved, but they don't run our profession,
okay? Is it a gang or just two dealers I can't say, but they're around and
some are buying salons. But, they get in trouble, and it's hard to keep that
kinda thing undercover for long. They don't represent the average salon in
the city. That don't mean we're all angels. but we ain't dope fronts either.
That's important to remember, we are for the most part, clean cut, hard
working women and men in business in Detroit trying to make a honest living. Now, there lots of silly people who try and start a salon who think it's
easy, lots of so-called businesswomen and they can't cut it, cuz they try far
out silly and crazy tricks like hot tubs and champagne with valet parking in
the ghetto. That's those women who wanna be white, live out in the suburbs. But they ain't necessarily dope money, just foolish with their money or
some investors. If I had a dollar for all the investors I've heard about over
the years. This is a tough business, and dope money can't make you a successful salon owner"*

Do you know of any girls in gangs coming into your shop as customers?

*You don't meddle in your customers' business, but you know and there are
shops that cater to that clientele. I never did, didn't have to because my
clients are from the past thirty years. But lots of girls and boys getting out of
hair schools are hungry, and they go for what they think is the big money.
You know, the real money girls come to the shop two, three times a week.
The girlfriends of dealers have money and lots of it, the poor girls are always
trying to get it. Gangs, well what kinda gangs are you talking about? The
poor ones, they just get whatever they can. . .lots of girls in the neighborhood just do whatever they can to make it. Most of the girls running with*

gangs have their own place to hang and it's not my place. I have school teachers and professional women, church women. It's unfortunate but some young hairdressers go for the quick money and they pay for it. Thank God I don't have to get involved with those types. But, it's not just hair people— the dope people are all over the world.

I had this young woman who worked for me a couple of years ago. Good worker, 23-years-old, she wanted the money real bad. We had words about nasty talking girls, I don't know if they were in any gang, but her customers were very loud. She was doing all the latest styles, coloring and cutting crazy things into their hair. It's no big thing, they're young, it's always been that way. I tried to lecture her about money and the kind of people you want for customers. She let me have it, and she was right. Long as they want to get their hair done, well it's better than some of these women, especially this new funny kinda woman who says later for the beauty shop. Women who say they don't need to be looking good, well they usually some ugly frustrated woman.

It's the one thing, the only thing, I like about the dope crowd, they know how to look good, real good. So my ex-worker reminded me of how she likes their money and making them look good. I understand her joy, but it's the danger I worry about. I told her to be careful. Now, today she is doing great, she ain't living with dope people, but she does the tough dope girl type hair. He whole business is built around fast young girls, some ain't in the dope scene, but they know that in her kinda shop the talk is nasty, the television and radio both are playing loud at the same time. It's her thing, she likes her customers and I like mine. . .the dope girls, the gang girls, all of what's out in the street comes into somebody's shop, we're like everybody else, I try not to judge, but it's hard today, the shootings, the killings...you just try to make it.

DRUGS ON CAMPUS

The following interview is with two seniors from Detroit who attend a Big Ten university. Their interview took place on campus and in Detroit.

In your experience, are there females involved in gang activities?
Carmen, 21, speaking,

Sure, it's everywhere, girls is getting it on campus and in the city. Lots of girls don't call it gangs, they say their crew or set, but it's all about getting paid . . . money.

Lee, 22,

> Girls are more involved in finding who the real money guys are, but girls
> want the same things guys want . . . money.

Are there females at universities who are interacting with drug dealers in the city?

Both answering with laughter,

> In the city? They're up here in school and you never know who they are.

Carmen continues,

> There are girls up here from the ghetto on dope money, lots of girls need
> money and aid is short, so lots of times you'll see girls with fellas in the life
> supporting them. That's just the way things are.

Lee,

> If you from the hood, it's no big surprise to know or have grown up with
> some fella who didn't go to college but is making it in the street. You don't
> just stop being friends with somebody because they're rolling.

Isn't this strange, that co-eds would date or talk with young men selling narcotics?

Carmen, frowning and sharply replying,

> Co-ed's need money, they want to live large like everybody else. What's so
> surprising about wanting to get over? And these college boys are arrogant
> and disrespectful. They take us for granted; they treat us like dogs. The drug
> dealer wants us and is willing to pay you . . . dope man G ain't trying to
> screw me and my best friend like the frat boys. Lots of people say shit to me
> 'bout being with dope guys, but if they treat me good, what do I care? Any-
> way, there lots respectable boys whose families think they so rich and they
> caught up in selling dope. Don't think it's just ghetto boys, lots of rich black
> kids is illing and you would be surprised who's out there! Some of the little
> white boys be selling dope, I know some white boys who is getting it on,
> and some white girls is copping cocaine from fellas rolling. See, y'all think
> it's the blacks, but mommy and daddy should check their kiddies from the
> suburbs, they in the mix, trust me.

Would you date someone who is dealing dope?

Carmen,

Like I said, y'all think college boys is nice, but they treat you like you're dirt. Now, the few I know that are cool, they get taken real fast, girls be on them with a quickness. It's hard to get a good man, and girls grab any fella that treat you special. Most of the college boys feel like you ain't no big thing, 'cause they're in college just like you.

Lee,

College boys, especially the athletes, think they is supposed to get their ass kissed. I know this big football star, and I used to have a thing for him and we was in the same class. Now this fella wanted me and my homegirl in the class to do his homework and just give him the answers on the test. Half the time he didn't even come to class. Then the fool come over my place one night to study, he said . . . yeah, right, he came over at two o'clock in the morning without books, paper or nothing but his nasty little mind. I don't know him, told him there ain't no ho's over here. He don't speak to us now; I don't know if he passed but he didn't even care. Now, Dope Man G, he's so proud of me being in college, tells his boys, my girl is smart and he wants to give me some of that money!

Three more co-eds from colleges in Michigan, Sherly, 18, Brenda, 20, Beverly, 21, gave their views of interacting with the life of illegal narcotics.

Brenda discusses the shortcomings of dating dope dealers and college boys.

Dope boys is trouble if they got real big paper 'cause they think they is the only thing in the world. I like their money, but you got to be real careful, 'cause they can trip. The only difference between the dope boy and college boy is one got money and the other one don't. I would prefer to have me a quiet little guy with some sense. I want the money but not if I got some crazy boy ready to kick my ass if I don't do exactly what he says . . . my sister got pregnant by a dope boy, and it's been hell for our family. Dope guys is ignorant, they can't get to "class" if you know what I mean. Money can't buy you class, or they think that everybody in college is acting white. I like college and I know I am black. When I graduate I won't have to listen to no man or anybody else telling me what to do. I'll be on my own.

I like Public Enemy and Minister Farrakan, and I wish blacks would listen to them. . .the dope thang is getting out of control. My sister is just one of the college girls who done got caught up in the street thang. Most of the young guys in our set is either rolling or trying to get it on. Girls is just trying to hang on; it's so hard to make anything out here in this crazy shit. But if you ask me, it's better to leave the dope boys alone. The college boys is dogs, but I can handle them lots easier.

Florence,

Dope fellas is everywhere, everybody I know is rolling. Maybe some nerd guy in the dorm is not out there, and you never know today, it's just tight out here, the campus is fucked up 'cause we ain't got nothing but girls, girls, girls, girls, and the guys got their pick. We just start fighting each other over the same guys. Dope guys is straight if they think you ain't dissing them. They got coin and they will spend on you, and that's better than getting messed over for nothing. At least dope guys will buy you dinner at some-place besides Mickey Dee's. Word, we ain't really got lots of choices. It's so bad sometimes I just want to go home and forget the whole college thang.

Sherly,

Well, it's not like it's no fellas for you out here, it's just the way fellas dog girls. I date whoever is treating your girl the right way. Dope fellas can be cool if you know how to treat 'em. My brothers told me that cuties will go to college and start acting real fucked up. Me, if a guy got some paper well, it's okay with me. I like fellas that's rolling, least they making it. It's better than some fella in college who just wants what he can get. That's why I go home so much; if my peoples knew I was coming to Detroit to see some fella who's out in the dope thang they would scream . . . but if they got the paper, well, it's straight with me.

Why risk getting involved with someone in the street life?
Brenda,

It's easy, the street guys got money, cars, and they willing to buy you things. When I was a freshman, my roommate was from West Bloomfield. Girlfriend mother and father were teachers. She was cool, she didn't dis me 'cause I was from the city. She was concern 'bout paying for her college 'cause it was so high. She was always talking 'bout how I got some help for my school, and she didn't 'cause her parents were making okay paper. We got along real good, even talked 'bout men being dogmatic. My second year we wasn't roommates, she moved into a single room, but I stayed in her room lots of times. We would eat fried chicken from my grandmother, and she would have pies and sweet things from her grandmother. She said her grandfather hated blacks, but her grandmother said people were people. Then one night her family called and said that her grandmother had died. Girlfriend went out, I cooled her out. She was out of control and I felt bad 'cause her grand was real *straight . . . she was real cool, I liked her grandmother 'cause she always spoke real nice to me, like I was her friend. . .Her grandfather died about three months after that. Finally, my girl tells me that her grandparents left her some paper. Girlfriend was on full, got a new car and was dressing like she was on full. My girl is looking real good, she's living large. She says she would rather have her grandparents, but since they left her on full, she is gonna party . . . she got all kinds of boys chasing her and she got money for school.*

Now, my grandmother died and we had to get money for her funeral. I mean my grandfather died when my mother was little. My grandmomma was living on G.A. and Social Security. She was cool, she always gave me little things but she had to take care herself. She died last month and I was thinking about my old roommate and how she got paid, and me, well . . . it's just tight for us, if you ain't got no paper it's real tight. So, if the dope man got some change and it looks good, a girl got to go for it. 'Cause, nobody is gonna leave me shit, and if I want it I got to get it myself . . . that's why girls is out in college or in the street getting paid. It's the best way we know how. If you ain't got nothing for us, shut up!

Sherly,

Sometimes I just hate men, and I think maybe I am turning into a funny babe, you know a lesbo . . . men make you hate 'em, that's why lots of babes end up working for themselves, they get tired of men controlling or playing silly mind games. You want your own things, dope boys and college boys all try to make you do what they want and when and how they want it! I am like Janet Jackson, I want control! I know that's why some girls ration out the sex, that's all you got and the dogs be sniffing and you got to let 'em smell it [laughing]; they want them boots, and you got to keep 'em as long as you can. When men get what they want then you never get what you want if you didn't play it right.

Brenda,

Word, my best girlfriend is at another university, and her man is this big time roller. My boy got big paper and will spend it on her with a quickness. But she's 'bout a dumb bitch, she wouldn't kill 'em you know, she's nice, right? He's driving the big Benzo, and she's driving the little Geo convertible, fuck that! I tell her take all his paper, all of it, 'cause it's just a matter of time and he's gonna do some rotten dog shit to her . . . take all his money while you can. If he's driving the big benzo then your girl got the big benzo too, it's the only way I see a girl out here! Got to get it when you can. You never know when it's gonna stop and you better get much as you can while you can.

Regina, 20, roommate of Brenda who is not from Detroit, has another viewpoint,

> Dope guys are trouble and I wouldn't give 'em the time of day. Y'all let 'em think they the kings. My mother and father would die if they thought I would go anywhere with dope people. I belong to a sorority and we have nice guys, well, they are not killers and dealers. They come up here with their money and act like they can just buy a girl. I didn't come to college to have some dope guy tell me what to do . . . later for dope people.

Brenda snaps back at her roommate,

> Don't even try that Detroit dope guy thing . . . and that soror shit ain't making it either. We all know more sorority girls is getting it on with dope boys than you can count. Girlfriend likes dope boys when they like her [laughing], she wants some of that paper . . . . Are you saying you ain't never been in one of the dope fellas car? Or you never been out for lunch with some of the guys from the hood . . .oh, oh, oh, you thought that big Beemer was some frat boy whose daddy gave him that paper y'all was spending out at the mall after homecoming? Please! Girlfriend is down with the program, Bren is just perping for you; she loves roller's paper, but she won't let her daddy know it, but trust me, she would get with the right rolling guy if the cash was large, she would be there just like rest of us. Her daddy can't give her the paper that the dope guys can, and I don't know too many people turning down paper.

Sherly adds,

> What's the deal, anyway, half the fellas we know is rolling and the ones that ain't is either trying or acting like they rolling. Most people from the hood know somebody in their hood, family or friends that is in the life, that's how thick the shit is today.

MIDDLE EAST AND ARAB AMERICANS

There are six members present having lunch with the investigators at this interview in a downtown hotel. This is one of several meetings during the month with this all-female group. The interviewer asks Arlekka, 18, how she feels about the invasion of Kuwait by Iraq. She is a member of the Red Gucci Girls. The other members are Gail, 18; Patricia, 16; Harriet, 23; Natrina, 19; and Vellicia, 19.

Arlekka is very outspoken and speaks for the Reds. All of these young women are wearing sweatsuits and expensive jewelry. They have been downtown all day getting their hair done and have agreed to meet at the hotel for lunch and interviewing. The investigator has known several of the members over the past seven years.

Arlekka, looking puzzled, answers the question about Kuwait.

What's up with Kuwait? I don't think shit 'bout Ku-wait or anybody that ain't in my thing . . . what is this shit 'bout anyway? I don't even know what you talking 'bout . . . you are asking me shit that ain't got shit to do with us. What difference who invades what? Is they the HOOK? Now ask Ms. Thang, she knows everythang 'bout everythang . . . bet she knows 'bout Ku-wait or invading shit. This girl reads the papers and listens to the news all the time! Tell 'em 'bout the world girl, tell 'em girl . . . . [The group laughs loudly, all except Vellicia, who is considered the brain of the group. She has attended community college on and off for the past two years. Her brothers are successful narcotics dealers in Detroit.]

Vellicia responds sharply,

Lick me bitch, all you dumb ho's can't read, and if the television ain't show-ing ya some video, ya can't comprehend. Kuwait is about getting paid, probably taking over their oil . . . these bitches don't know where gasoline come from. Arlekka thinks gasoline is growing in her backyard, dumb ass ho. I know some of the A-rabs in the hood, and they're Iraqis, they tell me shit. The invasion is about getting paid, it's just like out here in the streets. The Iraqis say the Ku-waitis dissing them and they done talking 'bout the shit. They got this fella named Sa-ddam and he's stupid, and he wants his money, it's just business.

Arlekka, frowning and eating her hamburger, warns the group,

Those A-rabs stank, they talk 'bout niggahs like we ain't shit. I hate going into their stores and they always trying to get on yo ass. They charge two dollars for a pop . . . now V always talking nice to 'em, fuck 'em; me and the crew was in there last week and this little short A-rab named Hassan told some fellas to get the fuck out and don't let him see them in the 'hood or he and his brothers would fuck them up. Now, who in the fuck is he? The fellas look at us, and you know what time it was? One of the fellas is in the Dick-heads Crew and they is crazy and they got 'bout thirty young boys in that crew. They gonna fuck my man and his store. It might take some time, but trust me, that store is gonna get popped, 'cause those young boys is serious, and they ain't taking no shit off no little ho ass A-rab. Might take a few months, but trust me his ass is gone. V think 'cause they don't dis her they alright, but they do business with her brothers and they know that those guys ain't no little crew boys . . . the A-rabs is dissing anybody they think they can dis . . . Anyway, have you seen they way that Hassan muthafucka been looking any black girl's ass, the man is so horny. The man is fucking ya with his eyes, he's a nasty little mutha-fucker!

Room service brings in soft drinks ordered by the leader. Harriet has her hair pulled back into a ponytail and is wearing an expensive gold necklace with her initials in diamond letters. The waiter is a young man no older than twenty. He seems to be in awe of the young women, in particular Hunetta, who is paying him from a large roll of money. The girls, sensing his surprise, tease and flirt with him . . . Gail and Patricia jokingly ask his name.

What's your name? What's happening when you get off, want to ride in my convertible? Tip my boy, he's cute! Got any friends in the hotel, hey bring some Pipers back, or can you get off early and maybe me and the girls might stay over night and show you some fun? Want to get high?

Vellicia is still defending her association with the Arabs in the neighborhood. The crew is arguing about who is against the Arabs.

That Hassan bastard told me that Minister Farrakhan wasn't shit, now V, you know the Muslims stick together and here this Hassan is dogging Minister Farrakhan. And you know the Minister is straight, and this smelly muthafucking A-rab is dogging us. And he told the fellas that he likes to get black pussy. He ain't shit . . . You know he is always at the crackhouse getting freaks to dog . . . . Fuck the A-rabs, if that Hassan say anything to us he'll get some black pussy in his face with my heater blasting him!

Vellicia shouts back,

Silly bitch, Hassan is a Chaldean, he ain't no Muslim. And he's just one asshole, his brother Joe is straight, they know 'bout Hassan. Hassan is just a horny little punkass guy, he ain't getting paid and he just fucks everything up for everybody. The A-rabs ain't killing nobody like the crazy niggahs in the Dead Crew, and you bitches ain't saying shit 'bout them, and the Bongo Boys is raping bitches and ya ain't ready to shoot them. It's just ignorant little silly ass Hassan, and he don't count. He ain't getting over on nobody but them sack chasing ho's in the 'hood. What does he know 'bout Minister Farrakhan? The A-rabs ain't my jammie, but they're no different than everybody else out here. Some 'em is punks, and others is straight

Arlekka interrupts,

*They ho's, and if Hassan say shit to me, I'm just gonna smoke his little ass
. . . they jest some more muthafuckas dissing us. They all want to fuck you,
that Joe is jest slick, he serve up perpetrating Hassan, setting you know-it-all
ass up for the kill. He ain't gonna give yo ass none of that stupid paper.
And, anyway, that Hassan told me and Pat that if he was my man he make
us wear a veil and long dresses covering up our ass . . . fuck that shit.*

CLARENCE THOMAS AND ANITA HILL

Andrea, 23, Joy, 22, and Maxie, 20, are debating the merits of the
Clarence Thomas hearings in their living room. They are members of a
small cadre of women who are involved with young drug dealers.
Their home in suburban Detroit is filled with several young people
who are watching the hearings with great interest. The following discussion took place:

Andrea:

*He did it, look at 'em, he's a freak, looking like he's so straight. Nasty ho,
bet he done freaked everybody in his office. All them nasty old white men at
that big table is full of shit. Kennedy looks worried, he's a ho, big ho . . . my
grand said he got his picture taken with his naked ass out in a boat with
some young babe [laughing]. Clarence Thomas is an ugly muthafucka;
reminds me of this preacher I know, he's full of shit, too. What's so fucked
up is that Clarence Thomas is still gonna get away with this shit, he's a ho,
and nobody gonna get with my girl . . . Watch what I say, they gonna
make him the big time. He is so fake, looking all mad, fuck him and fuck all
'em at that big table, they all fake, they think black women is for fucking.
Why ain't no babes at the table? They just showing this shit for TV.*

Joy:

*Black women, shit, them ole nasty white men are fucking over white women
too! I bet they get with those freak parties, old men love to freak young
girls. Clarence is a freak, look at him, he's so fake, he's a ho. Fresh looking
Anita with her stiff ass, she probably like it, got mad when he got that ugly
white ho. Anytime you see all those straight teachers they is illing and freaking. He's a ho, straight freak. Look at him with those glasses, talking 'bout
hairs in his Coke can, right, bet he likes little girls and having girls do shit
like those freak movies. Big fella, you like freak movies like Clarence? Talk all
that judge shit, and he watching girls getting poked. He ain't shit, you can
look at his stiff ass and tell he's a freak.*

Maxie:

Hey, don't he look like those old nasty men that come to the dope house and be buying crack ho's? The people that be fronting in schools, church and on television 'bout how shit is so bad is the ones that be illing the most. I don't like him, he's lying his ass off. Look at his wife. That bitch know Clarence is a freak, fresh out of them movies like he ain't into the kinky shit. Clarence is lying and so is that ho Anita. Anita got big lips, and so do Clarence . . . Know what I mean, Joy? We see Clarence Thomas everyday, know him like all the other perpetrators in the city. The fag at the bank, he's always talking to me, he's the manager, oughta say his name and let his wife know that he's always looking at us when we come into the bank. He treats me real nice. He looks just like Clarence, stiff and ugly. Got big glasses and he talks real proper; fuck him, he wants to get with us, you know when men want you. Clarence is one of them, just look right at your ass, see right into yo clothes; sometimes in the summer, you go into the bank and wear some shorts, please, he be almost ready to get on you on the floor. Probably Clarence's brother . . . this shit is stupid, ain't shit gonna happen to him, he'll get the job, and still be slaying babes. Once a freak, always a freak . . . Anita is probably a ho, she got dissed for that old ugly white babe and just busted his mouth piece out . . . anyway, this Washington shit ain't got nothing to do with us. Clarence ain't down with black people, he's with those fellas at the table, and that ain't our crew.

Andrea adds,

We just got back from the Bahamas, and they gots lots of nasty men down there. They look in your shit, look at your titties and in your stuff and be smiling like they just wanna eat ya . . . ya know that boys and men is nasty dogs. I like to train my dog [laughing], make the dog do tricks. That's what lots of fellas do with babes, make 'em do tricks for the paper. Now me, I ain't with the shit of doing freak shit. Clarence Thomas looks freaky, looks like he wants some freak shit, don't he? He's so straight looking and reading all that bullshit; he's lying like a muthafucka, he done talk some nasty shit to her. Look at 'em, all his boys at the table they be doing shit just like him, ain't no women at that table? Wassup, they don't let bitches talk? Anita should tell everything she knows 'bout his monkey ass, fuck him talking 'bout he never did anything, he probably said some real foul shit to all them other ho's, talking 'bout he never did nothing . . . look at them ugly ho's, especially that fat bitch who is his secretary. All secretaries protect their boss. When I worked in this doctor's office, he was freaking all the patients and nurses. Nasty old dude, he would feel your ass or titties with a quickness, be talking 'bout oh, excuse me, I am so sorry. The secretary heard the nurses talking 'bout they was tired of his tired nasty ass and she was almost crying, saying he was a good man. One day I was in the supply room and heard somebody moaning oh, oh, so good and it was from the vent over the doctor's office. It was the secretary getting her big ass, busting them boots [laughing hard], my girl came out and she looked happy and didn't know we had heard her and Dr. Nasty in there . . . another Clarence Thomas. Half the time his black ass wouldn't even speak to me and the receptionist . . . ya think it's some old pervert out in the street, it's Clarence and every stiff dude out here trying to freak ya, that's the way it is on the block. Fuck everybody, Clarence Thomas is a lying ass dog, and his wife knows it, and President Bush knows it. Clarence is a nasty freak and they gonna let him be on the Supreme Court and everybody in America is gonna have a freak for a judge . . . it's fake, it's fucked up and ya know we right. Call us ho's but ya be illing with shit like this, a freak who's a judge, a lying muthafucka who likes freak movies. He's just like the dope boys who like fuck movies; a low down freak for pussy.

MIKE TYSON

These interviews started with the charges in the summer of 1991 that former heavyweight boxing champion Mike Tyson had allegedly raped a contestant in Indianapolis at the Miss Black America contest.

How do you feel about the rape charges against Mike Tyson?

Jolie, 20, member of a scavenger gang,

> He did the shit. My girl is gonna get paid in full. She probably could have gotten out of his hotel, but when men like him want, they just take your stuff; my girl just gave up them boots. I feel bad for my girl, hope she gets paid and he gots lots of paper. She get that cash, her life will be alright.

Honey, 23, member of a successful commercial gang, laughs and shakes her head.

> Silly bitch, she probably gave him the ass, then she changed her mind and hollered rape. Ain't nothing gonna happen, she some little silly college girl and he got bank, bank enuff to make her shit go away. Everybody knows that when fellas got bank it's their world, and if Mike Tyson got big bank, well, it's his word against hers and whose gonna listen to her? Wassup? Girls get taken off everyday in the hood; boys with bank know they can do what they please. The only way a girl gonna get respect is to have her own bank. Mike is rough, you know, raw, he's the man and she must be piping if she didn't know wassup. She know now! Anyway, lots of babes wanna give Mike them boots. Mike done had more babes than most fellas. Anyway, babes is always trying to mess with Mike, remember that fake ass bitch

Robin? If the bitch got taken off, it's her fault. Mike ain't no little soft ho, he's hard, gotta stay hard and black, that's the way it is.

Renae, 18, a senior in high school, has no gang affiliation nor any relation to illegal drugs.

Mike Tyson used to be my boy; but after the way he did Robin Givens, I have my doubts about the boy. He acts so rough and he is a boxer, so if she said it, I think it's possible. My friends and brothers think the girl is trying to get money, that's all they talking 'bout, she's a skeezer after his money. Well, Mike has gotten other women in ways I wouldn't want to be treated . . . . I used to think he was kinda cute, but if he treats women like they're his property, well it's not what I want to hear about a black man, especially a famous one like Mike Tyson. You know, men just treat women bad. Look at the way everybody is talking 'bout Clarence Thomas; and the Kennedy boy, he did his thing. Why is everybody so mad at this girl, she might be telling the truth? Every guy I know is dissing her, calling her bitch this and skeezer this. Give the girl a break! She might be stupid for trusting Tyson, but she might be telling the truth.

Myra, 17, a gang member in an integrated, covert operation,

Later for the girl, she should have known. Mike is notorious with his shit, he's just like any dope boy out here. They think if they got bank they can do anything. And old men is the same way. If a man want to bang ya, well, the only way to stop boys like Mike Tyson is to pop'em, put some holes in his ass with your gun. Bet he wouldn't fuck with me, 'cause I shoot his little ugly ass. Fuck his ass up. Got to let a boy know it's gonna be some shit if you grab this ass . . . . I got brothers and I know how fellas think. They can do whatever, later for that . . . Pop a niggah, shoot him and don't even think 'bout, shoot his ass and then watch how fellas start treating you straight. The ho is just working for the white people, she ain't shit if you ask me. If a man calls you in the late night you know he wants some boots. And if he got juice like Mike, well, you gonna bet it's time for kicking them boots. Mike is one of them silly muthafuckas that think girls is fo their pleasure. I know if Mike Tyson wanted to kick my boots I would let 'em [laughing] but if he got rough I pop his ass so quick, he wouldn't know what hit his little funny talking ass. You got to make guys respect you. Some guys need little help, like sticking yo heater in their ass [laughing]. Shoot 'em, smoke 'em, pop 'em, that's all men understand is getting slapped and told back off boy, step off nasty muthafucka, get back before I smoke yo nasty ass!

Ginger, 23, is a member of a successful all-female crew.

The bitch shoulda known what's happening. He did the shit, and ya'll know it, he's just another dog, a big dog, but he's a dog. That's why I refuse to be anybody's bitch. Look, how many times Mike done heard the word NO? He ain't hearing nothing but yes, yes, we wanna kiss yo ass, we wanna suck ya little dick, and he got that slick-talking Don King fronting him off, and them preachers talking 'bout Mike is a Christian, pl-lease, Mike is a ho, a big nasty ho, he would snatch any girl's shit, he's a maniac, but my girl is the silly ho. Later for that little silly college ho; saw her on television with all them white kids. Bet my girl thinks she is white, just like that ugly Clarence Thomas ho with his white kiss-ass wife. This girl gave up them boots and the next day she's out there dancing and singing with them beauty queen ugly ho's. I know plenty of fine black girls who make them ho's look like shit. That beauty queen shit is fake. All the men in that beauty shit is just like Mike Tyson, they want yo boots . . . there some little silly boys in Detroit who got a magazine and be taking pictures, talking 'bout getting you in movies or on television. Right! They tell some girls they want take their pictures and the ho's fall for that shit; they want to get them boots, they out cold. They all want to get them boots with a quickness. The girl is a little baby ho, crying, with her momma talking 'bout she can't sleep, and she'll never be the same again, right . . . they shoulda talk 'bout all the boys, I mean all the boys my girl done gave them boots up. Fuck Mike Tyson and fuck that little lying ho, she shoulda got fucked, she was looking to get it, she wanted to get paid and he did what fellas always do, they fuck you.

POLICE

The subject of forfeiture to the government is the subject of a *60 Minutes* show.

Valerie, 24, a member of a covert narcotic gang, is furious with this program:

This is such bullshit! Look at 'em, they robbing fellas and they call that shit the law. How can they take yo shit, saying it's made with dope? It's bullshit, that's what it is, stealing from you 'cause they say it's like that? The po-lice be out here robbing fellas and now this for-fei-ture shit means they can jest do us, 'cause they the law. I say, fuck the law, it's some made up shit. They don't grab the white boys buying the dope, they don't take their shit. It's jest like when they used to arrest the ho's; they don't mess with the old white devils buying the pussy.

You ain't got no rights if you out here in the street. The po-lice can tell lies and nothing happens to them. They beat us, kill us and they sell dope. Look at the Chief [Chief William Hart], he done got paid [referring to the indictment].

They beat down that Rodney King dude and nobody does shit. Cops shoot niggahs and nothing happens. Fuck the po-lice, fuck 'em, if they ain't trying to rob you or kill ya, they'll try and get them boots. Now, how can they do that shit, and they ain't showing no black people in this shit. You know why? 'Cause they kill the niggahs when they want. The hooks, all of 'em, I know it's the po-lice, FBI, the DEA, how come they always fucking with niggahs? Everybody hates niggahs, and them sell-out niggahs should get popped first. I hate the po-lice, especially the black po-lice. Ya don't never get no white boys; they sell dope too! They buy dope all the time and it's us on television getting busted. The street is raw, it's buck wild, and if you're soft get the fuck outta here. Boys be getting smoked 'cause they think they can't be touch; you ain't untouchable. If it's tight you'll get dusted out here. Lots of perpetrators and they jest talking; it's that time fo anybody if they in the way. Well, it's tight and sometimes you jest have do whatever it takes to make that paper. Now, here comes the lying sneaky ass snakes trying to stop you from making that paper; it's so fucked up. Got to take care yo thing, it's yo thing, do what you got do . . . but I done worked too hard to let some snitch bitch or some silly black Robocop take me or my people out. It's all bullshit . . . trust me.

Risse, 21, another member, continues,

It's real. Jest make that money, get paid, that's what my momma told me when I was real little, she said, 'girl, get somebody and take all their money.' Do what you got do, but get paid. No po-lice is taking shit from me. I been in the joint, I didn't let them big black bulldyking ho's squeeze me. Nobody better not fuck with me, 'cause I will pop a motherfucker, oh, yes, with a quickness. I may look little, but I will get something and get busy. I would shoot anybody if they try and take my shit. I ain't with it. Like my girl Val says, we gonna shoot somebody and that means if it's a man so what? If it's the po-lice, so what? Don't fuck with us, and everything is straight. That's the biggest shit the hook done tried, they gonna let some dog smell my car or house and then take it? Right, if that ain't silly. You taking my shit and I done worked hard fo it, and some dog smelled it. Shit, the dog might smell some girl dog and go out. That's the way the men is, they get that scent, I, my aunties used to say, they smelling them girls' tails. A dog smells my car, and they talking 'bout impounding it? Nope, I jest killed the dog and the silly ho's trying to get my monay.

THE RODNEY KING INCIDENT

This interview took place during the showing of the video tape of the beating of Rodney King in Los Angeles, California. It is two days after the incident. Male and female gang members discuss what the incident means to them.

LaMekka, 19, a member of a covert male/female gang, is eating with three members of a younger female posse and two male independent drug dealers at a local restaurant. This interview takes place about one hour after the newscast.

LeMekka says,

They beat my boy down, that was scandalous. They was kicking him in the head. That shit was unnecessary, I got tired of seeing that shit. They show it fifty times a day; Rodney King is on everythang. Man, it was fucked up.

Manfred, 21, a male gang member,

If anybody beat me like that they better just take me out, 'cause I am gonna get them back, I am gonna kill them. They was out cold. The po-lice ain't nothing but some beastmasters and if they the white hook, they like beasting on black boys. Hope my boy gonna get paid, 'cause they beat his ass real bad.

LaShea, 20, a female member of the same gang as LeMekka,

What you think the po-lice gonna do? They always beat ya down, and they was white, but even black po-lice will beat ya down. That's what they do, they love beating people. That's what po-lice do, they love being Charles in Charge. Fuck the po-lice, they ain't shit, pop 'em, shoot their asses if they touch me. My boy shoulda jest took his heater and smoke their white asses . . . if his crew had been in there they woulda got busy and took care their boy. They beat him down! The only reason everybody is crazy is 'cause they got the shit on video. Po-lice beast on niggahs everyday, everyday, and nobody cares. Later for Rodney King, fuck him, they shoulda beat his ass, beat him down. Fuck him for letting them beat his ass! White po-lice be talking shit, and the black muthafuckers who ride with 'em will beat you down right with them and laugh. I remember, long time ago, the Gang Squad niggahs came to this teen club on the Westside and beat down the Tony Boys when I was 'bout eleven. They bloody this boy real bad, fuck up his mouth real hard; they didn't take no shit. The Tony Boys was clever, real sharp, until the hook beat the shit outta them. They kick their ass real bad, and I knew then that the po-lice was the dog muthafuckas. Everytime I see them I was scared until I got older, then I just hated them. Rodney King just another niggah that got in the way. I done seen lots of Rodney Kings up on Mack. Me and my people will fight and shoot anybody who tries to dog us. Me, I hate the po-lice, always and always will. Fuck 'em if they black or white, babe or dude, the po-lice ain't my people.

LeMekka continues,

> My uncle talked 'bout when the po-lice was taking niggahs out during the riots in '67, and my grandmother says the hook was killing lots of niggahs when she first came up from Mississippi. The po-lice will do anything they want to you, they just dog niggahs and nobody says shit. They the biggest crew out here but ya don't talk 'bout that shit. Po-lice take little boys' monay when they first start rolling, they jest dog ya until you learn how to trick'em or shoot back at 'em . . . the only way I like po-lice is stanking dead.

Hari, 20, a female member of a smaller, scavenger-type crew, laughing, adds,

> When I see the blue I book out, the po-lice ain't nothing but trouble. Me and some of the fellas from the GWY crew was just hanging out at this club and the security fella came out and said for us to take a walk. We was feeling real fly 'cause the GWY had this dope tracker with the sounds kicking hard. We got in the car, and just said to the fat security guard that we might smoke him for illing. The fat ho called inside and three drunk niggahs came out flashing their badges, talking cash shit. Before you could take off a squad car with two white boys pull up and jump off into our shit. We was cool, but one of the GWY boys said he knew one of the white cops and he was always calling people out, niggah this and niggah that . . . they start talking 'bout if we wanted our little black asses kicked like Rodney King. Shit, everybody in our Humpty had heaters, if they had stepped off they would have got fired up real good. Shit, if they try to take us out like that video beating, they gonna get surprise from these girls . . . [laughing].

Freddy, 23, same crew as Manfred,

> Ain't no Rodney Kings here; just start some shit and we'll finish it. Nobody scared of the po-lice, they jest some badges with heaters. They got theirs and we got ours. The po-lice is crazy if they think we gonna let'em just beat us down. If I was Rodney King I would have grabbed one 'em and beat their ass.

LeMekka, in disgust,

> Right, they would beat yo dumb ass worse than they beat his big ass. I would have got busy soon as they stopped me, shoot them right in their face and drive off; they wouldn't never see shit after jumping off with us . . . if they treat me like a ho, I'll show them that I am in charge out here on the streets. Later for that John Law, it's street law. The strong survive and I am nobody's ho or little soft bitch. I am strong and in charge and when these here young fine babes grow up they wanna be like me . . . [laughing].

AFTER THE KING VERDICT

This interview takes place a year later after the verdict that acquitted the white police officers in the Rodney King trial.

LeMekka, responding four hours after the verdict.

Wassup? They don't care nothing 'bout niggahs, they just said fuck him, he ain't shit. They like doing that shit when you got no bank, got no juice; it's just like everyday life out here. Now, them niggahs is out of control, they is buck wild, they gonna fuck somebody up. Lots of silly boys running 'round beasting on people. They should get it together and just shoot all the white boys that beat him down. Later for all that burning shit up, I hate that shit, when it's Halloween I have to protect my grandmother's garage from all them silly boys. I just get my people and tell everybody that we down with Tyrone's crew and if anybody start burning our shit we gonna get busy. Fuck the riots, I just shoot 'em, bet they would stop burning up shit then. Justice? What's that? Justice is this here Uzi, justice is when a muthafucka ills you, blast his ass, justice is when somebody steps off in your life you jest blast them in their face. The white people in Detroit is the same ones that let them ho-ass police go free. Rodney King shoulda jest got busy; fuck a lawyer, fuck the judge, if he wants justice he should find them po-lice and smoke 'em. Now, that's justice. Look at them white people getting in those stores with all the Mexicans and black people . . . bet they blame the niggahs for all the shit, everybody is out there, but they'll say it's all the niggahs' fault . . . . Everythang is our fault; it's our fault for beating Rodney King and it's our fault for rioting. The verdict don't mean nothing to us, it's just some more bullshit. Things ain't changing 'cause some white po-lice beat a niggah down, that's what po-lice do . . . beasting is their job. They got their jobs and we got ours.

Freddy adds his feelings,

Can't believe this shit. Well, lots of niggahs is mad 'bout getting fucked over. I am pissed when they beat him half to death and they talking 'bout it's their job; well my crew gonna do our job and start fucking the hook up before they do their jobs and kill us. Look at this shit and they still talking shit 'bout it's okay 'cause he wouldn't stop getting up. Man, the po-lice is wacked if they think niggahs gonna take this kinda shit. I am gonna never stop for the hook now, let them beat me like that, and then they say it's alright.

Two days later in an interview during a newscast on the jurors from the Rodney King trial . . . LaMekka, in a very serious mood, listens as a juror from the trial defends her choice of supporting the police.

Listen to this ho, she's sounding all big time, listen to this shit. How is my boy Rodney in control? The bitch is a racist, she talking 'bout the riot ain't her fault; oh yes, it's your fault and all them silly muthafuckers who let them po-lice free. Listen to this bitch, and you know what, I know this lady out in Grosse Pointe where my sister used to work in a catering service. This bitch talked just like this wacked out ho, she said blacks liked welfare and being dirty and poor. She said that all blacks were lazy, said we needed to stop having so many babies. She sounds just like this ho on the television. You know, this ho thinks she's better than us. They think they're better than us and that we're some kinda dirty low down people. That's why I love fucking over them ho's at the mall. When I buy shit I let 'em smell my paper. Fucks them up to see a black babe with bank [laughing loudly]. Boom, see all them George Washingtons and Ben Franklins, all that green, it's like, let 'em see my bank.

Fellas do it all the time, that's why the hook be so pissed, po-lice hate to see it when you living large. They hate it when we getting it on . . . one thing I know for sure, the po-lice love to be in charge. I hope the niggahs burn the whole city down . . . nope, I ain't burning shit down, and I don't riot or loot . . . and I ain't down with welfare. I got a job, and it's paying and the fellas, we always say it this way . . . a bird [a kilo of cocaine] in the hand is better than a Bush [George Bush]. Me and my girls got too much paper to make, we ain't got time for looting. Looting is for poor people, people that's upset; the only thing that I am upset about is not making my paper. They right to get mad. But fuck Rodney King, look at him in that sweater, looking like Little Richard, he's a ho, talking all soft, pleading for us to get along. Go talk that shit to those muthafuckers that beat your ass. He's soft, looking like he gonna cry, little bitch, can't even talk; if that was me I be saying burn this bitch to the ground for letting them po-lice off. They should burn that little town where they had the trial down, that's why that ho is talking all that shit about "they" shouldn't be rioting 'cause she don't know shit and she don't care. I hope they catch this bitch and burn her house and car [laughing], she just another muthafucking whitie talking shit, like the ho out in Grosse Pointe. They gonna get theirs one day, and when it comes they'll be illing, why us, we were good to the blacks that work for us. Fuck 'em, blast 'em . . . let 'em stop me, they done fucked us over too much, it's our turn to get 'em.

. . .Robin, 19, and Chip, 22, two members of the RJH Girls, give their view of the King verdict. Robin states bluntly,

Rodney King or Rev. Martin Luther King, the po-lice hate niggahs and they gonna get us anyway they can; if everybody gets a video camera then we can make movies of the po-lice beating us . . . get a video camera or get a gun.

. . .Chip continues,

Look at those Koreans, just like the A-Rabs shooting people and the police ain't stopping them; they just let those Koreans shoot us and they got Uzis and ain't no police arresting them. If we had our Uzis they would be smoking us with a quickness . . . ain't no justice for the black man, just like Minister Farrakan says. The black man can't get no juice, he can't get no respect . . . got burn or kill, that's the only time whitie listen to us.

ABORTION

We took the reactions from several gang members and individuals concerning how they feel about women and abortion, Malika (CEO, high school graduate, 23), becoming very angry, (Note: This response is during a television newscast on pro-life demonstrations)

It's my business, how somebody gonna tell me if I want a baby? Fuck all them protesting ho's, the real tip is that they hate niggahs, and they think we the only ones on welfare and having all the babies. They don't want no niggahs in their 'hoods, but they gonna tell me to have a baby, then they gonna say you can't get no welfare, and go to work at McDonalds . . . the girl ain't having no crazy alley doctor up her ass, no way! If I needs an abortion I am going to a real doctor, 'cause the girl got the paper. If you is poor, you're out of luck . . . having a baby is crazy, but if you get fucked up, what you gonna do? Having a baby ain't for our crew, and like I said, it's my business. Now, some of these tramp ho's, they need to get their shit sew up 'cause some is making babies 24/7 (24 hours a day, 7 days a week). Me, I would want my baby to have all the best shit monay could buy . . . but having a baby is dumb, rope a dope babies is for somebody, but it ain't my thang.

Mona, (CEO, former corporate member since early teens, would not give age) is direct as usual,

Abortions been happening since I can remember, what's the big deal? It's up to you; if a woman is having problems and they don't want no crumb snatcher, you best know it's ways to get rid of it. The girls in crews don't have babies 'cause they clocking dough. Who needs babies when you getting paid? I buy my nieces all kinds of shit, and they love me, that's all the momma shit I need. Kids cost monay . . . . Have you been to the stores, and seen what clothes cost for kids? Now, lots of silly bitches be buying shit from that little Footlocker, buying Nikes, Reeboks, and little itty bitty sweatsuits from the same ones that make Michael Jordan and Magic Johnson . . . Lots of bitches need abortions. The people crying 'bout welfare is the same silly mugs stopping abortions. Well, what's up is these tramp ho's on welfare is the ones that need to abort, so if there ain't no welfare, no abortion, there's gonna be plenty of little rolling, killing muthafucka's, 'cause all these white people think not having abortions and welfare is gonna stop this crazy shit from jumping. . . It's too late! Plus, it's lots of white girls getting abortion. It's outta control.

Some respondents felt that the subject was racially inspired. Frankie, (territorial gang member, high school dropout, 23, elaborated with anger.)

It's a black thang with whities and us, they hate us and I hate them. They just want to see no blacks, like Minister Farrakan said, either they sending us off to fight their bullshit wars or they killing us. I don't trust no whities 'cause they hate us. Y'all talk all that pro-life shit, but them same whities be talking 'bout saving lives and they won't give a black person a drink of water. I used to work at this country club, it was for whites only. Sometimes a stuck up niggah would show and they be illing more than the whities. I would clean up tables and the stuck up niggahs wouldn't even speak, they act like I was nothing but some old dog. Anyway, this white bitch was my supervisor, she used to tell me and this other black girl that we could eat in the back, but the college white girls could eat in the dining room on their breaks. I hated the way they would treat us. That old ugly no ass bitch told me and my girl we was lucky that she let us eat. She made my girl cry one day, the bitch didn't have no man and she would just fire you up for nothing. I think the bitch like fucking over anybody, but especially niggahs.
When I get on full, I am going out to that place and say to her ugly ass, Hey Bitch, how you like me now [laughing]! Lots of whities would just stare at you, look at you like they ain't never seen somebody black. And you feel like saying, what's the deal, whitey? Them little white girls would be smoking weed, fucking the young college boys that was caddies and stealing shit out the kitchen. Some of those little cute babes would be busting out those old men, you know, the ones that was married and had big paper. One white girl was straight and she would tell us who was kicking boots with the married men. They was the bitches that acted like they was some kinda Barbie Doll, the ones that didn't speak to us. But if shit was missing, me and my girls would be the first ones asked, did we do it? When it comes to abortion people think it's us, you know us, "the blacks!" But my grandmother told me lots of young white girls get abortions, they always have. My grandmother said in her day lots of black girls would get sent away if they got bumped, or they got married. Now, some niggahs be talking trash 'bout no birth control pills, or they will take care of the baby . . . not me, ain't falling for that line. Nope, no babies for the girl. All I'm saying is that the white people where I used to work hate black people and they don't mean us when they talking 'bout saving babies' lives . . . like Minister Farrakan say,

it's our race they hate, they know its gonna be more niggahs so the pro-life bitches ain't going to adopt no black babies, they only want some white babies, or some babies from anywhere but Africa [laughing].

Shameka, scavenger gang member, 19, explained her views and the gang's feeling on the subject. (She calls them her set; they are known in the neighborhood by their gang name.)

Babies, well if you want one I guess it's alright, me . . . na, not me, but if you get busted out you might need to get rid of yo problems. My sister got three babies and it's crying and baby shit all the time. I kept telling her to take some control pills, but she like having babies and it's money from welfare. Most of the girls in my set don't really talk 'bout no abortions or babies. They ain't worried 'bout things like that. How do I feel 'bout abortion? I don't really care 'bout it, it's just some bullshit that ain't really got nothing to do with me. I'm trying to git paid, and babies don't help you git paid, now do they? Now some ho's will want to drop down with the baby, if they been scheming to git some niggah's monay by gitting busted out. When the dude finds out and kick 'em to the curb then the smart ho knows that baby is gonna be trouble. Then they want to git rid of that muthafucka. Lots of boys will leave when you git bumped [pregnant]. Old men, they be scared of having babies so lots of girls will git bumped on purpose or they be lying like dogs to git paid. Sometimes the shit just blows up and you done got yo self a baby [laughing].

Marsha, 17, non-gang member and recent high school graduate, addressed the abortion issue.

Well, girlfriends shouldn't get pregnant today if they know what's happening . . . but me and my girls feel like it's our business what we do with our bodies. My preacher at church gets excited talking 'bout unmarried mothers, but my set ain't worried 'bout no baby 'cause it's just too crazy. I want to get a good education, get a job and travel before all that baby business. My sister is in college and her girlfriend just graduate, got a job with some big company in Los Angeles, now suppose she had a baby? Abortion is crazy and you can check it before it get too far crazy . . . But it's my perogative, okay?

Gail, 18, a non-gang friend of Marsha's, who attends community college, laughed and continued,

Abortion? Huh, my father would have a baby if he heard me say abortion. Lots of girls we know had babies real early, like in middle school. Can't relate, it's just so out there. Having babies is the worst thing I could do, it

would ruin my life. Abortion is something I just don't even think about, naw, not with my mother and father. If that happen to me, and it wouldn't, I would do what is best for me, and that is my decision. But, like my daddy says all the time, he and my momma take care of me, and I am not ready to go it alone, so there is no baby for the girl or abortions!

Nancy, 18, non-gang member, reaffirms her friends' position.

Having babies is crazy, guys don't help when they get you pregnant. I have seen too much of that excitement, it's no way I am gonna get tied up with a baby. Most guys I know are going to leave if you get bumped; giving up those boots will cause you nothing but diapers and no guy to help out . . . abortion is something you need if you didn't take care of business up front . . . most girls I know ain't with it. Anyway, lots of guys like having babies by different girls, so you best keep your boots tight until it's right. My set is tight and we know who the dogs are, so it's straight. When you know they just want the sex, later for all the smooth talk; no job, no respect, one girl, all that is required for my attention, okay?

SAFE SEX

The interviewer asks the gang how they felt about safe sex. The Fendi crew responded while watching the Arsenio Hall show with guest Dr. Ruth Westheimer.

Dana, 19, responds,

Do you use rubbers? Most fellas talk 'bout they can't feel it, they don't want no rubbers. Me, I ain't kicking it with nobody right now, but if I did they would have to use something; ain't with no babies and definitely ain't down with the HIV; nope with OPP out and boys will fuck anything, that's the truth.

Sue, 19, and Mara, 22, express another view.

Lots of girls think they man ain't down with nobody but them; ain't no man seeing one babe. Some boys is getting off with other boys. Nobody likes to talk 'bout that shit. Girls be watching out for skeezers and it's some sweet booty boy kicking boots with their man. We know lots of boys, lots of fellas be sucking each other. Boys like other boys in crews. We know some real cute boys who be getting babes and fellas. You can catch some nasty shit out here from girls and boys. Fellas is skeezers. Skeezers be nasty, and boys who is skeezing be spreading all kinda diseases. Make 'em go to the car wash and wash their nasty asses off and spray their nasty dicks [laughing]. Naw, seriously, we tell each other to watch out for nasty babes and boys . . . call it safe sex, but we always look out for boys who try to kick boots with the whole crew. Jest 'cause they look fine don't mean shit, they can have HIV, and kill yo ass. Nobody is that fine, ain't no dick worth dying for. Fellas think they can look good and get the whole crew, that day is out. Now some babes wanna fella that bad, well, it's okay, time out, can't get the dead dick. Fellas think being a tramp is straight, they don't think fellas is ho's like women. Girls is the only ho's far as fellas think.

We got a girlfriend and my girl is the biggest ho in the world. Girl is knocking boots with everybody, y'all done probably hit her up. She thinks she ain't a ho 'cause she go to the university and she's in graduate school. She runs with these white girls and they is big ho's for the football players. College kids is the biggest ho's we know; they will kick boots when they drink that beer and pretend they don't remember shit [laughing hard]. The ho is wacked and she is with everybody, we call them kinda ho's, undercover ho's. They the worst ho's, lots of ho's in college, lots of freaks. The college boys is always trying to kick boots with us at parties . . . . That's 'cause college girls from the hood ain't got no time for 'em. Girls in college go with dope men. That's why it's tight out here, college girls got our men [laughing] and now we gonna take their college boys. The best way to protect yo self is to keep yo stuff, 'cause boys will be tramps, it's their way, and undercover ho's is everywhere. They is kicking in schools, the church, at yo house and in the street . . . safe sex is hard with all the undercover ho's in the street, read hard.

DOMESTIC ISSUES

Pat, 24, and Malika, 21, members of a covert entrepeneur organization address the subject:

Do you do dosmestic chores in your house? Should women do housework, or should men do those things also?
Pat responds,

If you fucked it up, clean it up . . . I am in business, I am not some cleaning ho. If a niggah think he got a maid he better push on, 'cause the girl ain't with it . . . Fuck that shit, clean up yo own shit, I'm getting some niggah to clean up for me, got it! . . . That's one of the things fellas tell me and I get mad and want to fight . . . Why, huh, why is it that bitches got to wash, and clean up, or change the diapers. That's another reason I don't want no babies. Its always the woman, the girls; it's pick up behind the nasty ass man, well, fuck that!

That's like this dumb silly bitch on television talking [Guide for the Black Man, S. Ali] this yang 'bout the black woman got to do what the black man say do, or he should kick her ass, [throwing down her bottle of pop, violently] right, kick my ass, and they gonna find yo ass somewhere stanking. This 'bout a silly bitch, dress up looking good, then the bitch started illing and Malika and the girls started screaming, we was ready to shoot that ho on the screen. I know if any man tell me some shit he better get ready to get his ass kick, or shot . . . 'cause we ain't with that shit. Is that bitch crazy?

Malika coolly responds,

If you got the change I'll clean your house, wash your clothes, and cook your food [laughing real hard]. But you better have big monay if you want me to clean after you . . . now, if some fool think I am his bitch, well he better get a grip quick! See, I am 'bout taking care myself and if you got your own change, well some things ain't a problem. What I am saying is that if you got monay you can tell anybody to clean up. With monay you the boss, and fellas might hate it, but you ain't got to listen to their shit, they hate it . . . get yo own change and you become the boss.

We asked the same question of Glenda, 20, Netta, 19, Marsha, 18, and Rhonda, 23, members of a small, unsuccessful scavenger gang.

Glenda, speaking on the subject,

What's up? Clean up? Well, if it's 'bout getting paid I'm gonna do whatever it takes. I don't mind if I'm getting tore off, long as he ain't beating my ass like I'm some dog or something; well I'm in the mix if there is some paper, okay?

Netta, disagreeing,

Later for some nasty boy making the girls clean up, fuck'em . . . my nasty brothers use to make me clean and wash for them. Nope, not the kid, it's wacked to clean up 'cause you the woman!

Marsha, continues,

Well, it's like this, if I'm cleaning up, what's he doing? I use to work for this old lady in the 'hood and she would pay me to clean up and her lazy ass husband use to just fuck things up the more I clean up . . . that's what I like 'bout dope boys, you git to go out and eat at Ram's Horn or Red Lobster, no cleaning up. Living at the hotel is straight 'cause whatever you mess up they clean it up . . . now that's living large, ain't it?

Rhonda snaps,

You ain't nothing but a silly ho, fuck Red Lobster. Get a old man, 'cause a dope boy will own yo sack chasing ho ass for a dinner and a screw . . . a old man will buy me a house or get me a car and be glad to get some pussy once a week. Young dope boys want to fuck you, and then let his boys dog you out for a Red Lobster dinner. I use to have this old factory man; his wife died and he loved me. He was the best thing I ever had happen to me, then he just got sick and died and I am back out here with you ho's looking for another one. Get me an old man, later for those young, crazy, dope boys.

Gertie is a grandmother to four young sisters who are part of a successful male\female gang that specializes in selling not only drugs but stolen car parts. The gang has been together for three years with few problems because of their size and their knowledge of the narcotics trade in the city. They are trying to sell heroin and crack cocaine because their main connections have been busted and they no longer have a supply of crack. The grandmother is discussing only her view of why young girls are involved in this gang.

The reasons these here young girls is doing wrong as you call it, is because it's what makes sense for them. My daughter has been on and off drugs for the last twenty years. The girls' father is out in the streets begging for a living. They provide me with things and I take 'em, and why not? I did day work all my life, that's all I did was clean up behind white people. Talking 'bout 'they' is my family or I was in their family, right! I was their slave. I did day work for nineteen years 'til my grandchildren got me out. You think I care what you or they ofays think 'bout me? My so called family used to give me leftover food. Sure I took it, they was paying me under the minimum wage back then, shit, I stole their salt, pepper, and anything else. They had this old mammy bitch for a cook; that fool loved white people so much she slept in the basement. Those little white kids use to make me work harder 'cause they loved to make me look stupid. They had six kids and all of them was little devils.

I remember, in 1969, my son George was killed in Viet Nam. I was so depressed it seemed like my whole life just got worse everyday after that. Well, Ms. Thang had the nerve to call me two days after the funeral . . . they didn't even come to my boy's funeral. The bitch had the nerve to tell me if I didn't come right back to work she would have to let me go . . . she said she was having a graduation party and she need me to serve the party. The fool said that spending time home wasn't gonna bring my George back.

I can still remember her saying, work is good for you, and it will get your mind off George. That's when this "family member" knew that I was gonna have to get another job. This woman and her nasty old husband told me that I wasn't a nigger like the ones that destroyed Detroit in the riots. I took that bus out to Grosse Pointe with other black women and I hated every day of it.

Now, my little grandchildren is looking at this world the right way and I love it! My grandson Tyrone is out in the street and he's a tough little guy working 'round the neighborhood. This neighbor of mine said to me last year, "your grandson sure is young to be driving all them fancy wheels." I just smiled and said, "its better than having no daddy, and anyway, what business is it of yours?" His daddy was my son George, and Tyrone is the one that looks out for his cousins, the girls. They're good kids, and long as they respect me, I don't care what they do. Detroit ain't the same today, jobs is hard to get, and the white people are after Mayor Young all the time. Hell, he didn't make this mess, it was them white mayors before him, but all them bastards like that ole ugly cracker Bill Bonds talking 'bout Detroit ain't shit is the ones that hate us. My granddaughters ain't never gonna have to clean no white bastards house! I told my girls don't end up like your momma on that dope, and don't clean no houses for nobody, ever [laughing]. The way these kids is making money it wouldn't be long before they get out to Grosse Pointe and start buying their own homes and have whities doing day work . . . . Domestic means being somebody's flunky, and these here girls of mine is working for themselves and I am happy to see it that way!

Lydia, 26, has been involved in selling narcotics for the past thirteen years with her brothers, and cousins.

Domestic work is what? Cleaning up for myself or somebody else? Look, all that cleaning up for a man is old stuff. Clean up yourself. I can remember in the dope house, when I was real little like maybe thirteen and the fella's would pay me and my cousin Teri to clean up the mess from making packs, those young boys would always tell us to clean up the mess . . . later for that. A man just wants to tell you what to do, it ain't bout being clean cuz most men is dog nasty [laughing], it's 'bout being in charge and making a woman the ho, you know the one who does what she's told, and I ain't hearing it. That's why I run my own shit, I am in charge of my thing, it's 'bout letting boys and old men know that you're in charge of yourself. Let the man be domestic, let him get the cleaning shit, let 'em do the ho work, I got paper and I'll do the hiring and firing and let somebody else clean up. The only clean men is the funny ones, you know the fags, now people dis 'em, but the fags is much cleaner than most men. We got a sissy that keeps house with our crew and he is the one, cooks and cleans and don't take no shit. He will shoot a fool if he has too, but you can count on him to keep it clean and fresh. My silly brother, the youngest one, is always talking shit 'bout Ralph, but when you want it done right, get Ralph. I am clocking too much dough to be cleaning house, and who said it's for the woman to do the domestic shit, probably some dickhead man.

WHO ARE YOUR ROLE MODELS?

These females are in a crew or have worked in some type of crew with males and females. There are all types represented in these interviews: scavenger, territorial, corporate, commercial, and covert entrepreneur.

DeAnn, 20, reflects,

I like Queen Latifah, I like Mayor Young 'cause he will tell a muthafucka what's up; he is fine, too! The mayor don't take no shit, and that's the way its got to be!

Vicky says,

I like me and Pat, we the role models for the girls in our hood . . . shit, fellas want to be like us, we crushing all the cuties. I remember this old stuck up bitch from some program came to our school, talking all that African shit, we laugh that bitch right out the room, huh? Africa? Right, I ain't no African . . . this bitch was acting real fucked up talking we didn't know who we was, and that we hated ourselves, say what? This ho was out of control and she had the attitude, bitch said I was ignorant. Me and Malika got with the bitch, if it hadn't been in front of the whole class we would have popped that ho. She was wearing some funny looking African shit, bet that ho ain't never been to Africa. But trust me, we told the ho, you better get booking when school is out 'cause yo old funny ass, wearing all this African shit, is gonna get beat down, coming in here calling us ignorant!

Pat, cool in her delivery,

Vic gets upset over little silly things. We just don't think that some of the ho's everybody else thinks is down is our kinda thing. Look, Jesse Jackson is straight, and so is fine ass Minister Farrakan. The girls that I like or, you know, kinda think they straight or is large is like Aretha Franklin, 'cause my grandmother loves that bitch, and she can sing. I like some of my girls on Bill Cosby, but you know life ain't like that . . . but most of the bitches we see is on television is talking like and acting like they don't know what it's like in the real. Now, Malika loves some television, with them stories. My girl was mad like crazy when they took off that Generations. *But television is like Cosby, it's make believe, that just ain't the way we catching it down here. Like Mike Tyson's bitch; she be fronting with the whities, she's a ho, but look at the bitches on television in the city. I can't get with it, them ho's be sporting them weaves, wigs, and their faces be packing that make up on like they Michael Jackson [laughing hard]; its fucked up, them ho's ain't like me and my girls.*

I likes real people, not fake hair and fake attitudes, you know, talking 'bout us like they ain't just like us. The only bitches like us is on 62, like RJ, but that ugly half white bitch Gina makes me sick, she's a ho. You ain't gonna see no people like us on TV, less they taking us to the joint. Now, Opray is large and she getting it on. I am glad she gained that weight back, 'cause my girl is larger than some little white bitch size . . . my girl is getting paid and she is running her own shit, ain't no man telling my girl shit. And she got that fine muthafucka and you know all the ho's want his ass; she's the only bitch that got her own real hair, and running the thing like it's gotta be.

Myra, 17, continues the discussion of role models,

My role model is me, all dressed down with my Fendi, and sackchasing earrings, with lots of paper, ready to buy plenty of shit at Northland. That's the only role model I need. Who needs some role model? That's y'all world. The preacher gonna tell me, the hook gonna tell me, the teacher gonna tell me, well it's like this, let my monay tell you . . . I don't want your model and your mentor shit is lame, it's out cold . . . . Some young babe working for the phone company came to this class and started illing 'bout we was women of Africa and needed her for a role model. The ho couldn't take her eyes off my Fendi bag, and the bitch was scared and you could tell it; now how is this ho gonna do anything and she is scared of us? I don't need nothing but paper, doughski, lots of monay, that's all I need. I ain't listening to all your bullshit 'bout what's wrong with me; what's wrong with you . . . . I done heard it all before, same old story.

Jody, 27:

Role models are what? I mean, who can show me anything if they ain't in our thing? I am so tired of hearing 'bout how we need role models. I think we got the role models, y'all is just mad we understand what role models mean . . . it means the best role model is the ones that is getting paid. Later for all that go to school, work in the Burger King. I am gangstering just like the fellas. Men want me to role model and have some babies, keep my legs open and my mouth shut, [laughing] and the hook want me to get off the street and not make no monay. Fellas in crews want us to work for free. I done did that shit already for White Castle and Sister's Chicken. I am getting paid. You asking me if I am with a crew, it don't matter 'cause I am a Gangster Bitch; I am getting paid because its my time and nobody can stop me, I am ready to get paid, and I don't need nobody and that's the way it is.

Janelle, 16, speaking of the hardships of being in the city with no role models.

Me, I want somebody that can tell me what to do. I had this counselor at this home and she was real nice, I liked talking to her. Then I got put into another foster home; the lady was old and she didn't know what time it was. Her husband and her older sons were all trying to kick them boots, and I hated it. She didn't care 'bout me. You need somebody to talk it over; I would like to kick it with some kinda woman, a black woman, but I have had white counselor who cared and it was better than talking to some fake, perping, black woman like the one at the social services. The crew that I am with is 'cause my brothers is down with 'em and my brothers said to leave the fake foster home. I need something, you know? I like talking with y'all, why can't everybody just chill? I met this policewoman and she was cool, but my brothers went out, said that the hook was the enemy and never get near them . . . it's hard out here. The crew is what's happening for me right now, but I would rather live just like other girls and just go to school and go to dances or roller skating. Its tight for me, I can't wait to just get up and get out on my own . . . this really ain't my style, it's just for now, have some monay and my own place."

MADONNA

Andrea, 19, member of a small, commercial gang that is gender integrated, is discussing her younger brother's and sister's individual gangs. Her sisters are arguing with each other over the HBO concert of pop singer Madonna.

Andrea:

My brothers are in this gang called the Mack Daddies, but it's my little sisters who keep shit started all the time. Listen to 'em, they talking shit about the concert.

Paula, 13, explains her admiration for Madonna's dancers, she seems to be enjoying the concert and becomes angry with others in the gang when they attack Madonna,

Madonna got it going on, her dancers can step . . . she's that girl.

Saqueita, 16, interrupts,

> She ain't shit, that bitch is fake to the max, she's nothing but a ho, a big skeezer, look at her with all them faggot dancers, she is that HO . . . . She the kinda bitch that tries to get all the fellas and want her ass kiss all the time.

Paula snaps back,

> You wish you had her shit, she is in charge. She got all them boys working for her, it's her show, she's the one!

Henri, 14, adds to the growing protest over Madonna,

> Girl is you hitting the pipe, Madonna is a little white ho, trying to dance with niggahs, fucking niggahs and acting like she the one, the bitch is out of control. She ain't blond, her titties is them plastic ones, she is perping like crazy, fuck the white bitch. She like that little white college girl at the Center. Bitch talking like she one of us, then one day this bitch tells us "we are all sisters, we're all in the struggle against men, it's 'bout women's liberation." We look at this crazy ho, say what? Look here white bitch, we checked this bitch real hard. Bitch, naw, white bitch, who is you talking to, we ain't got shit coming with no women's liberation. Liberate what? We fire this college girl up real fast, she didn't come with that sister shit no mo. Fuck some perping ass white girl, what she know 'bout us, she jest visiting. She was always throwing her hair round. Paula wanna be white, that's why she was listening to all that silly shit. Look at this ho Madonna, why she got all them faggot boys in the bed with her. This bitch love to be in the middle of everything, see she ain't got no girls round her, she think she that girl.

Paula, angrily refutes the charges,

> The girl got plenty shit, and what you know Henri? I like her cuz she knows how to make it happen, she is the one.

Andrea intervenes,

> Madonna is a tramp, and she done did it with everybody, she is one tramp ass ho, bitch can't sing, can't act, and she is always dissing folk, like she did Arsenio, the bitch need her ass kick . . . look at that bitch swallowing that bottle like it's a dick, nasty ho, on television sucking dicks in front of everybody . . . this ho likes to freak other bitches, me and Carol saw her in this video and she was kissing another bitch in the mouth. Now, tell me she ain't scandalous, she is the biggest ho in the world.

Carol, 17, member of Andrea's crew, adds her disdain for Madonna,

Selling pussy is her real thing, Madonna is selling pussy . . . if a black babe did what she did, everybody would be illing. Madonna kissing another babe is freaky, white people like that kinda shit. Paula is a little freak, she is illing like she some Madonna girl. Bitch you is black, and when we sell pussy it's just another black ho, we can't get on MTV or get no records sold . . . that ho been dissing the church and they eat the shit up, white kids, especially little white girls think Madonna is God . . . that white college girl was talking 'bout Madonna like she was God. I just looked at this crazy college girl and laughed. Madonna don't mean shit to me, she just some white babe getting paid like stupid. . .she ain't my girl and I sure ain't illing like silly ass Paula. Madonna don't mean nothing to me or this crew, she ain't got nothing coming and she ain't looking out for us, she only want the dancing ho-boys, the fags, black fags dancing with her white blond ass out front. The bitch ain't from the street, she acting like she hard, and she is in control . . . who cares, just another white bitch.

MOVIES

What are their favorite movies? The four groups represented are: A) Organized gang; B) Unorganized gang; C) Covert Entrepreneur gang; D) Non-gang and non-criminal groups and individuals who represent regular students or young females in the city. These young women ranged from ages 13-27.

Group A: Organized Gang

Margo, 19, speaking for her crew, described her favorite movies and entertainers.

I like movies with fine men like Denzel Washington, Eddie Murphy, and boy off Bill Cosby named Theo. We like movies that give babes some play. Hate that shit when babes git called bitches and make 'em fuck everybody and then ice 'em. We saw that shit 'bout Silence of the Lambs. The man in there was a freak, and the babes were too soft; that dumb bitch trying to help that muthafucka with that couch, now that wouldn't happen in our hood, we would have smoked that bullshit freak asking for some help . . . we went 'cause Elaine wanted to see that little Jodie babe. That movie was full of shit. Letting some crazy guy put you down some hole in the ground in the basement, fuck that! That's white people, trusting some freak in the night, just like trusting some dumb-ass crackhead, later for that kinda shit. I would have smoked my boy if he had said shit to me in the middle of the black ass alley, in the night? Trust me, he would have been dead with a quickness. I loved that fine ass Gregory Hines, any movie he's in I'm going to see it, the girls love them some "LA Law" boy, he is fine!

Group B: Unorganized Gang

Dorothy, a dropout from high school, works for the local grocery market as the lottery clerk. She recently left her crew over a dispute about working for a drug dealer.

> Movies, we like anything with Wesley Snipes, and Spike Lee is my boy. I like movies that don't have all that kissing and hugging like everybody is in love; I likes the movie with the shooting and fronting like New Jack City . . . we rent movies whenever one of us gets over and we stay in the big motel with the VCR. Sandra was going with this guy who worked midnights at Mazda, and go over there and watch all his old black movies, they would be funny with those big Afros and those funny pants and babes would be wearing some crazy shit. I like some of the white boys in the movies and the girls dis me, say I am a whitey loving ho, that ain't it, just when the white boy is cute, it just be that way . . . actually we will watch anything at the movies, it don't matter, long as it's at the movie.

Group C: Covert Entrepenuer

Michele, 23, Nicole, 21, Georgie, 20, responded to the question about movies. Michele,

> I like movies with Eddie Murphy, or something with Spike Lee. I don't like those jit pictures with girls getting sexed, and killing or beating babes. I go to the movies with the fellas that want to take me out and buy me things, movies is just a way to relax and chill.

Nicole,

> I don't go to movies because you might get taken out, my fella is worried 'bout getting robbed by some ignorant fool trying to get paid, we stay home. If the girls want to go see a movie, it's during the early day when nobody is in the theater. At night it ain't safe with nobody, the carjacking shit, or trying to avoid the crazies out here. Keep a low profile, never know whose watching or ready to bounce on your ass. If you look clever it's tight 'cause some crazy will try to rip you off, rape or kill you. Stay at the homefront, get a video, it's safer and you can just relax like Mic said.

Georgie,

> I go to the movies and later for being scared or careful, if some fool wanna die then get with me. I love the movies and the malls. I take my little cousins

and my momma, we go see whatever is playing. I like scary movies or sex movies with Mel Gibson or Denzel Washington. I love Denzel and Eddie and Arsenio or maybe that cute ass Michael Jordon should do movies. I go to see the Pistons and see my baby, Du-Mars, he's so sweet. Movies, malls, and the Pistons, that's my life, if y'all think I am staying inside because these fools is illing, no, no. Girlfriend is out here and is loving this monay, let's go shopping at the mall.

Group D: Non-gang

Lisa, 17, Naco, 18, and Nece, 23, discuss the movies and their social lives. Lisa,

Well so much of the movie things is silly, I like some of the rappers that do videos and Ice Cube is straight, but his shit with the 40s is out, so much of the movie shit makes blacks look like savages or silly. Me, I want to see strong blacks and the movies is always 'bout us as ho's or dope people. It's some smart bloods out here doing plays and rapping about positive or real black life. Most of the movies that some kids like is so silly—like that Freddy Kruger shit is out . . . I like that Oprah movie ["Brewster Place"] 'bout the projects when she is the old lady helping everybody. Or that fella on channel 50, "Roc." He did some movie with that ugly monster from outta space [Aliens 3] . . . . How come the monsters always black and ugly? Have you ever seen a white monster? Nope, but most movies is silly to me, they don't make me look good. I am black and I don't know the silly bloods on the screen, do you know anybody always singing and telling jokes, like we just make white people laugh. . . .

Naco,

We rent videos, its cheaper and it's safer, last time I was in the movies some niggahs started shooting and everybody hit the floor. It's like that anytime some good picture is showing, I just decided to wait until it's on video, it may take awhile, but it's better than having to duck them guns. I like action movies like Action Jackson and Boyz in the Hood, sometimes it's a funny picture. But I hate that skeezer Madonna and Robin Givens. My favorite movie is Sparkle, and I love me some Wesley Snipes with his pretty black self, strong black man. Everybody says it's Denzel, but for me it's Wesley. I like me some Branford on "The Tonight Show," all them brothers in that band is getting it on, and you can tell Branford knows he's the one.

7

The Twins

The following interview is actually a series of interviews taken with two sisters (twins) from Detroit. One attends college, the other has recently had a baby. The twins belong to an all-female territorial gang. While they do not sell drugs, they are familiar with the commerce of narcotics. They also show the diversity of young women involved in college who remain a part of urban street culture.

Do you see more men crews or women?
Randi:

I see more girls.

Some people say that there aren't any female crews out here.
Randi:

Yes it is . . . you know what it is, it's female crews but they don't necessarily have a name. Anytime you got three or more girls hanging, that's a crew and they all help each other fight.

You know what, we don't all wear colors but there are gangs out there and we don't necessary gang bang, like for a certain area, like they do in Chicago and in LA. The gangs here don't necessary call it gangs, they call it my boys or my girls. And everything is so drug-related, not that you can't say gang, you just say it's drug-related. It is more so that people trying to get over on each other than just flat out beefing.

It's over money or drugs or girls?
Randi:

Well guys don't fight over girls that much anymore. But girls always fight over guys. But I don't play that . . . . I'm not that type. I'll tell anybody if you can snatch him you can have him.

Are there a lot of girl crews in the city?

Gina:

> Yes. But they don't run into us, though. Yeah the Me So Horny girls. They all
> wear pony tails and I can't stand them. They all wear little biker shorts and
> the bra shirts and they all dance nasty . . . they feel on theyself and they
> dance off of slow songs by themselves.

Are they different from crews that are rolling?

Twins:

> You know what, I don't know what they do. They sleep for money. But,
> really, I don't know what they do, I don't know if they into dope and stuff,
> but they bummy, though. They the type that's into dope but don't spend it,
> they just do stupid stuff for guys.

Are you in a gang?

Gina:

> I mean, . . . far as us being in a crew, there used to be a lot of us, I mean
> just a lot. We done went down to the club with almost thirty deep before.
> We mainly get crewed up on Saturdays. It be ten of us in one car. We all just
> get in our cars. All of us got babies except her [Randi]. I say out of twenty
> girls we hang out with, four of us don't have babies. Me and her play the
> middle. We cool with everybody, but Mikki might not be cool with Lisa, but
> we cool with both of them. So that's how the crew broke up because such-
> and-such fell out with such-and-such and don't hang with us when the
> other such-and-such is with us. But now we go to the club with eight deep—
> eight or more.

Do you have a name for your crew?

Gina:

> Seven Mile Crew, they always say East Seven Mile Crew. I'm a tell you, this
> is how it be. All we doing is dancing, this girl looked at her watch, swung
> over [Randi]. I was seven months . . . all these girls swinging on my sister.
> So I had to get out there and do what I had to do. So the security guards
> picked me up and threw me out on my butt. Then, that next week, they
> gone say we got some fat ho's we want y'all to rush . . . we ain't gone
> throw you out.

Security guards said that?

Gina:

> Yeah, the security guards down there out cold. But we got some boy that's
> security guards and when we fight they help us. But we don't consider them

in our crew. We don't talk to nobody that be at the club. None during the week, but when we get in the club, we all family. We never went with anybody at the club, and all the guys would want to get with us.

All the guys wanted to get with us, we used to say, we got boyfriends. We keep it where we don't hang where our boyfriends hang, because that could 'cause a real problem. I don't have that problem anyway, 'cause Jason don't really go nowhere. But she try not to get with nobody from the club, but the guys in there see us fighting, they help us. It was getting to the point where we used to dance and give shows and girls would come out and dance on our time. We supposed to be dancing and they just come out and disrespect us. And we used to hang with these guys off Davison and they used to come out dropping girls.

Dropping girls?

Gina:

Punching them so that they fall, knocking them out, shooting at them. Then we fell out with them. See, we fell out with them 'cause they fell out with my boyfriend. And they came over my house with a gun for him, I said, wait a minute. You my friends but that's my boyfriend and he not gone come over here with his guns and his boys to see me. So, I said, y'all straight with me, but I don't want y'all over here no more. They get up to Persian and Osborn, had a gang, and all them thought they were going to rush my boyfriend, without me helping. I'm not saying I'll go head up with a niggah, but I had a big ole club and anybody that was going to swing was going to get swung on. So one of my friends called them and told them that I didn't get y'all, but I was prepared.

My friends out cold too. We've got into a couple of arguments and fight with them too. But we would always make up.

Is it better since she's [Randi] gone to school?

Gina:

No. 'Cause they don't do nothing but say, when your sister get back or when she come back she go straight to the club. And I love the club and my mother try to keep us from going, and I just tell them I don't know why they try to make up all these excuses, because we'll just catch a cab. We do not care. They think I'm a trouble maker but Randi has fought more than me.

We got banned from our graduation because she kicked the girl at the prom, and they had it on tape. So what my family was telling be behind her back. . . . This is how it is, they know me and her are close and my mother would always say, I think you would take your sister's side before you would my side and that's a shame. My mother think we'll rush her, because she think if she hit Randi, she think I'll jump on her. Because one day my dad slapped her. He never hit us, and when he slapped me she jumped up out of her sleep and she started hitting him all on his back and ran to get my mother. Then my mother always said ever since then they think we'll double team them, so they don't hit us.

Randi:

But, see, this what they did, my family would tell me to get away from my sister. They would say, your sister is pregnant, and she's wilder than she's ever been. That baby should slow her down, and while that baby should slow her down this is the chance for you too, since you missed your graduation, you have a second chance at you college graduation. I said, I'm going to Wayne State and I wanted to stay at home. They said, no, I think you should get out of town, and my uncle knew somebody at CS. I think you should get away from your sister. Your sister is pulling you down and she's uncontrollable.

Gina:

They said I wanted you to stay with me so you could get pregnant. They were just saying all this stuff behind her back and I told her don't say nothing but she went off. I told my grandmother for one, I don't appreciate you talking behind my back, and for two, anything you got to say about me, you can say in my face. They can have their opinions, they in the church, and they were talking about marriage and stuff. For one, I would never say Randi, girl, I think I'm pregnant, why don't you go out and get pregnant? I don't have no control over her stuff. We don't even be together when we with our boyfriends having sex.

They don't know if she's ever been pregnant, they don't even know if this is my first pregnancy. People kill me to sit up here talking that junk and say you must be the bad twin. I've been with my boyfriend a long time, and I did not plan on getting pregnant. But I wasn't about to abort it for nobody, and I take care of my daughter, and I don't put her on none of them. When I got something to do, he watch her. I very seldomly ask my mother. I ain't never held my hand out to nobody so far. I ain't say it ain't gone happen, but I don't plan on sitting on my butt.

Why were you banned from graduation?

Gina:

At the prom you know what this girl did, by me being the pregnant one, I was five month having time and this girl bumped me . . . she wanted to bump me, so I gave her a bump that she would remember . . . so they got it on tape and say, well, Gina magnified the bump.

Randi:

Guess how they trapped me into not going to the graduation? By them having it on tape, they had me on tape saying "chill out, Gina, we got to graduate, wait until after graduation." This how they got me, they said, Randi, you can't come to graduation because you suggested that you all would fight after graduation. And they banned. And my aunt told them that they will call the news, she said Bill Bonds will put that on the air. We found out on a Friday that they wasn't going to call our name at graduation . . . they wasn't even going to tell us. This teacher we knew told us not to go . . . they not calling your name and you're not walking across the stage. She told us on a Friday and graduation was on that Monday and wasn't nothing we could do over the weekend. So we missed our graduation.

They did not sign our diplomas and we just realized that about two weeks ago. And you, why, because they automatically put our diplomas to the side.

So you had a fight at the prom?

Gina:

No. The girl walked into me because I was pregnant. She was, like, she's pregnant, she ain't gone do nothing to me. She wanted to walk into me so I showed her what it was like walking into me. Then she said girl, I said bitch . . . I threw my stuff to Jason and tried to get her. Then Jason gone say to me that ain't just your child that's my child. Then Jason turned around and said, don't make me have to fuck up no ho's in here and started going off on the girl. So they said me and my boyfriend just couldn't get along with people.

Do you recognize that you are having conflict with. . .?

Everybody . . . this the thing, with teacher they would get upset because they could never catch us. They would hear we had a fight but could never catch us and the first thing when we go to the office, they would put out this big book with you grade and all, they would see is A-B-A-B, they would get so mad. You know what, the teachers we beefing with weren't our teachers.We have gotten away with a lot of stuff because of our grades.

You enjoy being trouble? I think you like it.

But, see, we don't get in trouble on purpose. That just the old stuff. But, you know what, the old stuff we sit up and laugh now. See it's easy to laugh now but back then we wasn't laughing. We just kept wondering why we kept getting in trouble. We get in trouble for our friends a lot too. Ok, like if we fight somebody, and say we was to lose, which we never lost, my friends is the type is to get her brother to shoot up somebody house. But what I tell her is, no matter what your brothers do they gone come back to me and Gina house 'cause everybody know where we lived. We told our friends, if y'all get in a beef, let us know what's going on so we will know what's happening. Because y'all liable to go beat up somebody and we ain't nowhere around and they send somebody to come shoot up our house because they know we hang with y'all.

And guys . . . two for one. Can I get two for one, I got two balls, one a piece. Guys say the nastiest stuff about twins. We was about to fight so many guys last summer downtown. It's to the point where we would be fighting all the time.

This guy tried to get with me, I was like, dog, I'm straight, he was like naw, naw, damn let me get that number. I was like, dog, I'm straight, I ain't got a number. So we get out the car . . . . Y'all ain't in vogue . . . . We went walking down Greek Town. We came back, all the windows was shot out, you could see bullet holes through the seat. They didn't shoot us but just think, they could of shot us, just 'cause we wouldn't give it to them. We was nice about not wanting to give them our number and I was like, man, I got a boyfriend, two of them, you know I tell guys anything . . . I be like, I got five kids at home, I need to get there. They ask me if I got a boyfriend, I say, yeah, I got three of them and don't need no more.

He shoot the windows . . . we didn't hear the gun shots but we came back to the car about a hour later, windows all shot out.

Did that scare you?
Gina:

No, because I didn't know they had a gun so I wasn't thinking like that, but when we came back and all the windows were shot out, I said, niggahs just ignorant. It made me think about how stupid niggahs are, because once we walked away and went partying they just decided to shoot our window because we didn't want to give them our number. This the thing, they just wanted us to pay for the windows. I ain't paying for nothing, it wasn't my car. My friend boyfriend paid for it.

This the thing, we got a heart. It's certain things we won't do. We do think before we act, we not just flat out, out cold and just do stuff. But it really take a lot to scare us.

But we used to be so silly. We used to get a whipping and run upstairs and laugh.

Did they whip you good?
Randi and Gina:

Well my mother would whip us and we would go upstairs and laugh and she would try to whip us again but we would laugh. Don't nothing scare us.

You know what . . . Randi that is a little scary that you would get a whipping and laugh. Some people might think you're hard.

Randi and Gina:

> You know what so funny, the look on my mother's face, like she really hurting us, "I-told-you-don't-do-this" and we wouldn't say nothing and sit there and then go upstairs and just laugh, laugh, laugh.

> And Susan would tell on us . . . but she would just cry. Did she tell you about when someone stole her car?

Yeah, the carjacking.

Gina:

> She just broke and cried and said, oh, I didn't mean to leave you. I just died laughing.

Where were you?

Gina:

> I went in the store and soon as I got out of the car and went into the store they made their move. She was crying and carrying on. Then she went off on the police. Did she tell you how the police don't like her? After she talked to the first police they were dissing her, so we drove to my house and the police we like, could you slow it down and she was like, Ok. Then she said, I can't stand the police. So he rolled his window down and told me to roll my window down on that little speaker and said, tell her I can't stand her either.

> I mean, police are so ignorant . . . I don't like women cops. Women cops think they tough, they try so hard to prove they so bad. Like one day this lady gone say search these broads, I don't feel like it. Then called me fat, she told my brother if he moved his head she was going to bust him in it then tried to intimidate my little brother. You know, pull him to the side, try to talk to him like he gone tell her something she want to hear. Then told her if she turned her head again her face was going to match her shirt. I had on a red shirt, 'cause they don't want you to see their faces when they talking all that trash. They did the same thing to me before when my boyfriend was in the house, this time he look and they slapped him down . . . they just kick his butt.

> Oh, you know what, speaking of crooked cops, the security guards at Northern used to set us up to fight. They used to pull us out of class and say do you really fight . . . and the girl said, I don't want to fight and locked herself in the classroom. Yeah, they used to say, if you see those twins fight let them fight so we can kick them out. Yeah, they was just trying to set us up.

How do you feel about the police?
Randi:

I can't stand them.

That's what everybody tells me.
Gina:

The only thing I like about them is that they get crewed up after the club.

Why there?
Randi:

'Cause this girl just pulled a gun on us about two weeks ago and police was right there. She walked up on my girl and said, "sucka punch me now" and pulled out a 45. I ran so fast, all I knew is she was aiming our way. That was enough for me. So it's gotten to the point I can't even drive mamma's car down there 'cause I don't want them shooting out her windows, I don't know if they remember the car or not. But, lately, when we been going, we been getting dropped off. My friend had a head full of weave that night. She took it out now and they don't know what she look like now, and she's had her baby now, but she told me she's going back 'cause she ain't worried. They were mad at her because she got into a fight with them. I wasn't around, they were on the other side of the club. I wasn't around, so when the gun came my way that was enough for me.

You know, this the thing, we been going to the club for five years, right? We think the club is our club, we got the one corner, we all be in and we don't like for a bunch of girls . . . like if six girls came in our corner trying to dog we wouldn't start nothing with them, but we all get on the floor and let them know to push on. We feel so at home at the club, and we walk around like we own it.

Do you ever see the day that you guys won't be so intense?
Randi:

Yes. But she is tripping with this baby, she is just so determined to be the perfect mother she is making me sick, because if her baby is crying I'll say, oh, Alexis, shut up and she'll say, don't talk to her like that. And she got the baby spoiled to death and it's hard when other people babysit.

Do you ever fight each other physically?
Randi:

Yeah, we used to. It's been a long time. We just want to fight my brother now. We waiting on purpose and I'm going to let everything build up 'cause *when I let him have it, I'm letting him have it. Edward makes me sick, he's still young and silly . . .like he took a pack of candy and smacked me in the back of my head today while I'm driving. He just do a lot of stuff that he ain't got no business doing. He will tell my boyfriend if I talk to another guy and he our brother. But he play too much.*

Who are you close to beside each other?

Randi:

Nobody . . . Well I'm getting close to my grandmother . . . we been talking and gossiping. We get along good, we can talk to our family like we can talk to you. I wouldn't say it's nobody in our family that we not close to.

When my daddy used to be out cold, my mother used to say burst out that bitch window. His lady friends' cars and if they got a daughter our age, oh we terrorize you until you leave my daddy alone. We burst the windows and he come cursing us out. But he knew not to say too much, just why y'all do that.

Has anybody ever struck fear in your hearts?

Gina:

Well that gun . . . I was running so fast and it wasn't really aimed at me so maybe . . . .

That's not scared, that's common sense.

Randi:

Ain't nobody never strike fear in my heart but it was a time where I say I could have been sitting down and something would just say don't do it or you gone die soon or slow down or . . . yeah something like that. I get those little feeling and thoughts but don't nobody scare me.

We've been in shootouts and raids. I've sat here and watch my house get shot up with my sister in there. I was across the street at my friend's house.

Who shot it up?

Randi:

This crazy lady, she sell dope. I was across the street at my friend's house using the phone, and I heard some shooting. I looked out the window and see three people shooting up the house. Everybody was in the house except me. So I called the police, and then I called these Arabs my daddy was cool with, and they all came over and crewed up . . . but didn't nobody get hurt. But that's just a crazy feeling wondering who's getting shot. Then, you call the police and they take all day.

What is your view on sex?

Randi:

> You know what, I'm going to be honest, everybody tell you, once you start you can't stop . . . it's nothing and the way young people have abused it now they make sex a bad thing, 'cause it used to be something beautiful. It ain't nothing now, it's too scary. How you gone have fun worrying all the time—who this niggah laying up with or what you gone have?

Gina:

> You know what, when I was pregnant I switched clinics. I took the AIDS test just 'cause I always said I'm going to take one and the doctor was like, are you on drugs and why do you want one? I said, that is a real scary thing . . . you just never know.

How do you think it is on the streets?

Gina:

> Everybody is getting scared. I've been with my boyfriend since 1986 and I ain't gone lie, we were using condoms . . . I didn't have my pill and I ain't buying it. Me and him use condoms now. My friends really crack jokes, well, it's something you ain't telling us . . . they'll say Jason fucked somebody and you knowing and you ain't telling us . . . why you making him use rubbers.
>
> I tell them they just think everything funny but I tell them that I don't want no more kids and my pills haven't kicked in yet, 'cause she only two months. I don't play that. It ain't bothering me, it don't feel no different to me but I don't know what he feel but I'm straight.
>
> Yeah, people say they scared of AIDS, but yet and still, they don't use condoms. I guess because for one, they don't want to break the mood.

Isn't it kind of hard to keep a relationship?

Gina:

> Not with me.

Randi:

> I ain't gone say I can't keep a guy . . . but it never works.

Do you think it's going to work with Keith?

Randi:

> Yeah because . . . this the thing, I have changed a little and it do have something to do with him because he really do try to get me to change. He tells me all the time, Randi chill out or just be cool. But, just being away in school period, I have changed.

Do you [Gina] go to school now?

Gina:

> No, I'm starting in the fall. I'm starting nail school, and I love being a mother and don't regret having her.

You love being a mother?

Gina:

> Yeah, I, man I ain't saying I want to make it a habit or hobby, but I love her and she ain't no problem. This is my girl for real. And then, in a way, I think God wanted me to get pregnant because I was using condoms. I knew when some of them busted . . . you know, so when I missed my period—I found out when I was five weeks. And I wasn't about to abort it. I always wanted a boy and a girl, but not this early.

Yeah, it is kind of early. Do you think you're going a little bit too fast?

Gina:

> No. See, you think that 'cause you on the outside. We were just brought up where nobody hid anything from us. You know, you got some kids that never knew anything until a certain age. We knew everything from the beginning. Yeah, 'cause for one my family is into dope.

Is that good?

Gina:

> In a way . . . . I think it's good that we can be streetwise and school smart. But the bad thing is that we sort of justify wrong things, without knowing it. Seriously, it's certain things we used to do that we don't do now, like we don't smoke or drink.

You don't?

Gina:

> Back in the day we used to hang on Seven Mile and help these boys that used to roll. We used to help them hide their stuff in the dentist office. Or we'd be the watch dogs. They pay us $50 a day to tell when the police would be coming. But this is before they started messing with girls. We were tomboys then and we would basically sit up there on Seven Mile on the garbage cans with our gold tooth and hat turned to the side, and basically look at them when the police came, to let them know. Or we would go in the dentist, and throw the dope under the mat. I got some girls over there on Mumford that when the hook would be coming, they would be doing little raps. They were real young, like twelve.

Randi:

> See, this thing, we always been bad as far as fights, but we always been on
> the honor roll. We get good grades. When rapping was in, we had a demo
> tape, we was gone make a record, things went bad. We cheered for about
> six years, I mean we always was active, but we still had fights. Everybody
> would say they think they bad 'cause they twins or again they got some-
> thing smart to say. They jealous. Like, when they call they say that "Y'all
> only fresh because of dope—if it wasn't for crackheads." You know every-
> body got something to say.

> We grew up going to church with my aunts. We would go to camp three
> times a year. A Christian camp, we would fight but you couldn't get us to
> say a curse word, we would say I'm gone kick your "A," or that "B." We
> would go to church with my aunts and everything would be fine, but we
> would go back home to the same thing and wasn't nobody in our house
> doing nothing. Wasn't one Bible in the house, but the one our aunt gave us.

> You see we were just going through so much growing up, and then only
> having that one day to be with my aunt was not enough. We fell out with
> the lady at church, we were tired of everybody in our business talking junk.
> We ain't been to church since. We go to church every blue moon and visit.
> We started going to church with my grandmother, after we stopped going
> to that other church. But we don't go to church on a regular basis, because
> people in the church are fake.

**Well, you know, you guys are really refreshing. I think it will be
interesting to see how you will end up.**

Randi:

> Yeah, I want to see how we end up too. Yeah, I know I'm going to make for
> the simple fact I know what type of guys I mess with, and I know they
> money ain't guaranteed and I don't never want no guy to leave and I have
> nothing, I want my own. That way, whatever he lose, I still got mine. You
> moving in my house, so when it's time to get out, I'm kicking you out.

> But, you know what, men are a trip, because, in most situations where I
> talk to my friends and they got stepfathers, the man always move in with
> the woman. So what kind of man is that who have to move in with the
> woman and her family? I don't really respect no man that got to move in
> and then try to tell the kids what to do and he living off his woman. Every
> girl that I know that got a step daddy, he moved in with them.

Do you have juvenile records?

Gina:

> No.

Have you been arrested?

Randi:

> I've been arrested twice. Watching a fight in eighth grade . . . they took me
> to the gang squad, took my picture and everything.

Are girls as violent as guys?

Gina:

> Yeah, worse. It be more girl fights than guys at the club. But it's more inter-
> esting to see two girls fight than guys. Because girls fight to the end . . . they
> scream, they kick, they bite, they pull hair. I just had a fight the other day
> and my shirt came off and this guy who is my boyfriend's friend said, let me
> see them titties and then called my boyfriend and told him.

You had a fight the other day?

Gina:

> Yeah, about two weeks. Yeah, it was this girl who was talking about me
> when I was pregnant and I checked her about it. I seen her and I got with
> her.

Where?

Gina:

> At this house party. Me and my girls went to the party and rushed the
> whole party.

Randi:

> Yeah when Gina was pregnant I had called her and these girls was playing
> on the phone and she 6-9 them and said, yeah, when I drop my load I gone
> get you.

What's 6-9?

Randi:

> Star 6-9 trace the last house that called you back. So, if somebody playing
> on your phone you can trace them.
>
> They like to call us and have us go off 'cause we know how to cap real
> good.

Cap, what's that mean?

Randi:

> You know talk about people, play the dozens.

Do you work?

Randi:

> We had a job, me an' all my friends worked at the same hotel—it didn't work. It was at the Knights Inn. I got fired. I worked at Little Caesar's. And they steal big time. But the manager just tried to dog me out.

Well, how do you get your clothes? You got a Polojacket, how do you get your money?

Randi:

> Well, my boyfriend bought me this jacket for Sweetest Day, he get checks and I get them all.
>
> How we get money? Well my mamma and daddy. When I went to school I had $700, I didn't plan on having $700. For one, this is my first time going to school out of town, when I had $700 I took it and I feel like I don't have no family down here, I'm on my own and I really felt independent and $700 wasn't enough for me but I settled for it. After being in school about four weeks, I realized I didn't need $700 so I came home and bought a big fat herringbone. It was my money, my decision—my family gone try and play me now that I have all this money now, which I don't, that was just a one time thing. I get my money from my mother, my father, guys, and I shoot dice sometimes.
>
> One day it had got so bad that I had to shoot dice just to get into the club. To come up with the $7.

Do you enjoy motherhood?

Gina:

> Well, it's not hard yet because, look, I don't have no bills but all I get is $70 every two weeks. Aid is sick, they ain't playing when they say this is just for you basic needs. 'Cause once I buy diapers, I'm broke. Only thing I can say, I'm glad I don't smoke cigarettes or on drugs because I couldn't support my habit if I tried. But whenever I get my checks I take care of her first, then my money go the club and Van Dykes, that's $18 every weekend.

You like school?

Randi:

> But I have changed for real . . . it's fun sitting up here kicking the old school stories with Gina, you know talking to you. But I have changed a lot, the stories I'm telling you now, I'm not, you know . . . .

What's your major?
Randi:

> It was Communication but I changed it to Social Work. I really do love school, I do and I always have.

What about the boy that got killed from Detroit?
Randi:

> Oh, up there . . . Keith was there. He had three asthma attacks, they was chasing him and boy, he was acting like I was supposed to be there for him. It wasn't nothing but asthma and he was in the hospital. My roommate went with the boy that got killed.

What happened? They said the boy that killed him was from Detroit.
Randi:

> Yeah, Bill. All week Bill had been falling out with people. Keith had been telling all week that this boy was crazy, he's scaring a lot of students and he supposed to have a gun. They didn't never do nothing, the day the boy snapped—he fell out with this African guy name Charles, he called up to Keith room and said that Bill is down here acting crazy, come down and get him before I kill him. Keith and the boy that had got killed, Joe. . .he was telling Keith that he was glad he came here to go to school 'cause if I would have stayed in Detroit I would have been dead somewhere or in jail. That's when the phone rung. When they went downstairs Bill was there. . .Joe roommate knew Bill and so when everybody was calling Bill crazy, Joe said, let me talk to him, because my roommate know him and I can probably talk to him and said, Bill, man, come here and Bill yanked away and said, I hate all or y'all, he ran out, got a gun, came back maybe two to three minutes later, kicked open the door and said, I hate you— pointed at Keith and pointed at Joe and just started shooting. Joe took all the bullets because he was close. He just started shooting while, he had a sawed off pump.
>
> They could not find the boy that did the shooting. Bill walked around from the time he killed Joe all the way to 2:00 that afternoon the next day with a long coat on and a sawed off. A girl in my dorm was hiding him, she hid him for about two hours and said she didn't know—he was just like hide me, hide me and he ran in there. When they found him at about 2:00 he was in a hotel called the Roll Away Inn. They never found the gun until this day.

Would you shoot somebody?
Randi:

> No . . . but I would shoot somebody before I stabbed somebody. Because, you know what, it takes a lot of heart to and a lot of evil in you to sit there and stab somebody. Because, you can easily shoot somebody and pull the trigger and be like, oops, but the damage is done . . . but to sit there and deliberately keep stabbing somebody to death.

What do girls mostly carry?
Randi:

> Knives. Because police don't look at knives as seriously as they look at guns and it's easier to carry a knife and not be noticed.

What do you carry?
Randi:

> I carry simple stuff like a fork, 'cause I'll poke you in your eye. I carry locks and I carry a bat because it don't go off in metal detectors. I get into courts with my bat.
>
> A girl pulled out a knife on me and I clunked her in the head with a lock and this was at school.

I'm really beginning to think that you like to fight.
Gina:

> No, I've slowed down.

8

Women in the Criminal Justice System

To gain a better understanding of the issues facing women in urban Detroit, I have sought to bring the cycle of interviews full circle. It is important that all views and voices be heard to have a complete picture of the streets on both sides of the law. During the last fifty years women have become a viable part of the criminal justice system—as correctional officers and authorities, probation officers, police officers, judges, court administrators, and attorneys. This chapter presents the views of women within the criminal justice system. Illegal narcotics have expanded the possibilities for females in crime. In direct contradiction to traditional female images, women have become both lawmakers and lawbreakers.

THE POLICE

The role of the female police officer has become more visible in recent years. Detroit has one of the highest concentrations of female officers in the United States. In the last decade, women have assumed many diverse roles within the organization. There are females in the ranks as patrol officers, middle management, special assignments, and deputy chiefs. The presence of female officers on the streets of urban America is a matter of fact in 1993. Women are well represented as police and have their own viewpoint of what is taking place in relation to crime.

Mary Jarret-Jackson is a thirty-five-year veteran of the Detroit Police Department who has worked her way up the ranks to Deputy Chief of Western Operations. This distinguished career began when Chief Jarret-Jackson attempted to seek employment in the criminal laboratory and was laughed at by the white male police officers. She was told that at that time there were no blacks nor females in the crime lab. The officer went on to explain that only police personnel worked in the lab.

In this city, Chief Jarret-Jackson is acutely aware of what lays ahead for young people. When asked how she felt the young females would fare in life, her response was, "I don't envy them at all, this is a very difficult time for young people."

This professional law enforcer, who has an incontestable reputation—both as a forensic expert and administrator—prescribed a caring, supportive, and interested society to meet the challenge of youngsters today. "They certainly need somebody who cares whether you live or die."

Valerie Wilton, a ten-year-veteran of the Detroit Police describes her feelings as an officer:

> We're out there everyday and its tough. On the streets you're just like the men. I am seeing all kinds of things out here. You see people who need your support and then there are those who hate you. Girls or women are part of life out here. Sure, I am seeing bad women and girls, just like the men and boys. Gangs? Well, I don't work with gangs, but I am certain that girls have changed today, a lot different from what it was like in this city when I grew up and went to college. Everybody is tough, the senior citizens are tough, its just tough out here.

Lesley Seymore, chairperson, National Black Police Association addressed the role of females in police work in the U.S.:

> Black females in police work are very aware of internal and external problems of police work. The expectations of working within a male dominated profession is one dimension, and being black is another. Seeing females as criminals is part of the job, it's not always easy, but it comes with the job. As we expect understanding within the black experience from black officers, women must extend that sensitivity in relation to females. The bottom line is that women must be included in working within police organizations. We are part of the problem and solution. Anyone leaving women out of the process of the criminal justice system has missed the point.

Avon Burns, coordinator of the criminal justice program at Mott Community College, gave a historical perspective of women in criminal justice:

> Historically in criminal justice, and law enforcement in particular, women were virtually excluded from the opportunity to compete for traditional uniformed entry level positions. This overall general exclusion of women seemed

to result primarily from a long-held societal perception and notion that larger males were more ideally and physically suited for the demands of the profession.

Some thirty years later, from the sixties to the nineties, it would seem that many of the historical problems of the sixties and before continue to be problems today, e.g., adequate pregnancy policies, high ranking promotions/chief of police. In terms of acceptance, are we really ready to accept a woman as a Chief of Police?

Given the "chilling effect" impact of government policies, and dollars for criminal justice and law enforcement, particularly in relationship to aggressive and innovative minority recruitment, the pool of interested, motivated, and qualified African American women, men, and other minorities may actually be declining. After all, such communities are generally hardest hit by unemployment, drop-outs, drug addiction, and other socio-economic problems.

THE COURTS

Brunetta Brandy, 35, an attorney in downtown Detroit has an ongoing battle over mistaken identity. She is forever being courted by young men who think that she is involved in the illegal drug business. She has been approached as a drug dealer simply because she drives a Mercedes Benz and wears stylish clothing. She is a young, African American female attorney but many of the B-Boys or B-Girls think she must be a participant in the "drug culture." Brandy had mixed emotions as she reflected on this:

It's rather sad that the young men assume automatically that I am part of this dope scene. Many people, black and white, in this nation, jump to the conclusion that selling drugs is the only profession you could possibly have if you are African American and driving a Mercedes. The young men are brainwashed; even when I inform them that I am a lawyer they assume that I am a dope lawyer. It's like the only successful role for a black is that of working in the dope business. My private practice is based on hard work, not on the drug culture. The females I see in court are just as hard as the males. This drug scene has produced some very negative conditions not only for Detroit, but also this nation. The females that watch or admire my car, or clothing, have the same distorted models of success. The whole imagery of these youngsters, including females, is very distorted.

Those who are in this business of selling drugs have the worst attitudes I have encountered for clients. The difference is hardly noticeable whether male or female. Females who are involved deeply in this culture are, in my

opinion very different from what has been seen in the criminal justice sys-
tem. There is no doubt that females I am seeing day in and day out are
tougher. What has made them tough is life in these times. The coldness of
some of these females is scary. . . . What is really scary is that I am being
hassled in the middle of the day. It's very scary to be identified as someone
in that drug scene, when you realize the constant threat of violence that
comes with their lifestyle. I assure you that I am not ingratiated when these
young men flirt with me and assume that my car means that I am part of
their culture. Some may think of this as flattery, I am not flattered in the
least . . . I am scared of the potential, and disgusted with the attitude.

As a former member of the Michigan Correction Commission as well
as someone who works with young women in the community, she
seems to sense the tragedy for so many young women in Detroit.

It's hard knowing that so many young women, girls, are making mistakes
that will erode not only their lives, but society. I worked as a correction offi-
cer when I first came out of college and it's disheartening to think that so
many young women are entering this segment of the criminal justice system
. . . I want to see more women lawyers, judges, police . . . not more serious
criminals.

Wendy Baxter, a judge in the circuit court of Wayne County, has
viewed the problems both from her juristic position, and as a native of
Detroit. She indicated that she personally has not seen any significant
female criminal activity in her court. However, she is very aware of the
societal issues facing young African Americans in urban centers. She
indicated that parental guidance and involvement were the corner-
stones of youngsters being able to make the right choices for the
future. "The child is usually reflective of the homelife, you are what
you see . . .," said Baxter.

This young judge is very aware of the attitudes that women face.
The difference between women or girls with fathers in their lives is significant, in the young judge's view.

The young women who have had fathers at their sides are not as aggressive
and independent in some cases. Yet, young women, girls, who have had to
fend for themselves are more independent, bolder in some areas, but defi-
nitely not waiting for some male to correct or assist them.

Judge Baxter's point is interesting since Detroit, like other urban
cities, has a very high concentration of female, single-headed house-
holds. Homes without men. The question of independence, tough
perceptions nurtured by women and society, have perhaps come
home to haunt America.

Izetta Bright, Chief Magistrate of the 36th District Court, has found females taking on a more serious attitude as criminals in her court. Bright, who has lived in Detroit all her life, is acutely aware of the drastic change in female attitudes and behavior.

There have been more assaultive-type crimes in recent years. Traditionally, females had been more represented in the non-violent type crimes such as uttering and publishing [writing bad checks].

Bright indicated that the socioeconomics of urban centers like Detroit should not be ignored. The image of young women involved in crime has Magistrate Bright concerned that the media has sometimes placed too much emphasis on popular sensationalism, particularly in the case of the young women arrested during the 1991 July Fireworks celebration in downtown Detroit. A group of young women were caught on video in a confrontation and beating of two suburban white women. This video played nationally and is considered another blow to the image of the city. There were reports that the women were reckless, unruly, and showed no remorse in their hearing before Chief Magistrate Bright. She was very disappointed that the reports stated what she considered to be false. "They were very civil and I had no problems whatsoever. The reports in the media of confusion, inharmony, simply did not take place in my court."

Reports of gang involvement and past criminal records were aired repeatedly during the incident. However, there was no organized gang action with these five young women. While the video caught part of the melee, there appears to be much more to the story. One of the young women, Marie Springfield, had no police record and had never been arrested. Unfortunately for Springfield, she was tried with the group and not separately. With questionable legal advice, and an unusually speedy trial and conviction, this twenty-two-year-old, married, mother of two, who had never been in any legal predicament before, is suddenly in prison.

Two of the young women, who are twins, had, allegedly, extensive juvenile records. They have been identified as members of an Eastside gang named the Cross Conner Gang, aka "The CCs." Despite their denial, they have an infamous reputation as gang members and as terrorists in their own neighborhood. One neighbor, who demanded anonymity, summarized the twins.

They are the scariest folks on this block, they beat up boys, women, or grown-ups. They are bad, and I just knew sooner or later this was gonna happen. If you want trouble, those twins will give you plenty . . . they are

ready to fight over anything. And they are not scared of the police, or any-
thing else. It's scary to think what they will be like if they decide to get seri-
ous in one of those dope things and have real power. I bet the next time
they'll be worse on whoever is in their way.

The CCs were an integrated male/female scavenger gang. At the
time of the ordeal, there had been no reports of the CCs being active
in any particular manner. In surveys for this project there are reports
from field interviews that the CCs are capable of violence and negative
acts in their own communities. The reaction to violence and young
girls brought the public wrath and dismay rapidly. This reaction
addresses a much larger picture in this polarized region. There are
those in the black community that felt this fight was just another day
in the life of the ghetto. Its media attention centers on the actuality of
bad girls, women out of control that are no different from males.
While the twins are considered gang members, this was not a gang
mission. The feeling of some in the community was that these girls
were judged by different standards than a gang of white males in Ster-
ling Heights who kicked a young boy to death during a fight. Springfield was troubled by the double standards, and questioned why, since
they had murdered someone, they were still free.

In an interview in Scott Correctional Facility, Springfield explained
that she knew of the twins only in passing. She had only met them the
night of the event.

Yes, I was in the fight, but the video didn't catch the white women cursing
and throwing beer on us. I was trying to break up the women who were
fighting my friend who I had come downtown with, that was my girl, Keke.
Yes, I was fighting because my friend was being attacked by the other
women. But, I had absolutely nothing to do with any robbery. I understand
that the prosecutor had a job to do, I just didn't like the way she acted and
treated me like I was some kinda bum. I am not a gang member and I have
never been one.

Springfield, a graduate of Finney High School, was taking classes for
court reporting. She is concerned that the public know that she was
not some worthless welfare recipient; she had a life. She is aware of
girls in gangs in the city, and especially aware of the promise of the
good life from the drug culture.

If you live in the hood, you see the girls and boys who are making money,
and yes, it's attractive and tempting. I had seen the CCs and I have seen
lots of crews, posses in the city. That is not the type of life I had chosen, it's
there and you know it, but you know it's short. I just want the truth known,

I am not bitter, I hated the circus of cameras and people talking to you like you're nothing. The TVs shining those hot lights in your face . . . you have people making up things about you and they don't even know you. The police arrested me like I was some big drug dealer. This one police was talking bad to me, he had a hat and suit like he was Dick Tracy. When they came to my house they surrounded it, and when I came out it was like they had guns out, you could hear the clicks, what for? I came with no problem, and I didn't have no gun or weapon, I gave them no problem. When I got in prison everybody was talking 'bout, "Oh, y'all the fireworks girls." I just want to get out and get my life back. I don't hate anybody, I don't hate white people or anybody. Thank God for my family, they have stuck it out with me.

Eleanor A. Austin, Wayne County Probate Court Administrator, has worked in the criminal justice system for the past thirty years. Mrs. Austin understands the changes in attitudes of young females first hand from the daily experience of administration. She is aware of what works and certain that the juvenile justice field is capable of greater success if given the resources. However, she is concerned with the escalating change in young juvenile female attitudes. Historically, the primary offenses referred to the Court for females included Retail Fraud (shoplifting) and Truancy. Over the past four years, however, the number of assaultive offenses (felonious assault, aggravated assault, and assault with the intent to do great bodily harm) have increased while the number of referrals for truancy have decreased.

When asked if physical and sexual abuse was a factor in the delinquent activities of females, Mrs. Austin indicated that abuse is one of the critical issues that influences the shaping and molding of many young women today.

This veteran of the juvenile justice system was deeply concerned about the status of the family in the lives of young females in Detroit and Wayne County. The shift in the family structure, along with socioeconomic decline, has taken its toll on families in this city and Mrs. Austin cautions that society must be able to provide some social guidance in lieu of the changing of the guard. Many parents need assistance in the home; not just monetary, but concrete services that contribute to their ability to cope with the daily problems of survival. If our communities recognize the importance of investing in resources to service our young people now, we would realize significant savings in lives and money.

Judge Frances Pitts is presiding judge of the Juvenile Division of the Wayne County Probate Court. Pitts is an advocate of keeping families and youngsters together and endorses holistic community-based programs opposed to incarceration. This jurist is very concerned about the humanity of youngsters. In discussing the social conditions of Detroit, she underscores the harsh realities of the 1990s.

In response to the question of increasing female involvement in serious crime:

> I believe there may be an increase of young female involvement in acts of violence, but it may be some time before we have solid data on that. I do know there has been an increase in the number of girls detained in our Youth Home, which suggests the possibility of more female involvement in serious offenses.

Judge Pitts speaks of the importance of humanizing troubled youth:

> Society must keep in mind that some of these youngsters have not experienced bonding and family attachment, important as it is, in their primary relationships. There is the issue of basic trust that may be lacking in the earliest years of these children; a trust that most of us take for granted. However, even when youngsters are without these relationships as babies, for example, some of the void can be rectified with nurturing and a sense of permanency and love during their formative years.

Mary Janeley, a probation officer, and has worked as a correctional officer in the Michigan Department of Corrections. Janeley is convinced that the public has a limited understanding of what her department actually provides. The perspective of gender is important in her estimation of working within the correctional system. When asked if she felt that women have a tougher job winning inmates respect she responded,

> It's tough in the sense that women are tested not only by inmates, but in society it never seems to cease. Some of your peers, supervisors, and society in general tests women in an on-going sense. I am very aware of my surroundings, being a woman means that you must stay aware in particular when working in this field, period. It's tough for anyone working in corrections, the public expects so much of us, and at the same time our hands are tied. When you ask questions about subjects like the family situation with female inmates, it's hard because what can one say? What do I feel about it or how does it feel as an correctional officer? My job is defined very clearly; and yet, you see things that are difficult to explain to someone not working or walking in our shoes daily. My only answer is that females are having problems in the system as are males. I see problems being serious for women, and women incarcerated are taken seriously by myself and many of

*my peers in this field. Women are no different than men in this system, I
have seen plenty of tough and mean men and women.*

Kim Worthy, assistant prosecutor in Wayne County, has no doubt
about the serious attitudes of women and crime. Worthy prosecutes
homicides; before that she worked in juvenile prosecution.

*Women are represented in homicide more and more. I am not surprised
when I have a female perpetrator. The public has become more willing to
treat women in the same manner as males. In the beginning, women were
getting away with murder because of how society responded to the more
violent acts as unusual for women. Times are changing; I am seeing more
aggressive women, and they are their own person. It's interesting because
women are now involved in various criminal acts with men. That involvement is changing from the secondary, supportive, indirect type of experience.*

When asked if she is resented as a woman prosecutor, she says no, and
that she is, many times, praised by females in the court room.

*Black women, in particular, approach me and tell me they are proud of me.
In relation to crime, the jury is more in tune and wants results from the
criminal justice system. In doing my job, it's not unusual to have a woman
on trial for homicide. And it's not unusual for the jury to convict, if they find
her guilty. My only surprise is that the public or anyone is surprised at these
women who are as capable as males.*

The prosecutor, when questioned further as to what she meant by
females participating in crime with men, explained,

*One of the more disturbing cases comes to mind. A female and male team
raped a woman. Now, I have had women assist a man abducting another
female and perhaps watch as he raped her. But in this case, the woman
raped the woman physically. In other cases women are participating in the
crime directly, contributing equally as the men. Women are tough and I am
certain there are several reasons for this change. In my job I am seeing
women as the perpetrators. Not in the same numbers as males, but women
are involved.*

Worthy indicated that she has not seen any gang activity; she has
been in charge of some high profile cases such as the Tony Riggs,
Michael Cato, Anthony Riggs murder trial. This is the case in which a
recently returned army veteran was murdered by his brother-in-law.
The prosecution successfully tried Cato. The wife is expected to be
charged in an appeal.

CORRECTIONAL FACILITIES

As an attorney and former inmate,* Georgia D. Manzie is uniquely qualified to address the plight of women in the criminal justice system. While a prisoner, Ms. Manzie was a plaintiff and co-counsel on a class action lawsuit filed in federal court to challenge the inequalities of women prisoners. Ms. Manzie states that the judge ordered the Michigan Department of corrections to make sweeping changes in its treatment of women prisoners. However, she added that after 16 years of litigation, the court intervention only amounts to women being treated "equally as bad" as their male counterparts; generally speaking, the conditions in all prisons are inhumane.

Ms. Manzie discussed the isolation and poor treatment of women prisoners. She was acutely concerned with the children of incarcerated women. According to Manzie, the problem of termination of parental rights impacts women prisoners harder than men, basically because the overwhelming majority of them are single parents, and in many instances, fathers do not even formally acknowledge paternity.

Ms. Manzie states that prior to the lawsuit being filed in federal court, women received no paralegal training and the State did not provide women with a law library which met the minimum constitutional requirements for access to the courts. Therefore, in most instances, women lost their paternal rights by "default" because they did not even know how to get a writ signed for them to be transported to the custody hearing.

During one of two lengthy interviews, Manzie was asked if she observed any female gangs or gang activity during her three-and-a-half years of incarceration, she responded in the negative. However, she noted that many women formed "psychological families." In her observation, these "families" were more the result of "psychological needs as opposed to sexual needs for women inmates joining 'families.'" According to Manzie, these family structures are similar to traditional families with traditional roles. The male roles are dominant, and many times abusive, while the female roles are subservient. Our study has found traditional roles in these "families" such as fathers, mothers, and children, even elders who sometimes assume the role of grandparents. Manzie, however, states that throughout her incarceration she maintained strong ties with her parents and siblings and never felt the need to become a member of such a "family."

Marie Springfield, supported Manzie's description and explanation of the "family." Springfield indicated that she knew of it's existence

---

*At the age of 20, Manzie fatally shot a former boyfriend who had repeatedly assaulted and threatened her.

and had rejected joining. She also agreed that some new and young inmates did become involved with older "men" [lesbians] in the prison environs. While Ms. Springfield said there was no threatening factors to force a inmate into this lifestyle, she understood how it could happen easily.

If you got nobody coming into prison its scary. I had my family on the outside and they never abandoned me, thank God. It's hard coming into that situation and not having anybody to tell you what's going on.

Warden Joan Yukins, is in charge of two female institutions in Michigan. Warden Yukins understands the strain of motherhood and the dilemma of being incarcerated. Her background as an educator is sensitive to both mothers and children in this perplexing situation.

In relation to "families," I am not very knowledgeable, yet we are dealing with the problems of separation of women and their children. In this regard we are trying to bridge the gap, it's not easy for the inmates and certainly it's tough on children and families. Without any question I am concerned, and my feeling is that women incarcerated are human beings, and their motherhood is as important despite their status in the criminal justice system. We are concerned, and I am including those special factors in making positive decisions in meeting our responsibilities within the criminal justice system.

Marie Springfield spoke as a mother of two young children.

My grandmother saved my kids for me, it's hard being separated and it's tough on you even when they visit you in prison. Their so young and they don't understand what's happening, it kills you to see them in prison and then they leave . . . some girls don't have nobody bringing the kids to visit and you can see it hurts them to be left alone. I can see how girls get caught up in the family thing. When you got nobody it's real hard, and if you feel left out, you might do anything. Me, well it's hard being around all women, all the time. It's just hard to be separate from your family and it's really bad round holidays . . . just want to get out and see my kids.

The incarceration of women is just one more segment of the overall problem of this society and its focus. Women in prisons are part of what needs to be understood in dissecting the concerns and voice of women and the criminal justice system.

Angela Nevins, a probation officer, spoke of the troubled lives that both females and males have re-entering society after being incarcerated.

It's tough and you wonder how they're going to make it out in the world with no support. The families of these women have already abandoned them and once back home they have no happy reunions waiting for them. Their children have suffered the most, mentally it's hell on everyone. I just try to support them and listen, what are you gonna do? It's not fair, and the average person in this city never finds out how hard these ex-offenders have it. The poor women have it harder than the men. The men are celebrated by their peers both inside the correctional facilities and on the streets. Yet, women are treated like low class, dirty, second class citizens. Have you ever heard someone say something decent about a female ex-offender? Society is more tolerant of men ex-offenders, females are treated like refugees. And the crazy ones make it hard for those poor souls trying to do what we, the probation people, say to do. Its the no-good ones that you remember, not the good ones. The kids suffer the most when the women are in prison, and when they come out, it's mental hell for these women and men. My job is tough enough without trying to make sense out of this madness, everybody blames us, hell we just do what little we can do. The courts and judges make the rules and we just follow these poor fools around and wait for them to mess up.

SOCIAL PROGRAMS

Deborah Hodge-Morgan, a social worker in the Michigan Department of Social Services addressed the harsh reality facing many young women in Detroit who are attempting to start over after serious addiction to illegitimate drugs such as crack cocaine. Hodge-Morgan is part of the Families First Preservation Program. She has first hand knowledge of what happens when young women try to reclaim their lives after the devastating encounter with hard drugs.

The public may think in terms of middle class values, but I can't afford to be stunned by the situation, their reality is sometimes ugly, less than what many of us grew up with. The importance is to establish some positive, real communications—something of substance. To appreciate what some of these young women go through, their situations and families, you would have to see where they were before . . . the public would be shocked at how some people live. Some children are just existing, not being taught anything, and this condition is not merely confined to the inner city or Detroit.

Vernice Davis Anthony, director of Michigan Department of Public Health, offered her perspective of violence:

Violence and its related drug milieu is pervasive in all too many communities. It is frequently thought of as a problem of males, especially black males. However, the true picture encompasses, to a great extent, many young girls and children. In fact, in the city of Detroit, according to one study by a physician at Henry Ford hospital, homicide is the leading cause of death for children as young as age nine. Also, the Michigan Department of Public Health Child Mortality Review Report of 1991 concluded, "the numbers of children killed with firearms more than doubled in the decade of the eighties, these deaths are clustered in high-risk neighborhoods and most children are killed by someone they know." Violence is a "learned behavior. It is not an inherited disease or a virus that cannot be cured or prevented. Clearly, this is a family problem, and a community problem, even an attitudinal problem, and the solutions far outstrip the criminal justice system.

Cynthia Taueg, director/health officer of Wayne County Department of Public Health,

Family violence and drug use are significant predictors of behavior in children. We must rethink and reevaluate our approaches to reduce violence and substance abuse to achieve maximum results. This includes expanding on our strengths and the things we know that work, and to courageously acknowledge, and then seek to correct, our weaknesses. New approaches based on community leadership with government support will take us far into assuring future victory over the rising tide of senseless violence and loss of life so pervasive in our community today.

Karen Schrock, a native of Detroit, is chief of the Center for Substance Abuse Services for the State of Michigan.

There has been a negative stigma attached to women using drugs in our society. While many take pity on the children, women alcoholics and other drug users have been scorned by the public more so than men. I am concerned that both deserve treatment and concern.

Lynne Burdell-Williams, Deputy Director of Wayne County Youth Services, had this to say when asked if females are considered the same in youth services programming as males.

Females traditionally have not been included in the provision of services and allocation of resources beyond the "conventional" service delivery systems; i.e., ADFC, unwed/teen pregnancy, adoption, etc. Due to the historically small numbers of females in the juvenile/criminal justice arena, institutional, private, and non-profit organizations have not considered females in designing their service delivery systems. You may recall the old saying, "boys get into trouble, girls get pregnant." Obviously, the narrow focus of service providers has created the tremendous gap in services to females, the com-

plete disregard for addressing the gender differences and the lack of support services; such as day-care opportunities for females who attempt to access the limited existing services available. Systematically, these gaps, lack of specific gender needs, and, in general, afterthought approach to females has yet to be adequately recognized and addressed.

9

Conclusion

The debate over whether or not women are involved in gangs is influenced both by history and current events. The insistence of those who define gangs as merely reprehensible representations of society at its worst fall short of the reality of life on the streets. The isolation experienced because of racial barriers as well as gender barriers in American society must be taken into account in any analysis of these women. While the gang is the organization from which their socialization evolves, it is not simply belonging to one or not belonging to one that defines them. Their perceptions of being in a gang are not uniform. As it is for ethnic gangs and experiences within the United States, these gangs of females are as varied and different as their male counterparts. Their lives are integrated with and, at the same time separated from, males. The fact is that our perception females in gangs in the 1990s cannot and should not be limited to Fredrick Thrasher's rudimentary definitions or analysis. This is a new day, and the fact is that women in gangs differ from males in both thought or action. While there are female scavenger gangs, just as there are male scavenger gangs, their idiosyncrasies, cultural exposure, self-esteem, etc., dictate a different perspective.

Detroit has partially become imbued with what Barry Michael Cooper aptly named the New Jack mentality in the movie *New Jack City.* The New Jack era has emerged, displaying the attitudes of young men and women impressed with, and influenced by, the drug culture. The women in this study are from various backgrounds and have various attitudes. There are those who fit into the on-going drama of the narcotics business. Compatriot gangs and social and political advocacy networks address a complex multidimensional experience in the black community, including a Black Nationalist Consciousness. The reality is that an illegal underground economy has become the foundation for this new era of urban citizenry.

Young African American women are as invisible today as African Americans males were when Ralph Ellison wrote his classic, *The*

Invisible Man, more than thirty years ago. The isolation on which sociologist Robert K. Merton based his Strain Theory is a double strain for young, black, females in Detroit. This nation has not, as of 1993, brought the young Hispanic or African American female or male into the mainstream of American Society. The success of the Great Society certainly championed many minorities and propelled them into the middle class. However, since its abolition in the early 1970s, due to the dominant conservative philosophy, there has been no true policy to include the lower class or minority groups. Today, gangs provide many of the same support systems that the traditional establishment fails to provide. In Detroit, women, like men, have found that gangs can fill a void that grows daily due to the continued presence of homelessness and unemployment.

In Detroit, 80 percent of the African American families that live below the poverty level are headed by single women. This city can no longer provide the meaningful employment for unskilled laborers that the automobile manufacturing industry did for so many years. The recent dismantling of social service programs in the state has also devastated life for some urban dwellers. While there has been some media attention given to social conditions in Detroit, the city continues to fight a reputation it has not welcomed. One result has been that the entire issue of gangs has been dismissed not only by city government but also by most academicians.

The gang typology used in this study started with the grouping of those called scavenger gangs. Scavenger gangs are those that exist by whatever means possible. Scavenger gangs drift in and out of crime; their subsistence varies, and their world is one that is filled with uncertainty. While there are many individual scavengers in the city, there are also those who have formed themselves into gangs to better their chances of survival. This is a new twist for urban gangs in the U.S.; bands of young children, homeless families, homeless women, men who are mentally troubled, and drug addicts all are members of scavenger gangs. Women are scavengers both individually and as members of gangs. There has not been a great deal of attention focused on how these people or this gang type exists. These scavenger women have no advocates, nor are they regarded as important by politicians. For females, living below the poverty level in the inner city has produced a sense of hopelessness that can only be described as naked and raw. The mentality of many of Detroit's young men is that their existence must be carved out by any means possible. Today, some young women have adopted the same attribute as these men and in their disillusionment and despair they have become part of a growing group of poverty-stricken scavengers.

The scavenger gang is unlike any other gang in this typology. The plight of the scavenger has not changed over the past fifty years. It seems as if the scavenger is locked into an association with poverty. There is little doubt that the ranks of the scavengers have filled with those who do not feel part of a kinder, gentler America. When territorial gangs come to power, they have their real estate; when commercial gangs form, they have targeted a product, and corporate gangs have an infrastructure that mirrors the major mainstream corporations. Scavenger gangs have no property, no turf, and nothing of value; some have no homeland. Their existence is simple, as is their structure. There is nothing complex about their motivation; they are driven by, and bond for, one reason—survival. Other gang types present choices, scavengers have none. The territorial, commercial, and corporate gangs are fluid and mobile. If scavenger members are able to join another type of gang, more than likely, they will. Trapped in their desolate environment, it is difficult to break out or escape even if they can recognize the reality of what is happening. When comparing males to females in my earlier book, *Dangerous Society*, males dominated this typology in terms of actual numbers. Scavenger gangs of men were numerous. Yet, females were in scavenger gangs, and were abundant in homeless families; they did exist in scavenger gangs that were living off a barren landscape.

A small gang of six crack addicts gave some very insightful views on the structure of their scavenger crew. Montief, 25, explains their ordeal.

See, two of the girls here is my cousins. People think 'cause we like to get high that we ain't human. I have held jobs on drugs, it's not like what y'all think. Like that bullshit 'bout first time you hit crack it's addicting, that's bullshit. We're making it the best way we can out here. Hell, if we weren't beaming up, we would still be poor and black, right? Teke don't like y'all, she says y'all is the hook, y'all is up to something . . . I ain't worried, anyway I like your eyes, they look straight, they say you in charge. And I am in charge in this house. We all stay here and take care of each other. How? Whatever it takes, it's gotta stay funky [laughing] and we look out for each other. Look we just cut this fake ass faggot bitch out of our thing, he was illing and he was sick with that AIDS. Lying ass bitch would have gave us all the shit if we hadn't watch his tramp ass. Y'all might think we just some more down and out crackheads, but we living and making it, it's hell sometimes, but we doing it everyday. Sure, some days it's tight and we have to do some low down shit. But I've been on dope for most of my life. Dope killed my momma, killed my two brother,s and it's gonna kill my little sister 'cause she out here in a crew that's out cold . . . we all gonna die, just wait and see . . . . Crack is what makes us crazy, but it's the best high I know. This ain't the way I wanted things to work, but that's the way it is. We know, but what's gonna change? Nothing but that pipe makes things seem different. Crack is gonna get ya, watch out . . . [laughing].

How do we survive? Well last year this time we was selling yellow ribbons for the war, making a little paper [laughing]. I boost a lot, but it's getting hard, 'cause everybody watching black people and it's harder to get into the malls. But it's always something to do in the street. Right now it's all girls in this crew. Sometimes you sell your ass, safe sex [laughing]. Sometimes it's just stealing and lying for a dinner, not a hit. I love dope but sometimes it's just doing women and men. It's lots of scandalous ho's out in the street, used to be just men who were dogs, but today it's women and they is getting colder than the men. Do we have a name for our crew, well if I told you, the po-lice would be able to get us! [laughing] Well, we are the Stankhos, naw, we just the ho's off Linwood . . . who needs a name, that's like television.

The issue of class is one that is almost exclusive to the scavengers; they are mainly from Detroit's lowest class, the underclass. These females are undereducated, unemployed, and unable to see themselves in any other situation. Unlike the other gang types observed in this study, scavenger gangs have been in urban America since the beginning of urbanization. They also have been ignored more than any other group. In addition to their isolation, female scavengers might be doubly isolated, both as individuals and as gangs. The reality of female invisibility in crime statistics and the fact that they are not considered serious enough to be defined are products of elitist ignorance. This oversight is inexcusable; society is hurt by not having females included in a review of societal ills. The female experience may be different but that does not make it less important or irrelevant. The role of females in all-female scavenger gangs or in integrated male gangs mirrors similar struggles in the wider urban environment. Scavengers reside at the bottom of the social infrastructure and are locked into a social and economic caste. Whether it is fighting over a bottle of wine, for a sandwich, for some crack cocaine, or simply trying to find a warm and dry place to sleep, survival is what motivates these women. Gender becomes a less significant factor at this level of existence. The same is true when females join corporate gangs; success has its power, in the same way, poverty has its power working against females; it may not be a large-scale phenomenon, but their existence should be respected despite its simplicity.

The ugly reality of mothers with children moving in and out of shelters demanded that some women form alliances to survive. Gilly, 24, a young mother of three, explained how she banded together with two other young mothers to teach their children how to beg for food as people came out of restaurants. Their existence was Spartan at best;

their activities were unpretentious and without guile. Gilly laughed when asked if she considered herself a gang member.

If feeding my kids this way, yeah, we call ourselves the Stay Alive Crew. There is no way we can make it without hustling out here, and when it's lots of little kids begging it's better for us, 'cause people who just ate will always give the kids something. We ain't like no crews like selling dope, we ain't breaking no real laws, I guess. But Brenda, my friend, got four kids, and we all live by hustling. You sell your foodstamps for money if you can; some of the shelters are getting so filled up that you can't send your kids to school or you lose your place in line. Now, some women is selling their kids, selling their kids for sex, or money 'cause they messing with that damn dope. It's just four of us, and we make up ways to get money. This is the worst year ever, since they cut back and cut people off it's been hell. Our crew [laughing nervously], we just some young girls doing whatever we can. I was in this trade school and my mother was keeping the kids; now she got her aid yanked, and her medicine is stopped, now her worker says she will be back on after the new year, but she can't wait until next year. We stay with her when we have no other place. It's hard. I am looking for a place with the girls. But welfare is so hard and cold, they got so many rules and they just dis you for any little thing. One worker I had was really helping me, but she got bumped and I got this white bitch and all she says to me "How did you get yourself in this mess? How can you have all these children and no father?" I stay depressed, but one thing for sure if I don't work with Brenda and the girls here it's nobody gonna help us. It's the worst thing in the world to have to live like this.

The difference between females and males in scavenger gangs is their method of survival. The participants in the 1967 riot included many young scavengers who were rebelling against the injustice of the segregated society that had existed in Detroit for years. Ron Hunt, social worker and community activist, spoke of the changing roles in the 1960s, caused by the drug menace.

The dope, in particular heroin, created armies of zombie-like addicts. Unfortunately, women were in that wave of heroin addicts also . . . so yes, I would see women in surviving gangs, small gangs of junkies. They would be scheming to commit crimes such as break-ins, or con games. During that period I was working with drug programs, including methadone, and many of our clients were women. The females did not commit the same types of crimes as a rule. Women were more about the less dangerous crime, they tended to try and trick people out of their money.

Again, little attention has been paid to the lower class in the inner cities. Their isolation and neglect has created a breeding ground for scavengers from the rank and file non-citizens and anti-citizens. After the 1967 riot, little remained of what were once stable neighbor-hoods. After the initial blow of the riot, a heroin epidemic hit the com-munity. Small-time criminals rose out of the heroin epidemic. Property crimes became common, as did incidents of purse snatching and stick-ups. Women on heroin worked mainly in prostitution and boosting (shoplifting). It has been suggested that the first female criminal orga-nizations were composed of prostitutes. The problem with that exam-ple is that prostitutes worked mainly for men and did not see themselves collectively as a gang. The first scavenger, dope gangs with females, may have emerged during this period because of the nar-cotics business. Junkies would band together temporarily for the attainment of a hit (much like crack addicts today). Leadership would vary, but the motivation never changed; to obtain heroin and get high. Males, working as teams, did robberies. Females would work with men in a scheme that was parallel to the original Jack Roller from the 1930s. Traditional vice-crime became more serious with the spread of heroin in the late 1960s.

One of the tragic reminders of the demonization of illegal drug use is the ease with which the public can and does dismiss the deaths of those involved. I have called this the "Godfather Attitude," because of how well Mario Puzo's novel *The Godfather*, depicted the attitudes of America when it comes to segregating dope in this nation. When the media reports on the on-going war on drugs, the headlines usually read "gang-related or drug-related . . ." The buzz words are gang and drug; if Americans hear those words they think, it's okay, they deserved it, and it's dismissed. One young gang member felt strongly that America did not care what happened to junkies, the homeless, or to any other people down in the trenches of urban America. "Lots of girls know that crackheads ain't nothing, they know any girl out here on crack is liable to get popped, raped, or just beat down 'cause nobody cares what happens to 'em." Detroit has had numerous inci-dents of drug homicides. Women have been victims many times with-out much protest being raised; again the thinking is, well, what is a girl doing around that type of vice, anyway? This fact is clear in the case of the Highland Park Strangler. Benjamin Thomas Atkins admitted to raping and murdering 11 women. These women were prostitutes or crack addicts and their deaths caused little public concern.

It is interesting to note where these gangs reside and how they sur-vive in Detroit. Decaying, declining streets set the tone in many neigh-borhoods. There is but a remnant of the old, unique, mosaic pattern of Detroit neighborhoods. These regions are considered the most polarized of all the urban centers in the nation. The middle class has fled the city. Many of those who now live in the suburbs feel a sense of sorrow and resentment toward the residents of the inner city. Some local politicians, such as former Oakland County Prosecutor, L. Brooks Patterson, have advocated a get tough on crime policy in Detroit to cure the woes of the region. The unofficial line is "Let the blacks have the city." Some have spoken of the invisible wall that starts at South-field. With no economic or social foundation, it should not be a sur-prise to find gangs/organized crime filling the void.

The selling of narcotics in depressed neighborhoods directly follows from the conditions of isolation and the system that can only be labeled apartheid. While disgusted citizens debate the problems of dope, the fact is that open drug markets exist in certain communities. The consumers come from all over, but it is these outsiders who fuel the business. There are no neighborhoods anymore so there is no pub-lic protest from the community. Scavenger gangs live in abandoned apartment buildings, gutted-out stores, run-down housing. Survival in these streets is tenuous; violence is part of everyday life. These are streets that are controlled by war lords. These are business or commer-cial zones geared for the sale of narcotics, stolen cars, and murder for hire. One can look at a map of the city and see exactly where the vio-lence, brutality, drug trade, and poverty are concentrated. During sev-eral interviews a reputed young drug dealer explained that Mack Avenue was his place of business, but he lived in Southfield because it was safe. The young dealer went on to explain that most of his fellow dealers were moving or have moved to the suburbs, because it was much too violent in the inner city. With no support to hold on to, it's no surprise to find gangs, groups, and individuals forming their own rules, and their own government. The underground economy is not new, it is flourishing because that is where those who are blocked and not respected come to do business. It is also where they learn they are not part of an America that has ignored them.

The women described in this book are not part of a visible middle class. They are not part of the women's movement, they are not counted by Planned Parenthood or Right to Life. These women are part of another "silent majority" in the *other America*. It is not that they are ignorant or don't care about these issues. It is simply that they are on the firing line of a war. These are the daughters of African Ameri-cans and Hispanics whose oppression has meant that they have seen their mates suffer. White females have been oppressed by the success of male dominance. But within the African American culture, some women have been blamed by their mates for surpassing him or bene-fiting from their inferior status in American society. American apartheid symbolizes the struggle these women face to go beyond race and class. When they become part of corporate gangs, they shed the confining skin of second class citizenship within their world. They do not endorse the liberation of women in the same manner as NOW or Gloria Steinem. They have been regulated not only because they are black and poor; their gender is one more shackle. Sexism exists in criminal enterprises, as well as in legal commerce. In the streets, in the crack houses, in the bars, and in the correctional facilities, women are beginning to demand to be respected and acknowledged.

The confederation of young females in the illegal narcotics trade is growing. The influence of the drug culture on those in the inner city is remarkable. The numbers of actual participants in the drug trade can be misleading. The emulation of those in the drug trade by those who are not can be confusing. The empowerment derived from membership in corporate gangs is similar to that experienced by middle class Americans becoming members of prestigious country clubs, or elite professional organizations. The young Hispanic or African American who cannot see herself or himself successfully in other institutions can see opportunity in the dope business. Tough and dangerous as it is, it is visible in terms of the people they have grown up with and lived with daily. They can converse with these prosperous people. They can see the power of the gang, the celebrity status. This is real, it can happen to people just like them. These women can remember seeing "that girl" at school, in the shopping malls, driving a new Mercedes, BMW, Corvette, sporting Gucci, Louis Vutton, Fendi, and smelling of expensive perfume, going to Auburn Palace to see the Pistons, meeting John Salley at parties. Rubbing elbows with Thomas Hearns, smiling at Emmanuel Stewart. Meeting Mike Tyson, Michael Jordan, and shopping in the same stores where legitimate celebrities purchase their clothes. It is their time, they have arrived and they have a life.

Women cannot say who they are in this society. The interests of females in the inner city are no different than of those of women in the suburbs. Their goals are to be like the images constantly paraded in front of them in the media. It is the leisure of living the life of the rich and famous. Sgt. Anthony Holt, a consultant on this study, stated in dismay,

> These women are exactly like the men in their drive for independence. The younger girls are bent on taking charge of their lives . . . it's as simple as that, and no one should find that surprising. I certainly don't. My complaint is that they, like their male counterparts, can not expect society to support them when they choose to make it in the criminal enterprise.

Females from these corporate gangs come from various classes. The middle class segment, both male and female, are generally motivated by monetary gain. While the pressure merely to survive is not the same as that of the scavenger gang, there is the pressure to achieve and acquire. Acquisition for women in a minority culture is a reflection of what women in the larger society seek. Corporate females look down on the lower classes. The young women in organized gangs have little concern or compassion for those not making money like them. Their affiliation is based solely on monetary gain. Unlike scavengers, there is little concern for bonding or sisterhood. These young women have found their liberation. But progress is not perceived in the same way as feminist liberation. Just as male gangs in the business of narcotics, these females view themselves as capitalists. They refer to themselves as business women, and to selling drugs as just business. Attaining status is a fine old American tradition, the dream of living "the life" is alive and well in this nation. Illicit narcotics represent the means to an end. The failure of the traditional institutions to include these young women has led to their careers in crime.

There is an indication in the 1990s that corporate trained female gang members are, like some male members, investing in themselves. Their smaller, leaner organizations are the covert entrepreneurial organizations. The CEOs are like the commercial gangs of the old days. There are many commercial gangs and covert operations that are not concerned about monopolies like corporate gangs. This model of gangsterism is efficient and has proven to be more successful than the larger corporate model of criminal enterprise. Structurally, these gangs are a cross between "Amway-type" distributorships and covert guerrilla operations. Females have emerged as key players in this model. The product in this case is illegal dope. Women have found joining corporate gangs and covert operations to be rewarding. Despite public perception, most gangs are not drug-crazed terrorists. Women in corporate gangs as well as those who decide to branch out on their own do not, generally speaking, use drugs. This parallels the males who are successful in entrepreneurship. Historically, scavenger gangs have been poly-drug users. Women dominant in the leadership of territorial, commercial, corporate, and covert entrepreneur gangs have their own mores. The common sense of many of these young women contains an element of self-protection. The interview with the twins underscores their ability to survive, and to understand their underworld and their overworld. It is not simply the only avenue out for females, it is also the most appealing and, in their view, the shortest and most promising way out of the concrete reservations of urban America.

The other dimensions of gangs, groups, and social and political networks are entangled in a complex culture of which America is unaware. Perhaps the public is more comfortable with the demonization of girl gangs. Despite what people may think about drugs, gangs, and crime there is a closer common ground with gangs than many citizens are willing to admit. The thinking of many young women in Detroit is homogeneous on subjects ranging from music, clothing, church, violence, sex, education, dating, and other issues. Changing demographics are bringing a different kind of student into higher education, as shown in the interview with the twins. The public is anxious to find simple solutions, and rationalizations. Poverty plays a part in this whirlpool of social dysfunctions in America. Yet, the outcomes show clearly that despite theorizing by so-called experts, their formulas leave many unanswered questions. While there are social and political activists in the youthful population who abhor drug dealers, they share with drug dealers a common disdain for police agencies. The same is true of some nationalist's displeasure with drug addicts, who they feel are a detriment to and drain on the black community that should be eradicated.

Compatriot gangs are becoming more and more confused and frustrated in their quest simply to live in these trying times of urban life. For outsiders, what begins as a simple ride out to Belle Isle, a concert at Joe Louis Arena, or a house party may result in defending one's life, honor, or innocence. Theorists who point to law breaking, deviance, or criminal intentions know nothing of this environment. It is objectionable to label gangs criminal or deviants in a society where certain members (black males) have become endangered to the point of being classified by the Center for Disease Control. The task of separating the plight of females from males is as impossible as keeping compatriot gangs safe from erratic and unpredictable violence. When girls in this urban environment carry weapons or desire to attain wealth by means of selling narcotics, their activity is no longer marginal. Even the so-called aggressive fighting gangs may become tomorrow's freedom fighters, as has happened in other revolutions. A nation that sends young people to fight in a foreign lands should recognize the similarity of the foreignness of its own inner cities.

There is the threat of being caught off guard, or not prepared for adversity. There is the fact of arming oneself to meet conditions little different from those encountered by someone living in Beirut. The visual picture that many girls observe day in and day out is unknown to those who discuss the problems of the city. The conflict produces warriors of incongruous types. How this experience touches girls in the inner city is unexplainable. One girl joins a crew of narcotic vendors; another becomes active in a sociopolitical network that builds a better community via education. Does the ugly fact that a gun gives a female a security blanket in a dangerous environment make her a deviant or a criminal?

Epilogue

There has been no past theoretical analysis that addresses the African American female gang perspective. There is a great need to examine this phenomenon. The role of women in gangs goes beyond the auxiliary role that they held in the past. Theories about delinquent females simply do not address those posed by what we observed in this study. I asked the women to speak for themselves in this book. These are their words and expressions, recorded as spoken, and untouched by anyone. Perhaps the greatest injustice done in regard to research on female gangs is that the bulk of what has been gathered has been collected and interpreted by men. This is not to suggest that research must be restricted in order to capture solid data. The point is that women are more than capable of speaking about and interpreting their own experiences.

Writing this book has proven to me that past social theories created by white males have little, if any, relevance to African American female gangs. Black women have been abandoned and ignored in so many aspects of life. In particular, women of color have been stereotyped as wild women of the streets, completely lacking any humanizing qualities. The literature on female gangs does not reflect the black woman's experience as regards generational and class differences; hip hop culture is ignored. The academy casts women as second-class citizens possibly of interest as sexual objects or one-dimensional criminals. This is inexcusable. Social theory has raised questions that should be explored. Theorists should investigate the womens' position in the same context as the males' position in gang studies. Cultural aspects, demographics, and other social factors must include female perspectives. This study underscores the fact that research on females is not dependent on male researchers nor on male theories.

Every one of these women is worth more than society believes. Their worth is priceless and irreplaceable. The inner city has produced successful mothers, workers, and law-abiding citizens. It also has produced dope dealers, gang members, crime bosses and victims. Many of the females interviewed have not been part of the political-economic infrastructure. The extreme and radical role change of African American females in America is evident in Detroit. This city has one of the oldest and most powerful black middleclasses in America. The 1990s have started with full-blown violence and illicit drug culture well entrenched. The turbulence of young women living in these times has become matter-of-fact. The hardness with which they interact finds gang membership secondary. Whether one is a dealer, dope fiend, or simply existing in this urban frontier, life has changed dramatically.

Black women in Detroit are successfully employed as teachers, principals, administrators, entrepreneurs, auto workers, postal carriers, and highly world-renowned professionals like Dr. Alexa Canady, a neurosurgeon. Detroit has the largest concentration of female police officers in the United States. Black females are well represented in the professional ranks in the city. There can be no denial of the contribution of African American females in Detroit.

Still a radical change is well shown in the demographics within the city. The underground economy has emerged, not only in the streets of Detroit, but also on the campuses of major white universities. If universities are not willing to acknowledge the widespread erosion of our cities, perhaps the city coming to the campus will attract their attention. Some urban-based students are not gravitating toward the traditions of sororities and other traditional activities in the same manner as earlier groups. Some young co-eds in private and state universities are mingling with young men involved in the dope trade. Some young women in college are following in the footsteps of the radical political activists of the 1960s and 1970s.

Sgt. Anthony Holt, who has worked with this project since its inception, commented on the change among student types in this decade.

Without any reservations, I know we are experiencing a different type of urban student. The cross section is diverse along both economics and social class. Girls are dating young boys that twenty years ago they won't speak to on campus. Females that come from the community are now politically active or some are commuting by choice, rejecting living on campus in order to keep close ties to their neighborhood. One has to be very careful in labeling someone a dope person. Whites, Arabs, Hispanics and others are wearing the same baseball hats, sneakers, Starter jackets, and listening to NWA or Public Enemy. Everything has changed and it's different is the only way to describe it.

Hip-hop is the cornerstone of communication for urban youth. Research into the cultural dimensions of urban America must include the voice of hip-hop.

Whether or not one likes rap music is irrelevant. What is relevant, is an understanding of it. Rap is more than music. Rappers have taken music beyond recreational listening and made it a means of communication. This is the voice of the street and it is empowering a generation excluded from society before birth. Societal institutions have failed this generation of youth by not listening. This form of cultural communication is similar to the talking drums sounded in Africa and in North America. The academy may dismiss this as "ghetto noise" but one need only look at the Los Angeles riot to understand what hip-hop is communicating.

Those who choose to ignore the symbolic meaning and revelations of hip-hop culture cannot honestly give an accurate account of what is taking place in the urban environment. We cannot solve the problems if we do not know what the problems are. Rap music represents the evening news for many urban youth. The hip-hop movement is rich and varied; there are many different types of rap music. Some is hard, vulgar and violent, yet, some is educational, comical, and even romantic. It is anything but simple and cannot be dismissed as just a fad. When NWA or 2 Live Crew can sell millions of records without ever appearing in the national media, it should be clear that rap has permeated the culture. It is not only the undercurrent in young black lives; it is reaching into the homes of middle America. A grandmother of a gang member recently explained to me in an interview,

> My husband is dead, but in his life he loved Walter Cronkite and the six o'clock news. I loved Sonny Eliott doing the weather. I love Nat "King" Cole and the Ink Spots, Dinah Washington and Billie Holiday, Carmen McRae. My granddaughters listen to rap music all day, they love that LL Cool somebody, they like all them rappers or whatever you call 'em . . . they don't care nothing about no news on regular television, they got their own way of keeping up with the world.

The Nationalist movement compliments some of the young female rappers like M.C. Lyte, Sister Souljah, Queen Latifah, and Harmony who address the concerns of black females in college and everyday existence. The raw, tough points of urban life are expressed in the themes promoted by female rappers such as YoYo. There have been faddish groups like Bitches With Problems, and Ho's With Attitudes, who seem to display their rap as "hard core street" in the same vein as male risque rappers. The poetry of the street reflects not what black youths dream about, it's what exists daily.

The triumph of middleclass blacks because of the civil rights movement is obvious. To some extent the overworld has had its successes for women of color in Detroit. Yet, the problems of those who are not in the working class anymore or never were manifest themselves daily.

The failure and hopelessness is evident in the streets where there are homeless women with children in city shelters and women begging on the streets. Some of these women are in this book.

The decline of black women is attached to several glaring factors. The major culprit in the lives of many females in this study is oppressive hopelessness. Some women are taking drugs that have enslaved them and made them into zombies; others have sold their souls for material goods. The success of hard working black females in the overworld is only one dimension of urban life. Another dimension is the underworld which includes the success of young black men, and today the success of young black women as well. The fact is that some females, like their male counterparts, have become proficient in selling narcotics. That profession for females is no longer one of second-class status. Women are involved and they can fail or succeed given the opportunity.

Looking at the city from the point of view of a gang like the Seven Mile Girls is different than looking at it from the point of view of everyday citizens. What is apparent is that the city is divided and segregated into protected enclaves and colonies. The young females in this crew know the history and future of this region. They point out the big houses and money homes. They know where the police frequent; they expect nothing in the streets but violence and disharmony. It is their expectations that I find so disturbing yet realistic. The twins talk about going to church when they were younger, yet at nineteen they speak as if the church is somewhere off in never-never land. They're ready for and presume that adversity awaits them daily. They really seem to anticipate physical battles at any moment and almost relish the thought.

The common denominator for many young women interviewed was the hard, serious attitude expressed as, "I am ready for the worst life can present, nothing would really surprise me, because I have already seen the worst of everything." It didn't matter if they were in a successful commercial or corporate gang. The attitude was almost always tough and there was no apology for this display of hardness.

Colonies of former working class neighborhoods are now hollow and abandoned dope dens, crack houses, and worse, open drug markets. The women living in these blocks are surviving the war in the streets. Sadly, some critics defend the conditions of these neighborhoods, as if to anoint street culture as livable. Poverty, crime, and joblessness are issues of social significance. The bitterness and secession of these citizens is an indictment against this society. This is the harvest of America's social engineering during the past one hundred years.

The city of Detroit has the largest African American population in the United States of America (1990 census). The question is whether the city has become one large enclave of the havenots. Professor Ira Schwartz, one of America's leading scholars in social work, has presented groundbreaking evidence of the dysfunction of urban America. His research at the University of Michigan's Center for Youth Policy shows how young women have fared over the decades in Michigan. Detroit has an infant mortality rate that correlates with the Third World. If the infant survives, he/she may become a child in a dislocated family and be predestined for failure. Until America understands that the young women in this study are a part of the overall picture and worth saving, this erosion of precious human resources will continue.

The inability of society to recognize women or different ethnic groups as equals, translates into a distorted consciousness for Americans. Girls in gangs, women using or selling narcotics exemplify America's failure to humanize women in these urban colonies. Their disenfranchisement, secession from citizenship, and disinterest in the social and economic concerns of everyday Americans has not been weighed. They are, without question, as invisible in 1993 as they were in 1902 . . . in this city, young American women of African descent have no one to champion them nor humanize their plight. These females are not the ones fighting for parity in intercollegiate athletics, nor are they wondering about better roles in Hollywood. Corporate America is very far away, and their world is immediate; AIDS is upon them, their children are being murdered, they are being victimized daily by unseen forces. Women's issues are relevant. These women understand oppression better than most. This oppression means that they have been abandoned by nearly everyone in this society. They bear the burden of social injustice.

The de-sensitization toward violence in American culture seems to be growing yearly. The overall destruction has robbed the citizens of quality of life. The children of the city live in the shadow of evil, in constant danger. There is an on-going brutality, a sense of rage that has claimed so many that it's hard for many citizens to experience outrage. Violence is just a fact of life in urban America.

A young woman on the Westside succinctly summed up the reality of drugs paralyzing neighborhoods.

The problem for us is more than the crackhouses and gangs. You can't sit by windows at night, because you never know when a bullet may come flying in your direction. You teach your children to hit the floor if you hear gunshots. You would hear gunshots only at New Year's on this block. Sitting on

> the porch use to be normal for this street; everybody knew everyone else and in the summer it was normal for the whole block to sit on the porch and watch everything. It was peaceful and enjoyable. My father watered our lawn in the morning before he left for work and in the evening. Now, we don't have neighbors who sit on their porches; people are scared of getting shot, it's simple as that. I am worried to death. I have three teenagers; I grew up in this community and it's changed for the worst. We have some of the old people who try and keep their places up, but we're living in fear. This is hell.

There is an invisible city with its hub interlinking poverty, class, race, and gender. Its infrastructure is solid, and well-oiled. Citizenship in this city is not governed by political boundaries. Its educational institutions are advanced and graduating massive student bodies. This city grows daily. The walls of segregation, constant brutality and declining industrial centers have enclosed this separate, seceding, hostile nation. America's "Invisible Nation" rejects the traditions and mores of the colonial sovereign. This is not another country invading us. This is a homegrown city of despair, forced segregation, and disenfranchisement.

During the Los Angeles riot of 1992, one black man screamed on the NBC evening news, "mothers out here with their children looting and stealing . . . I don't believe it." The chickens have come home to roost. Listen to Public Enemy; their social commentary points out to urban youth that there is a significant difference between America and *You*. Street education explains and amplifies the unfairness of double standards applied to women and men of color. Keela, the savvy young dealer, laughed about education and her future,

> Right, people done game my people, perpetrating whities smiling, lying, and we're dying. Got my job; I don't want y'all welfare, I am here, I am making it, and y'all didn't help me, except when y'all bought my dope. The way I see it, white people got it made they think, but ya' know what? Everybody think it's a black thang. It's a monay thang. Ya' make the rules and when it don't work ya way, it's change time. Change the rules for the white people. So it's 'bout keeping yo thang straight. All that wacked out shit 'bout 'just say no' is tricks. Welfare is for sillyho's; I make my own way. Later for welfare checks and case workers. Out here it's way you make it, girls got to understand that it's up to you. One thang is for certain, nobody gives a shit 'bout me, nobody cares. Education is what I got from all the teachers, case workers, all the niggahs coming out the joint begging . . . begging out gets ya nuthing. I got mines, it's the dope, it's the only bank that lets a girl get straight. So do it for yourself . . . nobody is gonna do it for ya.

This city has citizens who are fighting to keep morals and traditions alive in many neighborhoods. Yet, block upon block is empty, young children are not in school, homicide rates escalate. There is a blatant disregard for life. A young mother who is trying to do the right thing loses her baby daughter sleeping innocently in her crib from a stray bullet. A father tells his children to come home during any confrontation and get the gun. A crack-addicted mother leaves her child in the crack house as if it is the day care center. An underground employed mother takes her child to work in a crack house. Grandparents raise abandoned children. Young mothers live homeless with their children in the streets. These all represent the signs of the times. This is reality. There is no moral leadership, only hopelessness for this generation. How will these children grow up? Will they make America proud? Will they register to vote and see themselves as Americans, or as Americans of African descent? Even if there were no gangs and no drugs, would these women still be isolated and oppressed? The future looks very bleak. America, the focus must include these women. This problem is in Detroit, not Bosnia, South Africa, or the Middle East. Ethnic cleansing, warring tribes, the focus must include the balance of our urban cities.

Appendix A

Field Questions

These questions were asked in the course of this study. The groups varied in size and type. The main focus was to gain insight into the feelings and thinking of girls and women on subjects that came up during other interviews by females. The key to the typology is included in the questions or sub-headings. Some questions did not relate because of age or other factors and will indicate not applicable (N/A) in answer. Ivestigators surveyed four groups; (1) Non-Gang, (2) Scavenger, (3) Territorial and (4) Corporate (commercial) gang members. Groups 1, 2, and 3 had 20 respondents, group 4 had 10.

		Non-Gang	Scavenger	Territorial	Corporate
1.	Your favorite music, the type you listen to most.				
	a. pop	—	—	—	—
	b. country and western	—	—	—	—
	c. rap	19	12	18	8
	d. classical	—	—	—	—
	e. rhythm and blues	13	17	19	9
	f. jazz	12	2	3	8
	g. blues	5	4	2	4
2.	Favorite or most frequented place you spend for fun or recreation?				
	a. school	18	3	14	10
	b. shopping mall	16	13	17	10
	c. fast food place	16	16	13	6
	d. friend's home; own home; neighborhood	15	19	20	5
	e. other	—	—	—	—

	Non-Gang	Scavenger	Territorial	Corporate
3. Do you attend any type of religion, church, mosque, etc?				
a. church	16	3	—	8
b. mosque	—	—	5	—
c. other	4	17	15	3
4. How much education have you received (formal)?				
a. K-6	20	14	18	10
b. 6-9	20	6	11	10
c. 9-12	19	2	12	9
d. college: including community or professional school	—	—	—	—
e. special education, vocational, GED, or other type of education	13	13	16	5
5. Do you know of women carrying a weapon? If yes, please indicate the type.				
a. Knife	16	16	19	5
b. gun	6	13	17	9
c. other (baseball bat, chain, mace)	12	16	19	3
6. Is there a weapon in your home?				
a. yes	14	19	15	10
b. no	—	—	—	—
c. no answer	—	1	—	—
7. Do you carry any type of weapon?				
a. Knife	3	17	17	4
b. gun	10	13	17	10
c. other (baseball bat, chain, mace)	—	20	20	—
8. If yes, why do you carry a weapon?				
a. protection	12	20	20	10
b. business	—	—	—	—
c. fun	—	3	8	—
d. not sure	—	2	5	—
9. Do you have access to a car?				
a. yes	10	1	—	10
b. no	10	13	11	—
c. sometimes	—	6	9	—

	Non-Gang	Scavenger	Territorial	Corporate
10. Do you know of someone personally that has been injured or fatally damaged by violence?				
a. yes	20	20	20	10
b. no	—	—	—	—
11. Have you seen violence in person?				
a. yes	20	20	20	10
b. no	—	—	—	—
12. Are you violent?				
a. yes	—	3	—	—
b. no	20	12	19	10
c. don't know	—	7	1	—
13. Are you concerned or worried about violence in your daily life?				
a. yes	17	—	—	10
b. no	—	16	18	—
c. don't know; don't care	—	4	2	—
14. Are you working?				
a. full-time	18	—	6	5
b. unemployed	2	19	14	2
c. part-time	15	1	3	3
15. Do you smoke cigarettes?				
a. yes	12	17	14	4
b. no	8	3	6	6
16. Do you drink alcohol? (If yes, continue)				
a. beer	3	14	13	4
b. wine	2	11	9	4
c. hard liquor; whiskey, gin, rum, etc.	14	9	9	3
d. all of the above	7	15	17	1
17. Have you used illicit drugs? (If yes, continue)				
a. heroin	—	9	3	—
b. cocaine	5	5	9	2
c. crack cocaine	—	6	2	—
d. marijuana	12	16	19	4
e. other	—	17	13	—

	Non-Gang	Scavenger	Territorial	Corporate
20. Are you worried, concerned about AIDS?				
a. yes	20	15	18	8
b. no	—	5	2	2
21. Are you concerned about safe sex?				
a. yes	20	10	14	10
b. no	—	4	2	—
b. don't think about it	—	6	4	—
22. Is society sexist to you?				
a. yes	5	5	7	7
b. no	—	—	—	—
a. no answer	15	15	13	3
23. Is society racist to you?				
a. yes	18	11	14	10
b. no	—	—	—	—
a. no answer	2	9	6	—
24. Have you ever been raped?				
a. yes	3	13	4	1
b. no	—	—	—	—
a. no comment	17	7	16	9
25. Do you know someone that has been raped? (including male or female)				
a. yes	20	20	20	10
(number of females raped)	20	18	19	n/a

People that you like, identify as being part of your world, that you respect or talk your language, play your music and dress, eat and talk like you or understand you

GUY	TLC
Eric B & Rakim	TEDDY RILEY
KOOL G. RAP & D.J. POLO	WESLEY SNIPES
KRS-ONE	JAMES BROWN
LL COOL J	MICHAEL X
HEAVY D	MAYOR COLEMAN YOUNG

MASON
JODY WATLEY
WHITNEY HOUSTON
SALT N PEPA
GETTO BOYS
QUEEN LATIFAH
X-CLAN
SPIKE LEE
DARREL DAWSEY
MIKE TYSON
ICE CUBE
YO YO
KAOS AND MAESTRO
DR. DRE
DJ QUICK
NWA
DAMON WAYANS
TOO SHORT
MARTIN LAWRENCE
PUBLIC ENEMY
CHUCK D
LUKE CAMPBELL
TWO LIVE CREW
TOMMY DAVIDSON
EPMD
SLICK RICK
KRIS KROSS
EASY E
BOYZ TO MEN
BELL BIV DEVOE
WRECKX N EFFECT
NAUGHTY BY NATURE
JODECI
SIR MIX A LOT
BOBBY BROWN
DONNY SIMPSON
MC BREE
HOUSE OF PAIN
ARRESTED DEVELOPMENT
JAZZY JEFF & THE FRESH PRINCE
HAMMER
MC REN

PRINCE
MARY J. BLIGE
POSITIVE K
GANG STARR
MARKY MARK
GRAND PUBA
EN VOGUE
SCARFACE
BRAND NUBIAN
DAS EFX
CYPRESS HILL
BDP
REDMAN
EDDIE MURPHY
BEASTIE BOYS
RUN DMC
SPICE 1
SUPERCAT
MINISTER LOUIS FARAKAN
LUTHER VANDROSS
DENZEL WASHINGTON
DOUG E FRESH
ARSENIO HALL
JOE DUMARS
MICHAEL JORDAN
KOOL MOE DEE
ROXANNE SHANTE
BIG DADDY KANE
SISTER DEE
MC LYTE
SHABBA RANKS
CHUBB ROCK
FAB FIVE FREDDY
AL B. SURE
JANET JACKSON
GEORGE CLINTON
FUNKADELICS
MC BRAINS
A TRIBE CALLED QUEST
PM DAWN
N2 DEEP
CHRISTOPHER WILLIAMS

Appendix B

Slang Glossary

24-7 — occurring on a constant basis
5-0 — the police

ace — to take advantage of someone

bangin — the act of fighting
bark — the name of the narco cops in New York
beaming up to scotty — the act of freebasing cocaine
beat down — to be physically attacked
beatin the pavement — walking as your major means of
   transportation
beefin — to have a long vendetta with someone
benzo — Mercedes Benz
boomin — to be at your peak; to be prosperous
booster — a thief, usually in a store, shoplifting expert
buggin — to act obnoxious
bum-rush — to physically attack someone

championship hour — the time at which you are selling the most
   narcotics
change — money
chillin — sitting around relaxing
chizel — money
click — a person's closenit group
clockin — the act of making money
creepin — the act of sneaking; doing something you shouldn't be
   doing

def — admirable
dope — something or someone that's very admirable
dissed — to be treated scandalously or boldly
dividends — money
doin um' — to be making large sums of money

earl — to vomit
easy — going

factors — car, jewelry, shoes, clothes
fakin — to be phony
flavor — style, person has style.
fluncky — someone who does everything someone tells them to do
fly boy — a boy who looks nice
fly girl — a girl who looks nice
fresh — something or someone that's very admirable

gaffilin — to take; to steal
ganked — to take; to steal; to con someone out of something
get busy — to get started; the act of commencing
got it going on — to be admired; doing very well in life.

heater — a gun
hip-hop — fashionable, in with the times
hit — the name of sexual intercourse
hold it down — to obtain respect from a group of people based on material
holla-holla — to say goodbye to someone
homie — a close friend or companion

illin — to act obnoxious

jack — money
Jack Roll — person who robs, takes advantage of a drunk or helpless victim.
juiced — when someone conned you out of something

kickin it — sitting around talking with your friends
kickin them boots — having sex
knockin boots — wanting sex

loot — money

marquettin — the act of staring someone down
moula — money

O.P.P. — Other People's Property; Other People's Pussy (sex)

peep this — listen to this; to get someone's attention
peon — someone who gets no respect and everyone looks down on
perpin' — to act phony; to pretend
posse — the group of people you associate with

roll call — when you see the police coming
rollin' — the act of selling narcotics

sac chaser — a female who uses men for money
scrappin — the act of fighting
scratch — money
short — when you are lacking in some way of form
skeezer — a female who sleeps with men for money; sometimes
    refers to women in general.
smoke — to beat someone up or to shoot someone
soft — the term used to describe someone who is gullible, wimpish
sprayed — to be shot more than once or shoot a house up
squares — cigarettes
squirrelin — the name of sexual intercourse
stack — money
step off — to demand distance from your being; get away from me
straight — you're taken care of; you don't need anything else
strapped — to be armed with a weapon
strongarm — to rob someone

the jects — the projects or low income housing in a city
tip — a piece of information
tired — when someone looks raggedy or is out of the times in fashion
toe off — to receive a *large* sum of money
trippin out — to have fun or to act obnoxious

undercover ho — woman who is whorish, and careful not to let it be
    known

wack — stupid; obnoxious
weed out — to smoke marijuana in excess
what's up — how are you; hello; what's new
what you thought — a phrase used when you want to know why
    someone made a particular remark or statement
wiggum — check

you down — you're perfect; you're taken care of; you're covered
you set — you're taken care of, you don't need anything else